The U.S. & Free China

How the U.S. Sold Out Its Ally

The U.S. & Free China

How the U.S. Sold Out Its Ally

James C. H. Shen

The Ambassador of the Republic of China to the United States

1971–1978

Edited by Robert Myers

ACROPOLIS BOOKS LTD.
Washington, D.C.

ACROPOLIS BOOKS LTD.
Alphons J. Hackl, Publisher

Colortone Building, 2400 17th St., N.W.
Washington, D.C. 20009

Printed in the United States of America by
COLORTONE PRESS, Creative Graphics Inc.
Washington, D.C. 20009

ATTENTION: Schools and Corporations
ACROPOLIS books are available at quantity discounts with bulk purchase for educational, business, or sales promotional use. For information, please write to:
SPECIAL SALES DEPARTMENT
ACROPOLIS BOOKS Ltd.
2400 17th Street, NW
Washington, D.C. 20009

Are there ACROPOLIS BOOKS you want but cannot find in your local stores?
You can get any Acropolis book title in print. Simply send title and retail price, plus 50¢ per copy to cover mailing and handling costs for each book desired. District of Columbia residents add applicable sales tax. Enclose check or money order only, no cash please, to:
ACROPOLIS BOOKS Ltd.
2400 17th Street, NW
Washington, D.C. 20009

Library of Congress Cataloging in Publication Data
Shen, James, 1900–
    The U.S. & Free China: How the U.S. Sold Out Its Ally
    Includes index.
    1. United States—Foreign relations—Taiwan.
2. Taiwan—Foreign relations—United States.   3. United
States—Foreign relations—China.   4. China—Foreign
relations—United States.   5. Shen, James, 1909–
6. Ambassadors—Taiwan—Biography.   7. Ambassadors—
United States—Biography.   I. Myers, Robert (Robert J.)
II. Title.
E183.8T3S525   1983   327.73051'249   82-13884
ISBN 0-87491-463-9

Dedicated to Winifred, my beloved wife, who was with me throughout my long and agonizing mission and without whose encouragement and help I would probably not have written this book.

Foreword

In writing this book, my only motive is to leave behind a record of my personal experience as the last Ambassador of the Republic of China to the United States. Those interested in the subject will therefore have an authentic Chinese version of Washington's "normalization of relations" with the Chinese Communists in addition to what former President Richard M. Nixon and National Security Advisor/Secretary of State Henry Kissinger have already written and what Jimmy Carter and his National Security Advisor, Zbigniew Brzezinski, can be expected to write.

I did not arrive at this decision lightly. To begin with, unlike their Western counterparts, especially the Americans, very few Chinese in public life write memoirs the moment they leave office. Confucian teachings on modesty may or may not have something to do with this Chinese tradition. Even in the case of those who do write their memoirs, there is usually a stipulation that no parts thereof may be published until many years have elapsed or until the writers themselves have joined their ancestors.

Another consideration often cited is that it takes time for dust to settle. What is the point of reopening an issue so soon after it has been closed and when no useful purposes can be served? I do not set any great store by this sort of Confucian philosophizing. By training I am partly American. My student days at the University of Missouri's School of Journalism in the mid-1930s and still other years in the United States, first as an information officer in the '40s and then as a diplomat in the '70s, have had a great deal of influence on my attitude. What I have put down in this book may or may not be the whole truth, but it is as best I am able to ascertain it.

The Republic of China was a friend and ally of the United States for many, many decades. When Carter decided to finish off in December, 1978, what Nixon had begun to do on the China question in February, 1972, the blow, though long expected, was nonetheless shattering for everyone in my country. As Ambassador to Washington at the time, I couldn't say that I bore no responsibility whatsoever. As a matter of fact, I came under quite a bit of censure in our representative assemblies for failing to alert the government sufficiently ahead of time to what was about to take place, as if foreknowledge by a matter of hours or a few days would have made any material difference in the final outcome.

My wife and I returned to Taipei on New Year's Day, 1979, greatly saddened by the severance of diplomatic relations between our country and the United States. After almost eight years of continued tension we were both physically and emotionally exhausted. The change of pace accorded "an ambassador on home assignment" was therefore a welcome one. At President Chiang Ching-Kuo's suggestion, we rested and traveled on the island of Taiwan. Everywhere we went we saw our people working hard, confident of the future, despite our greatest diplomatic setback since the loss of the mainland to the Communists in 1949. We felt inspired and soon recovered our spirits. The question was: What should I do next? The answer practically suggested itself: Why not write my memoirs?

Fortunately, I have kept over the years a file of all my important papers, documents, dispatches, and notes of conversations with key figures in the Nixon, Ford, and Carter administrations, as well as clippings of news stories, magazine articles, and seminar papers on Sino-American relations. It took me almost a year to finish the first draft. On the whole I have used the chronological approach, with such cross-references as make the account easier to follow.

In October 1979, after having reached the age of three scores and ten, I retired from our Foreign Service into which I had blundered two decades earlier. I did this partly to free the Foreign Office from any responsibility for what I was writing and partly to have more time to spend on the memoirs.

But I remained undecided about whether to seek publication while I was still able to observe the reaction in the United States and in my own country to my account of the denouement of Washington-Taipei relations. Then one day I heard that Chang Chun, an elder statesman in my country who was for many decades personally involved in relations with both prewar and postwar Japan, had published his memoirs. Already in his early nineties, he admitted that he too had hesitated to publish for fear that the contents would unavoidably touch upon living Japanese personalities. But he had concluded that, Sino-Japanese relations having been terminated a number of years ago, whatever was top secret then had already lost its confidentiality. Besides, he said, he was anxious to leave behind him a record of what had happened so that people in both Japan and the Republic of China would know what had gone wrong and take care not to make the same mistakes again.

This sounded to me like valid reasoning. Practically all the American officials I dealt with when I was Chinese ambassador are still living. I am not so concerned about their sensitiveness;

since they are good at dishing it out to others, they ought to be equally good at taking it. What worries me more is the probable reaction of critics at home. But I hope they will understand.

Though I am some twenty years younger than Chang Chun, I too have come to the end of my career. Just as he worked tirelessly for the maintenance of Sino-Japanese relations, I have done my part in the preservation of Sino-American friendship. He was overwhelmed by events, and so was I.

I sincerely hope that the publication of my memoirs, almost four years after Carter recognized the Chinese Communist regime and severed diplomatic relations with the Republic of China, will have the effect of enhancing our common conviction that the American people and the free Chinese are natural allies, that they both stand to gain from having normal relations, and that they both are bound to suffer through prolonged estrangement. May the present abnormal situation turn out to be nothing but a transient phenomenon!

Chapter 1

Beginnings of Endings

My name will probably go down in history as the last Ambassador of the Republic of China to the United States. What a dubious distinction indeed! My only hope is that it will be an ephemeral one.

China and the United States established diplomatic relations on July 3, 1844, when the two countries signed the Treaty of Wanghia, known also as the Cushing Treaty. China's first diplomatic envoy, Chen Lan-ping, presented his credentials to President Rutherford B. Hayes in September 28, 1978. His official title was Imperial Emissary. This was during the days of the Manchus.

Following the revolution of October 10, 1911, China became a republic, but the United States withheld recognition until May 2, 1913, and the new Chinese Government did not send a full-time envoy to Washington until April 1914. This was Hsia Chia-fu, who bore the rank minister.

The two countries did not elevate the status of their diplomatic envoys to ambassador until May, 1935. Dr. Alfred Sze became China's first ambassador to Washington, and Sze was followed by Drs. C.T. Wang, Hu Shih, Wei Tao-ming, Wellington Koo, Hollington K. Tong, George Yeh, and T.F. Tsiang—all able men, though differing in their qualifications. My immediate predecessor, S.K. Chow, and I were the only two plain "Mr.s" in a long line of Ph.D.s or LL.D.s.

When I was appointed in April, 1971, a friend warned me that I might turn out to be the last Chinese ambassador from the Republic of China. That probability didn't stop me from taking the post. I went to Washington in May, fully determined to do my utmost to help preserve and, wherever possible, strengthen relations between our two countries. However, I had no illusions about what might lie ahead both for me personally and for the country I represented, because Sino-American relations had already begun to deteriorate.

The spring of 1971 was a crucial point in world history. Richard M. Nixon was already half-way through his first term as the thirty-seventh U.S. President. Realizing his own country's relative weakness at the time, he was seeking detente with the Soviet Union. The Vietnam war was in its fifth inconclusive year, with antiwar feelings running high in the U.S. On the Chinese mainland the highly disruptive Cultural Revolution had largely run its course. Two years earlier the Chinese and Russian Communist armies had clashed on a small islet in the Ussuri River.

From his vantage point in the White House, Nixon and his National Security Advisor, Henry Kissinger, must have seen in the steadily widening Peking-Moscow schism an opportunity not only to extricate the United States from the Vietnam war but also to pull the two Communist powers further apart. In retrospect it seems clear that the idea of playing the "China card" had already begun to take shape.

Between the second half of 1970 and the first three months of 1971, Nixon took a number of steps to ease restrictions on U.S. citizens who wanted to trade with or travel to the Chinese mainland. The real tipoff, however, was his order that the

Seventh Fleet discontinue its patrol of the Taiwan Straits. Outwardly this was done for reasons of economy. The subterfuge fooled nobody, however, and certainly not the people in our Foreign Office.

It was against this background that my government decided to recall S.K. Chow, who subsequently became Minister of Foreign Affairs, and to send me to Washington as the new ambassador. What was in our late President Chiang Kai-shek's mind when he authorized this switch—whether he needed a new minister in Taipei or a new envoy in Washington—was never made clear to me. At any rate, as it turned out, Chow held the ministerial portfolio for only one year, while I remained in Washington for seven years and eight months. Such are the vicissitudes of official life!

To this day it remains a mystery to me why I of all people in our Foreign Service was picked for this post. I know it wasn't President Chiang's own idea, for according to the then Vice-President and concurrently Premier C.K. Yen, the *Gimo* had asked him that very question. Yen's answer, as he related it to me later, was that in view of Nixon's moves vis-a-vis Peking, it was time to send a new ambassador to Washington; and that as I had worked as the *Gimo's* secretary-interpreter for many years, I was better acquainted with his views on world affairs than anybody else available. By that time I had been holding the post of second Vice-Minister in the Foreign Office for three years. To support his recommendation, which the then Vice-Premier Chiang Ching-kuo endorsed, Yen probably also reminded the *Gimo* of my American educational background, my working experience in the United States during World War II, plus the fact that I had come to know many American personages, political as well as journalistic, in the five years I had served as Director-General of the Government Information Office. Yen may also have added that I was fluent in English, articulate, and generally affable. The *Gimo*, I was told, didn't pursue the subject any further. Personally, I had a hunch that I was chosen not because of any of my credentials, but because of the belief that I would take the assignment without asking any questions; somebody else might have hesitated to accept the post in view of the growing uncertainty in Sino–American relations.

Dr. T.F. Tsiang, a scholar-diplomat and one of my illustrious predecessors in Washington, once said that it could be taken as the wish of every young Chinese who has ever studied political science or international relations in an American Ivy League university to become one day China's ambassador to the United States. That, however, was never my object. All I'd had in mind was to prepare myself for a newspaper career, as evidenced in my choosing to spend a year at the University of Missouri, not of the Ivy League, which had a reputable school of journalism. But through a combination of circumstances I happened to be on hand and ready when my government needed a new ambassador in Washington in the spring of 1971. When Foreign Minister Wei Tao-ming told me of the *Gimo's* final decision, I didn't even go through the gesture of declining the post, as one would have done under normal circumstances.

I arrived in Washington on May 10, 1971. At the Dulles International Airport I told U.S. and Chinese media representatives who met me that I firmly believed our two countries, aside from sharing the same ideals about freedom and democracy, also had important common interests, among which was the maintenance of peace and stability in East Asia. I pointed out that the Republic of China and the United States were allies by virtue of the Mutual Defense Treaty concluded in December, 1954. This treaty was a vital link in the offshore chain of collective defense that the United States had forged in cooperation with countries in the Western Pacific following the cessation of hostilities in Korea.

On the morning of May 18, 1971, I presented my credentials to President Nixon in the White House. In our conversation that followed the brief ceremony I promised him I would do everything I could to improve the relations between our two countries. He was very cordial and reminded me of his great friendship for the *Gimo* and Madame Chiang Kai-shek. But subsequent events showed that at that very moment he was secretly planning with Kissinger ways to establish contacts with Peking.

My first task in Washington as ambassador was to urge the U.S. Government to remain firm in its policy of safeguarding our membership in the United Nations. This question had become a perennial one after our withdrawal from the Chinese mainland in 1949. But every year with U.S. help, and that of many other free nations, we managed to stay in. The situation, however, had turned critical again following Canada's recognition of the Peking regime in October, 1970.

A fortnight before I was to leave for Washington, Nixon sent to Taipei a veteran U.S. diplomat, the late Robert Murphy, to explore with us the idea of admitting Peking into the United Nations while keeping us in at the same time. This was known as the "Dual Representation" formula. To make it more palatable to us Murphy intimated to President Chiang Kai-shek that we could keep our seat in the Security Council simply by co operating with the United States. There might even be a chance, he said, that the Chinese Communists would refuse to come in; in that case our position in the United Nations would remain unchanged, at least for some time to come.

President Chiang indicated that he would be willing to go along with the American plan provided the United States refrain from being a sponsor of Peking's admittance and also provided the United States take the lead again in rallying all like-minded nations to support the so-called "Important Question" formula that calls for a two-thirds majority vote in the General Assembly to expel a seated member. President Chiang also took the occasion to remind Murphy of President John F. Kennedy's pledge to use the veto power, if necessary, to preserve our seat in the United Nations.

The United States delayed finalizing its position for several weeks. Then, on July 15, 1971, came Nixon's sudden announcement that Kissinger had just made a secret trip to Peking and that he himself had accepted Chou En-lai's invitation to visit the Chinese mainland sometime before May, 1972. This was instantly interpreted in chancelleries all over the world as a sign that the United States was about to execute a volte-face in its China policy. When, in October, the matter finally came up for debate before the U.N. General Assembly, Kissinger was, by coincidence or design, in Peking for a second visit. This was ostensibly to arrange Nixon's trip, which would not actually take place until the last week of February, 1972—fully four months away. At any rate, Kissinger's timing tended to confirm to many of the nations prepared to vote in favor of the "Important Question" resolution that is would be futile to do so; after all, its key sponsor, the United States, was already wavering in its policy toward the Republic of China. When the preliminary resolution to determine whether the issue constituted an important question was defeated by a narrow margin on October 25, and just before the Albanian resolution calling for our displacement by Peking was put to vote, Foreign Minister S.K. Chow and the delegation he headed walked out of the United Nations. As expected, Peking was quickly admitted, and the U.S.-sponsored "Dual Representation" resolution died aborning. The United States probably meant well, but no one has explained to our satisfaction why there could be such an unbelievable lack of coordination between Washington's U.N. Ambassador George Bush, who was doing his best to defend our interests in the U.N., and National Security Advisor Kissinger, who was then being wined and dined by his new friends in Peking.

After we left the United Nations our international status plummeted. Practically overnight more than twenty nations switched diplomatic recognition from Taipei to Peking, despite the fact that the U.N. action was clearly in violation of its own Charter and against the very principles on which it was founded.

Ever since the loss of the Chinese mainland in 1949 our foreign policy had two principal objectives: first, to maintain our position in the United Nations and, second, to preserve our relations with the United States. The second objective became all the more important following the conclusion of the Sino-American Mutual Defense Treaty in December, 1954. Though no responsible official in our government had ever put it in so many words, the consensus was that if it should ever become impossible for us to keep both, we would rather forsake our membership in the United Nations than let anything happen to our relationship with the United States. After losing our seat in the world organization, naturally our government concentrated all its efforts on enhancing our ties with Washington. Herein lay my special responsibility.

Compared with Nixon's "bombshell" announcement of July 15, 1971, his trip to Peking in February, 1972, came almost as an anticlimax. There had been so much publicity about the trip during the intervening months that, when it actually took place, most people were already conditioned to treating it as a news extravaganza instead of a diplomatic event with serious portent for people in East Asia.

Nixon boastfully called the seven days he spent on the Chinese mainland "the week that changed the world"—without, however, specifying whether the change was for the better or for the worse. The way he humbled himself before Mao Tse-tung and Chou En-lai reminded me of the tribute-bearing foreign emissaries of previous centuries who went to Peking to pay homage at the Chinese Imperial Court. Nixon's hosts must have laughed in their sleeves at his behavior during their meetings.

The Shanghai Communique which Nixon signed with Chou En-lai on February 28, at the end of the visit, presaged the "normalization of relations" between Peking and Washington seven years later. It was a most unusual document in diplomatic history in that it was signed between a U.S. president and the head of a government that had not been recognized. Normally, it would not have the force of even an executive agreement. And yet, as subsequent events proved, it turned out to be more binding on the U.S. Government than had it been a treaty ratified by two-thirds of the U.S. Senate. In the end it led to the abrogation, at the end of December, 1979, of the Mutual Defense Treaty with the Republic of China.

Besides stating the respective positions of the two parties, Nixon and Chou En-lai agreed to move toward the normalization of relations between the PRC and the USA; to refrain from seeking hegemony in the Asia-Pacific region and to oppose efforts by any other country or group of countries to establish such hegemony; and to refrain from negotiating on behalf of any third party or entering into agreements or understandings with any third party that were directed at the other side.

What is meant by "normalization of relations?" Though this expression appears no less than four times in the Shanghai Communique, it is nowhere defined in it. Probably Nixon and Kissinger kept it deliberately vague, but this subsequently played into the Chinese Communists' hands. Before long they were claiming the communique had committed the U.S. Government to severing diplomatic relations with the Republic of China, to abrogating the Mutual Defense Treaty, and to withdrawing all U.S. military forces and installations from Taiwan. Though Nixon did not stay in the White House long enough to do all this himself, he certainly paved the way for Carter, who did it with gusto in mid-December, 1978.

The Nixon visit and the Shanghai Communique naturally upset my government very much. I was instructed to seek clarifications as well as reassurances from Nixon himself at the earliest opportunity. This I did on March 6, 1972. Among the first things he said to me was: "Mr. Ambassador, between our two countries we have a Mutual Defense Treaty. Please tell your government that the United States is determined to abide by its commitments to the Republic of China."

Another remarkable statement Nixon made to me on that occasion was that "the communique is not a treaty but a joint statement in which each side stated its positions on various subjects without trying to reach an agreement." He added that there were no secret deals of any kind and that he was not one to negotiate the fate of other countries behind their backs.

On the question of Taiwan, Nixon said he had emphasized to Chou En-lai the U.S. Government's position: that the matter be settled by peaceful means, leaving the actual process or procedure to the two parties directly concerned to work out between themselves. "Did Chou En-lai promise not to use force against Taiwan?" I asked. Nixon's answer was "No."

The day after I saw Nixon for this unusual conversation, I flew to Taipei to report to President Chiang Kai-shek. He looked serious but was not visibly disturbed. By his questions I could tell that he had read my dispatches. At the end of the audience he said: "Henceforth we must rely on ourselves more than ever before." This reminded me of his warning in 1970 of coming storms, calling on our people "not to be upset in time of adversity but remain firm with dignity and strive to be self-reliant with vigor."

In the latter part of March, shortly after my return to Washington, the U.S. and Chinese Communist ambassadors met in Paris. As this was their first meeting after a lapse of many months, it aroused our concern, especially when it followed so closely on Nixon's visit to Peking. I was instructed to ask the State Department for a fill-in on what had been discussed, as had been done on all previous occasions. Their answer was a very vague one. I was told: "Only inconsequential matters were discussed." This further aroused our suspicions, so I asked to see Kissinger. He procrastinated until May 3, when he said that no political problems, but only matters pertaining to the exchange of medical and scientific personnel, had been discussed.

Early in June, Kissinger went to Tokyo to brief the Japanese Government on what had happened during Nixon's trip to Moscow in the last week of May. I saw Kissinger on June 13. He told me that he strongly suspected that the Japanese Government was about to recognize Peking. He claimed he had repeatedly assured Japanese officials that in its policy toward Peking the United States would not exceed the limits set by the Shanghai Communique and would maintain its diplomatic ties and Mutual Defense Treaty commitments with the Republic of China. If, as he maintained, he had urged the Japanese Government to coordinate its policies with the United States, his recommendation was completely ignored: The Tanaka government took the irrevocable step of recognizing Peking and breaking its diplomatic relations with us and—the following September—terminating its Peace Treaty with us.

Japan's switch was a most traumatic experience for us. Our people felt terribly hurt after what we had done for Japan at the end of the Pacific War. But to keep the record straight, the Japanese Government at no time kept us in the dark with regard to its intention to recognize Peking.

In February, 1973, Kissinger went to Peking again. Before leaving Washington he told me that he would not discuss the question of recognition on this trip. As it turned out, he took half a step toward "normalization of relations" by agreeing to an exchange of liaison offices, which were quickly set up that May, to function very much as embassies, except in name. When I called on Kissinger on February 21, the day after his return to Washington, he handed me a copy of the joint communique he had signed in Peking. He said the liaison offices would have absolutely no diplomatic status and their function would be limited to matters of trade and cultural and scientific exchanges. Future contacts of a diplomatic nature would be maintained in Paris, as before.

What about U.S. relations with the Republic of China? Kissinger said they would remain unchanged, Mutual Defense

Treaty and all. But for how much longer? "Till the end of 1974 at least," he said, but he quickly qualified his statement by saying that this did not mean there necessarily would be changes after that.

Our Foreign Office reacted very strongly to the exchange of liaison offices between Washington and Peking. Besides issuing a public statement reiterating our position, it instructed me to complain to Secretary of State William P. Rogers that this would greatly injure our national interests and damage Sino–American friendship. The U.S. move, I was ordered to add, would encourage countries in Southeast Asia to establish contacts with the Chinese Communists, thereby upsetting the balance of power in the area.

Rogers was somewhat taken aback by our reactions. He promised to ask someone in the State Department to brief me on details. He also revealed that while in Paris he had met Chi Peng-fei, Peking's Foreign Minister, and that they had arrived at a tentative agreement on the question of frozen assets, whereby Chinese assets seized by the U.S. Government on American territory following the fall of the Chinese mainland to the Communists would be used to compensate American citizens and firms for their properties seized by the Communists on the mainland at the same time.

In September, 1973, Kissinger replaced (or, to be more accurate, displaced) Rogers as Secretary of State, while remaining Nixon's National Security Advisor. In mid-November he was in Peking again and held wide-ranging talks with Mao Tse-tung, Chou En-lai, and others. On November 14 the State Department issued a communique officially declaring the expansion of the area "where both Washington and Peking would be opposed to the establishment of hegemony by any other country or group of countries from the Asia–Pacific region as mentioned in the Shanghai Communique to any other part of the world." On the question of "normalization of relations" Peking had included a subtle statement to the effect that this "can be realized only on the basis of confirming the principle of one China." What did Peking mean by this? No one could be sure at the time.

When I saw Kissinger on November 19, he assured me that there would be no dramatic developments in U.S. relations with Peking, nor would there be any changes in U.S. relations with the Republic of China, including the Mutual Defense Treaty of 1954.

This marked my first and last meaningful meeting with Kissinger after he became Secretary of State. After that, whenever I asked to see him, he referred me to his deputy Kenneth Rush and, later on, Robert Ingersoll. Why did he decide to avoid me? One possibility was that he had found it painful to keep up the pretense that nothing had changed in our relations even as the United States was moving closer to Peking.

There was little or no movement in Washington-Peking relations in 1974, the year that saw the Watergate scandal, Nixon's resignation under the threat of impeachment, the assumption of the presidency by Gerald Ford. Kissinger, who stayed on as Secretary of State, went to Peking again in November, 1974, and obtained an invitation for Ford to visit the Chinese mainland the following year. But he didn't get to see Mao Tse-tung this time. Was this Peking's subtle way of indicating displeasure at the lack of momentum toward normalization of relations three years after Nixon's visit?

In April, 1975, people in the Republic of China were in deep mourning over the death of their beloved national leader, President Chiang Kai-shek. In a deliberate move to downgrade Sino-American relations, Washington at first decided to send Earl Butz, Secretary of Agriculture, to attend the *Gimo's* funeral, but later changed its mind and sent Vice-President Nelson Rockefeller. Taipei was too grief-stricken to mind, but the free Chinese would have felt better had Rockefeller been chosen in the first place.

Before the month of April was out Cambodia and then South Vietnam fell into the hands of the Communists. The U.S. Congress, by withholding military aid, caused the South Vietnamese regime to surrender without a fight. As if to appease its own conscience, the United States started a large-scale refugee rescue program at the last minute. It had no idea that thousands upon thousands of Vietnamese—the "boat people," as they became known—would try to escape.

The betrayal of South Vietnam gave the Republic of China a breathing spell. People high in U.S. government were overheard to say that "selling one ally down the river was quite enough for one year without abandoning another—the Republic of China." Ford went to Peking before the year ended and obviously pleaded for more time. He probably asked Peking to be patient till he had won a term as president in his own right in November, 1976. But he didn't make it.

Throughout 1976 there was again no significant movement in U.S. policy to China. It was the year of the Bicentennial. Various countries were encouraged to send art exhibits, dramatic troupes, or singing groups to America to help celebrate the occasion, but the Republic of China was told to avoid doing anything of the kind lest the Chinese Communists be tempted to do the same; the State Department didn's wish to be placed in the position of having to say no to Peking. The reasoning was utterly illogical, considering the fact that the Republic of China had been a friend and ally of the United States for many, many years, whereas the Peking regime, an enemy in the Korean War, still had no diplomatic relations with the U.S.

In order not to disappoint our people, all of whom had the friendliest of feelings for the United States, our government did not publicize Washington's unusual stand on this matter. Since the U.S. Government looked upon us as poor relations who were unfit to help celebrate the American people's two hundredth anniversary, there was nothing we could do about it. To keep up appearances various public organizations in Taiwan were encouraged to go to the United States to offer felicitations. We also contributed a two-hundred-foot-long dragon made of Chinese silk for the Fourth of July parade organized by the District of Columbia (the city, as distinguished from the Federal Government or any of its agencies), which was given in the name of the District's Chinese community. Those who saw it prance and dance down Constitution and Pennsylvania avenues that day had no idea that the State Department had forbidden us to make any show at all of our felicity.

Another reason for the absence of movement in U.S.-China relations in 1976 was that it was the year of the presidential election. State primaries and then the two national conventions largely preempted everybody's attention for many months, leaving little to spare for demarches in the field of foreign affairs. President Ford apparently believed that Peking understood it had to wait till he became an elected president before he could act on such a controversial matter. As for Carter, he was still busy scheming with his Georgia friends about how to capture the White House from the Republicans. Had Ford acted on the China question, I have little doubt but that Carter, for political reasons, would have seized upon it as a campaign issue and criticized the administration for abandoning the Republic of China. Remember how Nixon attacked John F. Kennedy for the latter's willingness to let the Chinese Communists have Quemoy and Matsu in 1960, only to take the initiative himself in reopening contacts with Peking in 1971?

A third reason for lack of movement on the "normalization of relations" issue in 1976 was the ever-present political instability in Peking, made more serious this time by the death of Chou En-lai in January and that of Mao Tse-tung in September. This was followed in October by Hua Kuo-feng's preventive coup d'etat against Chiang Ching, Mao's widow, and three of her henchmen—the so-called "Gang of Four."

Chou En-lai was generally believed to have been the kingpin in the Communist regime for a quarter-century. By all accounts it was he who first realized the need of "reopening to the U.S." following the Soviet invasion of Czechoslovakia in 1968 and the Ussuri River clash in February, 1969. It was also he who hammered out the final details of the Shanghai Communique with Kissinger during Nixon's visit to Peking in February, 1972. He died a virtual prisoner of the "Gang of Four."

In the spring of 1976 there was information from reliable sources that staff work on "normalization of relations" went on without let-up both in the White House and the State Department. If Ford failed to win his party's nomination in August or the presidential election in November, he would move quickly to normalize relations with Peking so that he could claim the "credit" for finishing what Nixon had started in 1971–72. With Kissinger at his side, no one could say for sure what Ford would not do before he left the White House.

Although "normalization of relations" between Washington and Peking was not an issue in the 1976 presidential campaign, Carter did address the question twice during the campaign. In his televised debate with Ford on October 6 he said: "I would certainly pursue the normalization of relations with the PRC... But I would never let that friendship stand in the way of preservation of the independence and freedom of the people on Taiwan." Then in his news conference in Kansas City on October 15, he proclaimed: "We are bound by a treaty to guarantee the freedom of Formosa, Taiwan, the Republic of China. I would like to improve our relationship—diplomatic relationship with PRC, mainland China, hopefully leading to normalization of [diplomatic] relations sometime in the future. But I wouldn't go back on the commitment that we have had to assure that Taiwan is protected from military takeover."

If we harbored any hope that Carter might downgrade the Shanghai Communique, it was soon dashed by Cyrus Vance, the incoming Secretary of State, when he stated on January 8, 1977, following his first meeting with Hwang Chen, Peking's unofficial ambassador in Washington: "Insofar as our bilateral relations with China are concerned, they would be guided by the Shanghai Communique." Then in his speech before the U.N. General Assembly on March 17, Vance gave added significance to the U.S. goal of normalizing relations with Peking: "We will continue our efforts to develop further our relationships with the People's Republic of China. We recognize our parallel strategic interests in maintaining stability in Asia and we will act in the spirit of the Shanghai Communique."

Our apprehensions were compounded when I met with endless stalling in my requests to see the new President Carter and his top aides. I even had difficulty in getting an appointment to see Secretary Vance until September, 1977, a month after his visit to Peking, and it came about only after some friends on Capitol Hill had interceded on my behalf.

It was said that Vance's trip to Peking in August was for the sole purpose of holding "exploratory talks." According to Teng Hsiao-ping, with whom Vance did most of the "exploration," Vance offered to upgrade to an embassy the U.S. liaison office in Peking and to downgrade to a liaison office the U.S. embassy in Taipei. Teng rejected this on the ground that this would still mean government-to-government relations between Washington and Taipei. Teng also challenged Carter's description of the Vance trip as a "success." He said that as a result of Vance's visit, relations between Washington and Peking actually had moved backwards.

Nothing much happened after these August "exploratory talks" until Carter's National Security Advisor, Zbigniew Brzezinski, went to Peking in May, 1978. To allay apprehensions in Taiwan and possible objections on Capitol Hill, Brzezinski's trip was described as one of consultation "on a broad range of issues," and not one of negotiating normalization. In a dinner toast in Peking he told his hosts that the United States did not view its relationship with Peking as a tactical expedient; it was based on shared concerns and derived from a long-term strategic view "to resist the efforts of any nation which seeks to establish global or regional hegemony."

On the same occasion Brzezinski announced "three U.S. fundamental beliefs:" that friendship between the United States and the People's Republic of China is vital and beneficial to world peace; that a secured and strong China is in America's interest; and that a powerful, confident and globally engaged United States is in China's interest. He also declared that the United States had made up its mind on the question of "normalization of relations" with the People's Republic of China. In yet another dinner toast Brzezinski said he found his talks with his hosts "useful, important and constructive." He added that "only those aspiring to dominate others have any reason to fear the further development of American-Chinese relations."

Richard Holbrooke, Assistant Secretary of State for East Asian and Pacific Affairs, accompanied Brzezinski on the trip to Peking. I saw him shorly after his return to Washington. He strongly suggested I reread Brzezinski's two dinner toasts, as if they were not clear enough. This deepened my belief that the Carter administration had decided to normalize relations with Peking on the latter's terms, waiting only for a face-saving formula and an opportune moment to announce it.

Also contributing to this belief was the fact that Brzezinski chose to arrive in Peking on May 20, which happened to be the day of Chiang Ching-kuo's inauguration as the President of the Republic of China. All our efforts to persuade the Carter administration to change Brzezinski's itinerary were to no avail. Clearly the latter had decided already to go ahead on the matter of normalization, regardless of how our government and people felt about it.

Brzezinski's visit was followed by two other actions. One was the dispatch of a high-level U.S. science and technology mission headed by Dr. Frank Press, science advisor to the White House.

The other was to permit the sale of arms to the Chinese Communists by the Western European countries.

By November, 1978, information from various sources indicated that Leonard Woodcock, U.S. liaison office chief in Peking, had been in constant touch with Huang Hua, the Communist Foreign Minister and other officials. The State Department would not reveal to us the subjects being discussed. Nor would they say whether Woodcock was engaged in serious negotiations on the question of normalization of relations. Until two or three days before Carter's December 15 announcement, the State Department spokesman was still saying that no decisions had been reached on the timing and the modality for normalization of relations with Peking. Meanwhile, the administration had been keeping Congress, including its leadership, completely in the dark. Then, taking advantage of the Christmas holidays, during which no one was watching on Capitol Hill, Carter sprang his surprise. Judging by the way he broke the news, he was having the time of his life with it.

Before France recognized the People's Republic of China in January, 1964, President Charles de Gaulle sent a personal emissary to Taipei to inform us of his decision and to give reasons for the decision. When Canada was negotiating with Peking for establishment of diplomatic relations in October, 1970, its Foreign Office kept our ambassador in Ottawa informed all the time. Even Japan, the enemy in World War II, sent a top envoy to Taipei in September, 1972, before the Tanaka government, alarmed by the "Nixon shock" of 1971, switched recognition from Taipei to Peking. But the United States, an ally and a friend, did nothing of the kind when the Carter administration embraced the Chinese Communist regime, its Korean War enemy and behind-the-scenes Vietnam war enemy, and terminated its diplomatic relations and subsequently its defense ties with the Republic of China.

Chapter II

Rejoining the Government

My seven-and-a-half-year tour of duty in the United States actually began with a two-week vacation in Taipei in the spring of 1956. By training I am a journalist. After a year at the University of Missouri's School of Journalism in the mid-1930s, I went back to China. Soon the Sino–Japanese War (1937–45) broke out, and as a form of patriotic service, I joined the Ministry of Information. In 1943 I was sent to San Francisco, where I headed the Pacific Coast bureau for four years. Recalled in 1947, when the Chinese Government had moved back to Nanking from its wartime capital in Chungking in West China, I was put in charge of the overseas operations of the Government Information Office (GIO) under Hollington K. Tong. By the end of 1948 the Chinese Communist army was coming down from the North China plain to threaten the Nanking–Shanghai area. Tong decided to send me to Hong Kong to set up a new GIO office. The following spring, after the fall of Nanking, the GIO was dissolved. For the first time in about thirteen years I was detached from the Chinese Government, and I resumed my newspaper career. For the next seven years I made a living in Hong Kong by writing, translating, and radio programming, but somehow I wasn't happy with what I was doing. I felt stifled and was looking for a change. As many of my former GIO colleagues were in Taiwan, I decided to pay them a visit.

From Hong Kong I had kept a close watch on events in Taiwan. I was glad to see how quickly the government had got hold of itself there, using the breathing spell provided by the Korean War to reorganize the administrative machinery, develop economic resources, and, above all, implement a land reform program to help the farmers, who, at the time, constituted a great majority of the population. The Sino–American Mutual Defense Treaty, signed in December, 1954, had been in effect for more than a year, instilling in everybody a sense of security that simply hadn't been there in earlier years.

In retrospect I couldn't have chosen a better time to go to Taiwan. President Chiang, seventy years of age, was writing his memoirs. With editorial help from Tao Hsi-sheng, a scholar and political writer, the President was revising the manuscript one chapter at a time. Several people were enlisted to translate it into English. As different translaters had different styles, this was not a satisfactory arrangement. Tao was on the lookout for someone to do it alone when I happened on the scene. My friends urged me to accept the assignment. It was a challenge to my professional ability, and I took the job on a one-project basis. But instead of spending two weeks, as I originally had planned, I had to extend my "vacation." Working morning, afternoon, and evening, seven days a week for six consecutive weeks, I managed to rough out a full translation of the book—almost four hundred printed pages when eventually published by Farrar, Straus and Cudahy of New York.

I took my fee and was about to leave when the President summoned me to his office in downtown Taipei. He was curious to find out who had managed to translate his book in record time. He asked me about my background, and I provided the details right up through the last seven years in Hong Kong. Suddenly he stated that he wanted me to rejoin the government. I felt honored by the invitation, thanked him, and gave him a polite but noncommittal answer. I wasn't sure whether he had uttered these words out of politeness or had really meant what he said.

During the war with Japan I had seen the President several times, but usually at a great distance listening to his speech. Once I had actually shaken hands with him. But on none of these occasions did I have the feeling of being drawn toward him. This time, however, I was actually facing him across his desk in a simply furnished room, talking to him, and answering his questions. He seemed interested in hearing what I had to say. He was warm, courteous, earnest. I was greatly impressed by his benign attitude and moved by his sincere dedication to our nation. I decided there and then that if the President should really send for me, I would respond without any hesitation. It would be an honor and a privilege to help him in whatever small way I could in his effort to rejuvenate the nation after the debacle on the mainland.

Shortly after my return to Hong Kong I received letters and telegrams from my friends in Taipei telling me that the President had appointed me his secretary with a twofold responsibility: first, to help put the final touches on the English version of his book and, second, to serve as his secretary-interpreter whenever he had English-speaking visitors. In August of the same year I moved my family to Taipei and rejoined the government.

My first meeting with Madame Chiang Kai-shek, however, was hardly a reassuring one. One day, shortly after I had joined the President's staff, I was asked to see her at their residence in Shihlin (Scholars' Woods) on the outskirts of Taipei. I was told to carry with me my translation of the President's book. The moment I was ushered into her presence, and without any preliminaries, she asked me point-blank who had done the translation. I said I had. Then she wanted to know how she could be sure my translation was correct. I said I had exercised great care but that of course I couldn't guarantee that my understanding of the Chinese original was completely correct or that my English rendition was appropriate. After bidding me to sit down in a chair opposite her, she continued: The "Chief" (meaning the President) had asked her to check my translation. As she had so many other things to do, how could she possibly find the time, since it would take at least several weeks to do the checking even if she stopped doing everything else? She fingered through my translation, which came to six or seven hundred typewritten foolscap sheets. Apparently she was staggered by the amount of work that would be required. Then she dismissed me and went upstairs. She was obviously high-strung! Had I done or said anything to upset her? I couldn't help wondering.

A few days later I saw Dr. George Yeh, the Foreign Minister then, and I related what had happened. He told me not to worry. As a matter of fact, he said, Madame Chiang had in the meantime asked him about my background. The fact that I had been on Dr. Hollington K. Tong's staff (Tong was by this time our ambassador in Washington) seemed to allay any misgivings she might have had about me—my reliability and capability. Later on I learned that in the past she herself had picked all the President's English-language secretaries; this time she had not been consulted. In a way I didn't blame her for having any reservations about me. I was, after all, a total stranger to her. Anyone appointed the President's secretary-interpreter would necessarily be privy to a great deal of confidential information. She was merely looking after the President's and also the nation's interests. Not long afterwards Dr. Yeh told me that Madame Chiang was reasonably satisfied with my translation, and he told me not to give the matter another thought.

Before long the grueling editing sessions got under way. At first they were held in Madame Chiang's study in the official presidential residence at Shihlin. She had asked Dr. Yeh to sit in. We would meet every afternoon to check my translation against the Chinese text for veracity as well as language. We went over it sentence by sentence and paragraph by paragraph. Every now and then we came upon a sentence or two in which Madame Chiang thought the President had been too straight-forward and not diplomatic enough. In such cases changes were made with the President's permission.

These editing sessions usually began in the afternoon because in the morning Madame Chiang had to attend to her other duties as First Lady, and so the three of us really plugged away. There were times we would stop for a cup of tea, and if the President and Madame Chiang had no guests, we often stayed for dinner and then carried on well into the night. From time to time the President, clad in his Chinese long gown, would stroll in to talk to Madame Chiang or just to ask how we were getting along. Both Dr. Yeh and I would, of course, stand up right away, but he would bid us to remain seated. Obviously he was anxious to see his book published as soon as possible.

At one time the editing sessions were shifted to the President's villa at Sun–Moon Lake, a scenic spot high in the mountains in the central part of the island. It was one of the President's favorite places for rest and meditation. He would go there three or four times a year to think things over, especially when he had some important decisions to make. For several weeks Dr. Yeh had left his responsibilities in the Foreign Office to his subordinates and took up full-time work with Madame Chiang and me in order to get the text to the printer before the end of the year.

The book came out under the title *Soviet Russia in China—A Summing Up at Seventy by Chiang Kai-shek*. It was serialized in *Life* magazine as part of the publisher's sales promotion. Farrar, Straus and Cudahy publicized the fact that the English transla-tion had been prepared under Madame Chiang's personal supervision, and nowhere in the book was I mentioned as the translator. I didn't ask for any credit or acknowledgement, and didn't expect any. What I received was something far more substantive—cash, of which I was badly in need, because my salary as a presidential secretary was a mere pittance, not even enough to pay my monthly rent.

In the introduction to his book the President wrote:

> In presenting this record to the world, I am filled with mixed feelings. On the one hand, I am fully aware that my country has been a victim of circumstances which drove her to temporary alignment with Soviet Russia on more than one occasion in spite of the known treacherous character and the aggressive aim of International Communism. On the other, I can lay claim to the proud fact that I have incessantly fought Communist aggression and Communist ideas for the last thirty-odd years. Like Dr. Sun himself, who on signing the agreement with Joffe (a representative of the Third International) declared that Communism was totally unsuitable to the needs of the Chinese people and, therefore, could not be endorsed by Kuomintang (Chinese Nationalist Party), I remain firmly convinced that the only road open to the Chinese people is that marked out by Dr. Sun's Three Principles of the People (Nationalism, Democracy and People's Livelihood).

The President hoped that his book would prove instructive to countries and governments and especially those in Asia that were facing the same threat of Communism. "If this book can in any way help enhance the vigilance and determination of those who are defending the cause of freedom and democracy and to bring home to the avowed neutralists the realization that they are unwittingly serving the Communist purpose, my labor will have been rewarded and the great sacrifice that the Chinese people have made will not have been in vain," he said.

By its very nature the President's book was not destined to make the best-seller list. Though the sales were quite encouraging at the beginning, they soon began to taper off. In Washington, Ambassador Tong was asked to submit a weekly report on sales. When it seemed the first edition *would* be sold out, it was decided to bring out a second edition. The same editing procedure was followed, though this time Dr. Yeh was spared and Dr. Beauson Tseng, a former Christian college president and scholar, was brought in to take his place. The three of us sat down for several weeks, fine-combing the first edition with a view to improving its readability. Looking back, I really feel that the biggest reward for my contribution to the President's book was the opportunity to work under Madame Chiang. She is a most brilliant lady: an eloquent speaker, a superb writer, and also a talented painter. As she came to know me better she became very kind to me and my family.

Perhaps the President waited too long to write his memoirs. Had he written them shortly after the fall of the Chinese mainland in 1949–50, a time when the "Who Lost China?" debate was going on in the United States, the book would have found a much more receptive audience. But by 1956–57 the Western reader's interest in China had waned. And this interest was not to be revived until Nixon's "reopening to China" in the early 1970s.

Even before the President's book was out of the way I began to work as his English-language secretary. My duties were many. As he carried on personal correspondence with foreign chiefs of state and heads of government, I had to draft letters for his signature. Whenever he received English-speaking visitors—foreign ministers, diplomats, scholars, business tycoons—I sat in as the interpreter. If the subject of conversation was an important one, I had to prepare a resume for him immediately afterwards. Sometimes he would direct that a copy be sent to the visitor. Other times he just wanted to have it for the record.

Whenever the First Couple had dinner guests at their residence or in the Presidential Office Building in downtown Taipei, the male guest of honor would be seated on Madame Chiang's right and his wife on the President's right. I would be placed to the right of the lady guest so that I could follow the flow of conversation and provide a running translation back and forth. The first few times I had no time to eat anything and went home hungry; my wife had to cook a bowl of noodles for me before I went to bed. Later on someone on the President's household staff advised me to take one small bite at a time, chew, and swallow quickly whenever the host or the guest was talking. Before long I discovered that the dinner table conversation followed certain patterns, and often I could anticipate the topics.

What I found most difficult was interpreting after-dinner speeches. The President was accustomed to having an interpreter on hand all the time, so he would stop speaking after a few sentences to give me time to interpret. He was in fact easy to follow; each passage or paragraph was complete in itself. Some of his guests, however, lacking his experience, would go on without stop, completely forgetting that I was there to interpret for them. In such cases I had to take notes in my own form of shorthand and give the President a summary in Chinese. This was not a satisfactory way because many of the details were apt to be left out of such necessarily abbreviated translations.

Besides being a Confucian scholar the President was trained as a soldier. He was most methodical in his ways of doing things, and he had a highly disciplined mind. He believed in preparing himself before he received any important foreign visitor. He would read the biographical materials prepared by his staff (in the case of a foreign statesman or diplomat the dossier was assembled by the Foreign Office) and would even write out in Chinese longhand the questions he intended to ask and the points he wanted to make and show them to me half an hour before the meeting was to take place. This made my job much easier.

As was generally known, the President knew little English. Madame Chiang usually sat in on all important discussions and did not hesitate to interrupt the interpreter whenever she felt this was called for. This could be quite unnerving for a beginner. I know, for I was one, never before having done any interpreting. Simultaneous translation is not quite the same thing as translating an article or a book. There, one has time to choose words or expressions. In interpreting, one has no time to grope for words.

While the President spoke no English, he apparently had a definite idea of how it should sound. One day Madame Chiang told me that the President did not like my singsong tone when I interpreted. It seems that I tended to start at a low key and then move up the scale as I went on. This upset the President so much that he once asked a retired admiral who was educated in England to interpret for him while I listened in on the side. I thought that was the end of my job as the President's secretary. Again, I confided my fears to Dr. George Yeh. As before, he told me not to worry. A few days later Madame Chiang revealed to me that she had dissuaded the President from obtaining a new interpreter, because, as she put it, I was the most competent secretary–interpreter the President had had in all these years.

I went back to interpreting for the President, but I did try to minimize what seemed to have irritated him so very much. Throughout my ten years as his interpreter I gave the President no further grounds for complaint.

Did the President really know no English at all? I won't say so. After all, he had studied English for a year or two in his high school days, his teacher having been none other than Hollington K. Tong. Once at a dinner the President was asked whether he had ever studied English. He said he had but that he'd had a bad teacher and hadn't learned much. "Who was your teacher?" With a wry smile the President pointed to Tong, also present at the dinner, saying "There was my teacher!" What a sense of humor! I can still remember how Tong squirmed in his seat that evening.

I believe the President knew a sufficient number of English words to be able to follow a conversation. Several times while interpreting I left out a couple of points he had made toward the end of his passage-by-passage delivery, and he would repeat those very points without my having asked him for help. If he couldn't follow the conversation, how could he have known the points I had left out?

I worked as the President's interpreter longer than any previous secretary. During the first three years I had my office in the Presidential Office Building itself. For the following two years I was the Foreign Office spokesman and for the subsequent five years I was Director-General of the Government Information Office. During the entire period the President had a steady stream of VIP visitors. Among them were King Hussein of the Hashemite Kingdom of Jordan, Shah Mohammad Reza Pahlavi of Iran, President Dwight D. Eisenhower, Vice-President Lyndon B. Johnson, former Vice-President Richard Nixon, Vice-President Spiro T. Agnew. Then there were John Foster Dulles, Dean Rusk, and Averell Harriman, U.S. senators and congressmen, and top-notch journalists from the United States. They all sought the President's views on the world situation in general and the Asian situation in particular. Without mincing words he would comment on his favorite theme, namely, the insidious scheme of the international Communists to conquer the free world. Even after Moscow and Peking began to quarrel on ideological matters he doubted the reality of their quarrel. Till he died in April, 1975, he held onto the belief that despite their conflicts and contradictions the Chinese Communists had more in common with the Soviet Union than with the United States or other members of the free world and that the two could patch up their differences someday.

To return to the President's visitors. It was fascinating to watch how he talked to King Hussein of Jordan. There was a disparity of some forty years in their ages, they belonged to two different generations, yet the two hit it off very well, the President talking like an uncle and the young King as a deferential and respectful nephew. At the time, Jordan was faced with a two-front threat: from Nasser's Egypt on the one hand and from a burgeoning Israel on the other. The President's advice was that Jordan could not afford to antagonize both neighbors; the King must make a choice and act accordingly.

The Shah's visit was a formal and highly ceremonial one. There were exchanges of decorations, banquets, and toasts. With the black gold already gushing from his country's wells, the Iranian monarch did not show much interest in what the Republic of China had to offer in agricultural know-how, commerce, and cultural interflow. One day one of his aides hinted that the monarch, a man in the prime of his life, away from home almost a week, might welcome some relaxation. Realizing what the aide had in mind, our protocol officer politely suggested that as His Majesty would soon be in Japan, he would surely find things much more agreeable there. To our great relief this subject never came up again during the visit.

President Eisenhower's visit in 1960 was the climax of postwar Sino American relations. He was the first U.S. President to visit any part of China while in office. He came to Taipei more than a decade after the Communist seizure of the mainland and six years after the signing of the Mutual Defense Treaty. The Chinese Communists indicated their displeasure by bombarding Quemoy for several days. The visit was the biggest news event after the Quemoy crisis of 1958. Scores of American newspapermen and cameramen and TV and radio commentators came with him. As head of the Government Information Office, I sat in on the meetings of the two presidents and interpreted for both of them during discussions and at banquets. I also interpreted for President Eisenhower when he addressed a rally of half a million people in Taipei's Presidential Plaza. In between I held briefings for the local press while James Haggerty, the White House Press Secretary, took care of the U.S. media representatives. I had never worked so hard in my life. The U.S. delegation brought some silver coins with Ike's image on them and passed them out to many of our people, but no one remembered to give me one. It didn't really matter, for among my treasured possessions today are two pictures—one showing the two presidents leaving Taipei's international airport and the other showing me at the mass rally in front of a microphone only five feet away from President Eisenhower, whose words I was translating as he spoke.

During the same ten-year span I helped five American ambassadors in their conversations with President Chiang: Karl L. Rankin, Everett F. Drumright, Admiral Alan G. Kirk, Admiral Jerauld Wright, and Walter P. McConaughy, to place them in chronological sequence. Both Drumright and McConaughy knew Chinese, having been language students early in their careers, but not really conversant enough with it to hold a serious discussion.

Rankin, a career diplomat, was well liked and respected. So were the other two careerists, Drumright and McConaughy. All three were fond of the Chinese people and enjoyed being with them while carefully watching over U.S. interests and meticulously carrying out U.S. policies. The two admiral-ambassadors were themselves two worlds apart. Kirk, now deceased, remained very much a seadog in both speech and mannerism. He was curt and seldom smiled, while Wright, a bit hard of hearing, was always courteous. There is a Chinese saying: "One who does not know how to smile has no business to be in business." How much truer is this of people engaged in the business of diplomacy!

Rankin was the first U.S. Ambassador in Taiwan. He presented his credentials on April 2, 1953, almost four years after the day in August, 1949, when Dr. J. Leighton Stuart terminated his mission in Nanking. For a while the United States practically wrote off Taiwan. It was the Korean War which caused a change in its attitude. Rankin was warmly received in Taipei.

He and Mrs. Rankin soon were frequent visitors in the home of President and Madame Chiang.

In the summer of 1956 there was an ugly incident in Taipei. An American serviceman killed a Chinese and was acquitted by an American military tribunal. Applause by friends of the accused in the courtroom angered the local inhabitants, and many of them turned up in front of the U.S. embassy to demonstrate against such a "gross injustice." This developed into a riot, during which some of the demonstrators, mostly young people, broke into the embassy and ransacked some of the rooms before Chinese troops were brought in from outside the city to restore law and order.

It happened that neither the President nor Rankin was in town that day. The former was resting at Sun-Moon Lake and the latter was visiting in Hong Kong. Both rushed back to Taipei. When Rankin called on the President a few days after the incident, he was unruffled and did not raise his voice or show any emotion. He looked serious but spoke softly. The President apologized, saying it was due largely to a lack of understanding of the American judicial system on the part of the Chinese people. He assured the Ambassador that the Chinese Government would pay for the damage done to the embassy and to other U.S. buildings in Taipei. The two then went on to have tea. Not another word about the incident was said by either party before the Ambassador rose to thank his host for his hospitality. That, to me, was diplomacy of the highest order, and I was very pleased to have been the "human instrumentality" that provided the necessary linguistic link on that occasion.

In his dealings with American ambassadors the President was usually courteous and considerate. He always paid close attention to what they had to say and phrased his answers in a polite way. Only once in my experience did he show impatience or abruptness. This was at the time of the Lhasa uprising in March, 1959. He summoned Drumright to his villa on Grass Mountain, fifteen kilometers away from Taipei. The President had wanted the United States to airdrop some military and civilian supplies to the Tibetan freedom fighters, but the U.S. Government stalled, pleading logistic difficulties. Several other people were present at the villa and the conversation went on without getting anywhere. Suddenly the President rose, saying, "Sorry, I have to attend to something else. Will you please carry on with the others." Then he disappeared behind the screen. Drumright was embarrassed, of course, but, as a good diplomat, stayed on and talked to the other Chinese government officials present at the meeting.

Kirk, who succeeded Drumright, had an unusually short tour of duty in Taipei—only about a year. Despite the shortness of his duty, he left the impression of being an old sea captain who would have felt more at home barking his orders from the bridge than heading an important diplomatic mission. There was nothing civil or gentle about him, and even in talking to President Chiang he sounded gruff and blunt. I could see that the President really didn't enjoy the envoy's company, but he remained unperturbed and discussed in a calm and friendly manner whatever had prompted the Ambassador to seek the audience. Once I heard him remark half to himself: "How could anyone be so discourteous?"

Just to give one instance of how haughty Kirk was. One day I went up to the President's villa on Grass Mountain to be on hand for the Ambassador's call. My car was tailing his. At the down-slope approach to the villa a policeman stopped the Ambassador's car to avoid its meeting an outcoming one. I could hear the Ambassador shout at the policeman: "How dare you stop the American ambassador's car!" Did he think Taiwan was a U.S. colony or occupied territory?

Wright arrived in the summer of 1963 and stayed for three years—uneventful ones in Sino-American relations. it was during his tour of duty that U.S. economic aid in the form of grants and gifts came to an end, partly because Taiwan's own economy was picking up and partly because of the Vietnam war and its drain on the American economy. The Gulf of Tonkin incident involving an alleged attack on U.S. destroyers took place in August, 1964. Wright was instructed to brief President Chiang on the implications of the congressional resolution of August 5 that authorized President Johnson to take retaliatory measures "to prevent further aggression."

I remember that the President listened carefully to what Wright had to say and asked only two questions: Could this mean that the United States, aside from aerial bombing, had decided to send in its own ground forces?—to which he received an affirmative answer; and Would the United States stay in Vietnam and fight till the war was won?—to which he received an ambiguous answer. He suggested that perhaps the United States might arm the South Vietnamese to allow them to fight their own war instead.

McConaughy, the last U.S. Ambassador to the Republic of China in Taiwan, held the post for almost eight years, longer than any of his predecessors. He and his wife, Dorothy, were Alabama born. Their warm manners greatly endeared them to people in Taiwan. They went everywhere, talked to everybody, and showed interest in everything Chinese, from painting to shadow-boxing.

The Ambassador had a good working relationship with Chinese government officials, not only those in the Foreign Office, but in other key ministries too. He was popular among Chinese in all walks of life and often spoke before public organizations and service clubs on the island. When he left in April, 1974, there was a big send-off for him and his wife at the airport.

In the second half of McConaughy's eight-year tour of duty, Sino–American relations had already begun to suffer from Nixon's "reopening of China." Had it been left to the Ambassador to decide, he would have probably chosen to retire before this happened. It must have been a painful experience for him to see Washington–Taipei relations deteriorate steadily year after year.

The lot of terminating the U.S. diplomatic mission in Taipei, however, fell to Leonard Unger, who, like me, was fated to be the last Ambassador—in his case, from the United States to the Republic of China. Unger arrived in May, 1974, and his tour of duty ended officially on December 31, 1978. A career diplomat—but, unlike Drumright and McConaughy, without a background in Chinese—he made relatively few friends during his four years in Taiwan. He was detached and even aloof in his contacts with the Chinese people both in and outside the government. Unger should have left Taipei when the official relations ceased on December 31, but he overstayed his visit by a fortnight. When he departed at last, there were only a few people at the airport, among them a protocol officer, because by then he was no longer the U.S. Ambassador but an ordinary American citizen.

To retrace my own steps a bit. Three years after I had joined the President's secretarial staff there was a vacancy in the Foreign Office. The President asked me to take it "just to broaden your experience." Of course I did as he told me and thus became the Foreign Office spokesman. My principal duty was to conduct the weekly news conference and answer routine queries about foreign affairs from media representatives.

I was soon given to understand that the Foreign Office spokesman's job was, where possible, to avoid speaking and, when speaking was unavoidable, to say little. The weekly news conference was a very tame affair. My staff would canvass the newsmen who covered the Foreign Office for the foreign news agencies and the Chinese papers beforehand for any questions they might have in mind to ask. In the absence of any questions, my staff members would rack their brains to come up with pseudoquestions for the occasion; after all, the show must go on. Answers were first prepared in Chinese and then were translated into English. The manuscript was then submitted to the Vice-Minister for Political Affairs and sometimes went on to the Minister himself for approval. On the day of the news conference, mimeographed copies of the questions and answers would be distributed to those present. I didn't even have to read them aloud. The news people would take a quick look at the Q. and A. If they had any follow-up questions, I would either answer them on the spot or note them and prepare some appropriate answers for the next meeting. Sometimes the meeting would come to an end within a matter of minutes. As a courtesy, tea and cookies were always provided by the Government Information Office, where these meetings took place. There simply wasn't much earthshaking news coming out of those weekly exercises, unless something important happened elsewhere in the world and Taipei's reactions were desired.

One such occasion presented itself in the autumn of 1960, a presidential election year in the United States. The question of Quemoy and Matsu had arisen during the Nixon–Kennedy debate—an echo of the Quemoy crisis of August, 1958. Nixon took the position that the United States, by virtue of the Mutual Defense Treaty, should help the Chinese Government defend the two offshore islands, especially if the Communist attack really should be aimed at Taiwan itself. Kennedy, while opposing a Chinese Government "withdrawal at the point of a Communist gun," responded that the chances of the United States being dragged into war would be lessened if the latter could be persuaded to draw the line of defense specifically and exclusively around Taiwan and Penghu (Pescadores). In other words, Kennedy was in favor of the Chinese Government shortening its lines by withdrawing from Quemoy and Matsu even before the Communists could launch an attack.

The debate, for obvious reasons, created a good deal of resentment toward Kennedy among people in Taiwan. They had weathered a Communist attack on Quemoy and Matsu only two years earlier. Here was a junior senator from Massachusetts aspiring to be the next U.S. president who wanted us to give up the two islands without a fight. To whom did he think the islands belonged anyway? They certainly did not belong to the United States and, therefore, weren't for a U.S. presidential candidate to dispose of.

It was this sentiment, no doubt, that crept into a written question sent in by one of the media representatives. I drafted an answer merely to stress our determination to defend these islands should they ever come under Communist attack. The questions and answers were processed in the established manner. Hsu Shao-chang, then the Vice-Minister for Political Affairs, touched up the answer by adding a few words to the effect that "under no circumstances would the Chinese Government abandon a square inch of its territory to oblige anybody, including the Senator." Shen Chang-huan, the Foreign Minister (my name sake but no relation) initialed it as a matter of routine. The prepared question and answer was duly released. There was an immediate reaction in the Kennedy camp, and people in our Washington embassy also thought that the added personal reference to Kennedy was gratuitous and might make it difficult for them to develop a smooth relationship with Kennedy and his administration, should he be elected.

President Chiang was upset and sent for me. I told him that the "offensive words" were put in by the Vice-Minister for Political Affairs on my manuscript and were duly initialed by the Minister himself. The President wanted to know whether I had apprised either of my superiors of my own views after they had approved the text but before it was released. I said I had spoken to the Vice-Minister again, voicing my apprehension of unfavorable reaction in the United States, but that he told me he would take the whole responsibility. The President did not say another word, but apparently sent quickly for the Foreign Minister. Shen told me later that the President gave him a long "lecture" on where he had done wrong such as he had never received before in his many years of government service.

Shortly after this incident Hsu was appointed ambassador to a Latin American country.

In the summer of 1961 the Government Information Office directorship became available. I indicated to Madame Chiang that in view of my journalistic training and experience I would be interested in moving into that post. The President, possibly because he had me in mind already for the slot, readily assented. He sent for Foreign Minister Shen and asked him whether he thought I was the right man to fill the post. Shen, an extremely bright man, could tell by the way the President worded the question that I had already been mooted as the next GIO director. He quickly concurred. The President bade him inform Vice-President/Premier Chen Cheng, because GIO is a sub-ministry cabinet organ and a new director must be approved by the cabinet. Chen held up the matter for two or three weeks, probably because he had someone else in mind or because he was peeved at not having been consulted beforehand. Finally the cabinet acted and I was duly installed as the new GIO Director.

Chen Cheng was a very fine man. Though a soldier by training, he had considerable administrative ability. He was so close to the President that the latter had even arranged a marriage match for him. For many years it was generally believed that the President intended Chen as his successor. Chen was Governor of Taiwan during the critical years after the fall of the mainland and the removal of the Central Government to the island redoubt of Taiwan. It was Chen who had put through the land reform and nurtured Taiwan's industrialization.

A totally selfless man, Chen was also a courageous leader, never afraid to speak his mind on any major issue. He picked his cabinet carefully and also gathered around him a "brain trust" comprised of such well-known Chinese scholars as Dr. Hu Shih, President of Academia Sinica; Dr. Chiang Mon-lin, head of the Joint Commission for Rural Reconstruction; Dr. Mei Yi-chi, President of the National Tsing Hua University, founded on the

Chinese mainland in the early 1920s with a portion of the Boxer Indemnity returned by the United States; Wang Yung-wu, a self-taught scholar; and a number of others. Chen would meet regularly with these scholars over a simple meal and then hold a tour-of-the-horizon discussion on any subject he or any of his guests cared to bring up. In view of the educational background of most of these unofficial advisors, one could be certain that the input was largely liberal and progressive.

The Vice-President/Premier was a very good man to work with. He looked less severe than the President, and people who came into contact with him were less awe-stricken and consequently felt less inhibited in expressing their views.

I accompanied Chen on his only two trips overseas: to the United States in 1962, when he conferred with President Kennedy about the Outer Mongolia issue; and later in the same year to the Philippines, where he urged President Macapagal to institute a land reform similar to the one successfully carried out in Taiwan. On both trips he represented the President, who had vowed, after his trips to South Korea and the Philippines in 1949, that he would not take another overseas trip until the government had returned to the Chinese mainland.

On his visit to Washington, Chen received a cordial welcome from Kennedy. This was shortly after the Soviets had put their Sputnik into orbit, when everybody in the United States was excited, and some even worried, over the possibility that the Russians had overtaken the Americans for good in space science and technology. When asked by the U.S. news media for his reactions, Chen said he was not worried at all because he had confidence in American capability and resourcefulness to recapture the lead in due course. Subsequent events proved him absolutely right.

Kennedy wanted to talk about Outer Mongolia's wish to enter the United Nations. He knew the Republic of China could veto this in the Security Council. Chen assured Kennedy that we would refrain from exercising our veto on this issue. In return Kennedy gave us a private assurance to the effect that if, at any time, a veto was necessary and would be effective in preventing Chinese Communist entry into the United Nations, the United States would use that veto. (As it happened, ten years later the issue never came up before the Security Council at all).

Kennedy at the time was greatly concerned over reports that the Chinese Communists were secretly conducting nuclear explosions at Lop Nor in Northwest China—a sure indication they were working on atomic weapons. This was the period when Moscow and Peking were still close to each other, otherwise it might have been possible for the United States to devise a way to neutralize Peking's nuclear potential at an early stage. At their meeting Kennedy asked Chen many questions about Lop Nor. Could he have been thinking of a preventive surgical strike?

Kennedy also showed a great deal of interest in the Chinese translation of the word "crisis." He was elated when Chen told him that it takes two Chinese characters to do it: *Wei*, meaning danger, and *Chi*, meaning opportunity. He subsequently used this in one of his speeches.

During the visit Chen was asked to address a National Press Club luncheon, and I was his interpreter. He made a good impression on everybody by his obvious sincerity and particularly by his straightforward answers to the questions that followed his brief opening remarks.

At Kennedy's White House luncheon in Chen's honor I was seated on Allen Dulles's right. I knew he was the Director of the Central Intelligence Agency, but he didn't know who I was. Just to be social I tried to engage him in conversation. He smiled but said nothing. Seconds later he produced a small piece of paper from his right-hand pocket. After a quick glance at it he looked up and said, "So you are Jimmy Shen, an ex-newspaperman and now the *Gimo's* secretary."

Never a man of robust constitution and long suffering from a duodenal ulcer, Chen's health began to decline even further. As a result, he became ever more irascible. Finally he had to resign from his post as Premier but remained the Vice-President until his death on March 5, 1965. On the day of his funeral thousands of Taiwan's farmers, who had benefitted from the land reform, came from all over the island to pay homage to "Uncle Chen Cheng."

There was another memorable, and tragic, incident during my stewardship of GIO. In June, 1964, Taipei became the venue for that year's Asian Film Festival. The Central Motion Picture Company, of which I was Chairman of the Board for a very brief period, was the host organization, with the GIO furnishing the backup support. The three-day affair, June 18–20, went on very well until the last day, when Loke Wan-to, a Chinese financier and movie magnate in Singapore, his wife, and a number of his close friends went down the island to see the Chinese Palace Museum art collection, at that time housed in a small building near Taichung. On their return their plane, a commercial one, crashed, killing everyone on board. This instantly turned into a great tragedy what had started out as a happy event. One of my GIO colleagues was among those killed. The mass funeral for fifty-seven persons was the saddest thing I had ever witnessed in my life.

Henry Kung, President of the Central Motion Picture Company, was the target of severe criticism from all sides, for a scapegoat had to be found. Actually, Loke's own people had done the booking, while Kung had been busy taking care of the festival. At any rate, the matter came up at a Kuomintang Standing Committee meeting chaired by the President himself in his capacity as the *Tsungtsai* (Director–General) of the party. I explained what had happened and suggested that Kung was not to blame. After all, it was an accident; unfortunate and sad, but still an accident. No one was responsible except the airline in question. For my remarks I received a severe scolding from the President. Like everybody else, the President was greatly saddened and thought I was trying to shield Kung, who was nominally my subordinate. As soon as the meeting ended everybody rushed up to congratulate me. I was puzzled. Hadn't they heard what the President had just said? They explained that, under the circumstances, the President had to blame somebody for the incident. The fact that he had scolded me in public meant that he would not take any punitive action against me. And as a matter of fact he never did.

In the fall of 1965, four years after I had taken over the GIO directorship, Foreign Minister Shen Chang-huan had a brainstorm: He wanted to send me to Colombia as ambassador. Whether or not this had anything to do with the fact that my wife was then taking Spanish lessons I was never able to find out. Apparently he had obtained the President's approval and also that of Premier C.K. Yen, who had even interviewed a successor for my post. About the only person the Foreign Minister had failed to take into his confidence about this matter was me. I asked Madame Chiang whether she had heard about it. She had not but said she would find out. Later she told me that the idea had not originated with the Chief, but with the Foreign Minister. She herself thought that I, lacking any knowledge of Spanish, would be unable to do much in Bogota. Chiang Ching-kuo, the President's son and at this time Deputy Defense Minister, also thought poorly of the idea. The negative signal reached the Foreign Minister just in the nick of time, for he was all set to ask Bogota for agreement to my appointment. Columbia, I am sure is a beautiful country, but I would have been practically blind, deaf, and mute there, and by the time I had learned enough Spanish to get along somewhat independently, I would most probably have been recalled or sent to another country.

I didn't have to wait long before another opportunity knocked on my door. In 1966, Dr. C.M. Chen, our Ambassador to Australia, was about to be transferred to Tokyo. I became his replacement in Canberra in the summer (winter in the Southern

Hemisphere) of 1966. The Liberal-Country Party coalition forged by Sir Robert Menzies, Australia's master politician after World War II, was in power. Unlike the Labor Party, which was opposed to the Vietnam war and, therefore, also to the U.S. policy of ignoring Communist China, the Liberal-Country Party was quite friendly toward the Republic of China.

Wearing my morning coat and striped pants, I presented my credentials to the Governor-General, Lord R.J. Casey, an Australian appointed by Queen Elizabeth II as her personal representative in Canberra. I was told that the Australian Government had had to send my name to London before agreeing to my appointment. My credentials were actually addressed to Her Majesty, despite the fact that the Government of the United Kingdom had recognized the Chinese Communist regime in Peking as early as 1950. No one, however, seemed to notice the incongruity of such an arrangement.

Harold Holt was the Prime Minister at the time and Paul Hasluck the Foreign Minister. It was during my tour of duty that Australia appointed its first full-time Ambassador to the Republic of China on Taiwan, a post left vacant for more than fifteen years after the fall of the Chinese mainland. It was also during my tour of duty that the Australian Prime Minister paid an official visit to Taiwan, the first ever in Sino-Australian relations. Unfortunately, Holt was drowned in 1968.

In 1966 the Vietnam war was raging. President Lyndon B. Johnson came to Canberra to confer with the heads of seven governments that had contributed troops to the allied forces in Vietnam. The slogan of the Liberal-Country Party coalition was "All the way with LBJ." The Republic of China, because of the firm U.S. policy, especially with regard to our membership/ representation in the United Nations, stood to benefit from American-Australian solidarity.

I was in Australia for twenty months. My wife and I enjoyed the post. Although there was not too much to do in Canberra, we arranged to visit all six states in the Union. Our relations with the Australian Government were good. Year after year Australia's delegates to the U.S. voted to keep us in and the Chinese Communists out. The only jarring note was when Australia recognized Outer Mongolia in 1967. I got wind of this only a few hours before the matter was to come up before Parliament. I alerted our friends in Parliament and asked for an immediate appointment with Foreign Minister Hasluck. The contemplated move, I told him, would mar the newly created ASPAC spirit. He explained that in a few weeks' time Australia would be playing host to an international conference to which Outer Mongolia had decided to send a delegation; it would be most awkward for Australia if it did not recognize that country in advance. But he assured me that Australia had no intention of establishing diplomatic relations with Ulan Bator, let alone exchanging ambassadors.

ASPAC, the Asian and Pacific Council, had been established in Canberra in early 1966 to promote closer economic and social relations among its member nations—Australia, the Republic of China, Japan, Korea, Malaysia, New Zealand, the Philippines, Thailand, and Vietnam. The Republic of China, having been barred from the Southeast Asia Treaty Organization, was happy to join ASPAC. At one time we had hoped this would lead to an even more substantial, though subtle, alignment against Communist countries in the Asia-Pacific region. At every ministerial meeting the Republic of China representatives would ask for a strong anti-communist statement in the communique, but each time they were voted down by Australia, New Zealand, and Japan, sometimes joined by Malaysia and Thailand, which did not want to irritate Peking. Only Korea and Vietnam, because of their experience with Communists in their own countries, supported the Republic of China's position on this matter at the annual meetings.

In August, 1968, I was called back to Taipei for consultations. What was up? I was greatly mystified. Friends in the Foreign

Office said it was the President who had sent for me; and as it turned out, the President had decided to reshuffle the top echelon in the Foreign Office. He wanted to know how I would like to be the First Vice-Minister for Administrative Affairs, helping the aging Minister, Wei Tao-ming. Naturally I said I was entirely at his service and would do anything he wanted me to do. But I had been in Australia for only twenty months. Couldn't I stay on for four more months, or at least through our next National Day on October 10? The President thought it would be quite all right, but the Minister said he needed me to act on his behalf in the ministry within a month, because he had to lead our delegation to New York for the annual U.N. General Assembly meeting in September.

Sir James Plimsoll, Secretary of the Australian Department of External Affairs, had been very friendly to me during my tour in Canberra. I met him again in Washington, when we both were serving as ambassadors. Early on in Canberra he advised me to establish contacts with members of Parliament belonging to the Liberal–Country Party *and* the opposition Labor Party, which was headed by Arthur Caldwell. Since Australia has a two-party system of government, he said, one could never tell which one would win the next election.

I bade farewell to Canberra in August, 1968. Succeeding me was Sampson Shen (again, no relation), a younger man who, like me, had worked as the President's secretary–interpreter for a number of years. He stayed on until the end of 1972. The Labor Party won the election that November—an upset victory—and Gough Whitlam, the new Prime Minister, lost no time in recognizing the People's Republic of China and de-recognizing us. Since then Taiwan and Australia have had only commercial relations.

In the summer of 1969, a year after my return from Australia, Foreign Minister Wei Tao-ming confided to me that the *Gimo* wanted me to replace C.M. Chen as Ambassador to Japan. I immediately went to see Mr. Chang Chun, an elder statesman who had much to do with our relations with Japan for several decades. He said the *Gimo* had not consulted him about it. I told him that I could neither read nor speak Japanese and so would be useless in Tokyo. As Chang was then Secretary-General to the *Gimo*, I knew he would relay my reactions to him. And sure enough, the following morning the *Gimo* sent for me and told me he had changed his mind. This enabled me to stay on at the Foreign Office as a Vice-Minister for two more years until May, 1971, when I was given the Washington assignment.

Chapter III

Signs of Change

Nixon had been in the White House for just over a year when, as part of his evolving new Asian policy, he decided to have Secretary of State William P. Rogers invite the Republic of China's Vice-Premier, Chiang Ching-kuo, to the United States for an official visit. By then it was clear that the latter would one day succeed his father, the *Gimo*, to power in the Republic. In retrospect one can also describe the invitation to Chiang Ching-kuo in early 1970 as Nixon's way of saying good-bye to his "friends" in the Republic of China.

Preparations commenced in earnest in Taipei for Chiang Ching-kuo's trip. The Ministry of Foreign Affairs and other governmental organs drew up position papers on various matters to inform and guide him in Washington discussions. As Vice-Minister of Foreign Affairs, naturally I was involved in making some of the preparations for the trip.

The *Gimo*, having observed Nixon's initial moves to reopen contacts with Peking with considerable apprehension, attached a great deal of importance to his son's trip. The two must have spent long hours together going over some of the matters on which the Chinese Government would need the Nixon administration's assurances and continued support. Presumably the father did most of the talking and the son most of the listening. The *Gimo*, even had a discussion with U.S. Ambassador Walter P. McConaughy.

The Chinese Government was anxious to find out what sort of concessions the U.S. Government intended to make in the bilateral talks with Peking's representatives in Warsaw. One session, originally scheduled for January that year, had been called off by Peking because of Nixon's decision to bomb Hanoi and Haiphong in a desperate attempt to force North Vietnam to come to the conference table. Secretary Rogers openly regretted this cancellation, saying that he actually had a few "constructive" proposals in mind, including the conclusion of an agreement on peaceful coexistence. There had been earlier signs that the U.S. Government was prepared to relax some of the existing restrictions on trade with and travel to the Chinese mainland by U.S. citizens. But how far was the U.S. Government prepared to go? Would it consider abolishing such restrictions entirely to permit the sale of nonstrategic U.S. goods to the mainland and allow an exchange of mail, telegraphic, and shipping services? Would the U.S. Government actively seek an agreement on peaceful coexistence when the bilateral talks eventually were resumed? In this connection, didn't the U.S. representative at the 136th bilateral talks held in Warsaw on February 20 say that, after all, there was not much difference between what the U.S. Government had in mind and Peking's much-vaunted Five Principles of Peaceful Coexistence that Chou En-lai first proclaimed at the Bandung Conference of 1955? (Respect for the sovereignty and territorial integrity of all states; mutual nonaggression against other states; noninterference in the internal affairs of other states; equality and mutual benefit; and peaceful coexistence.) For if the U.S. Government should actually decide to enter into such an agreement, it would be tantamount to the recognition of Peking as the legitimate government of at least the Chinese mainland.

The second matter on which the Chinese Government needed reassurance was continued U.S. support for its seat in the United Nations—both in the Security Council, where the Republic of China was a permanent member with veto power, and in the General Assembly, where for twenty years there had been an annual battle over whether the Peking regime should be admitted as *the* representative of China and the Chinese people. Could the U.S. Government be depended on in 1970 to make the same all-out effort to keep the Republic of China in the world organization that it had made in previous years? As subsequent events proved, such concern was not entirely without foundation.

A third matter very much on the minds of the *Gimo* and Chiang Ching-kuo was how much help we could expect from the U.S. Government in case of another Chinese Communist attack on Quemoy and Matsu, the two island groups off the Fukien coast. Would Nixon honor the Formosa Resolution, as did Eisenhower in 1958, when U.S. naval vessels were ordered to resupply Chinese Government garrisons on these islands? Though the ships actually anchored outside the three-mile territorial sea limit, their very nearness did much to boost the morale of the hard-pressed defending troops in that major flare-up in the Taiwan Straits twelve years earlier.

Other matters on which the Chinese Government wished to have Chiang Ching-kuo present its views to the U.S. Government included the Formosans for Independence agitators, who were getting more and more vociferous in the United States; the situation on the Chinese mainland, where a power struggle brought on by the Cultural Revolution was still raging; and newer military equipment for the defense of Taiwan.

The Vice-Premier arrived in Washington on April 20 for his four-day official visit. He received honors and courtesies usually reserved for heads of foreign governments: military honors at Andrews Air Force Base, a stay at Blair House, tea with Vice-President Spiro Agnew, meetings with Secretary of State Rogers and Secretary of Defense Melvin Laird, breakfast with congressional leaders, and—topping the visit—a discussion with President Nixon followed by a black-tie dinner at the White House. The only thing he didn't do was to speak at a National Press Club luncheon. Instead, he invited a group of American journalists to have lunch with him at Twin Oaks, the Chinese Ambassador's official residence.

On April 22, Chiang Ching-kuo met Henry Kissinger for the first time. Initially the President's National Security Advisor had planned to receive the Vice-Premier in his basement office in the White House, where most other foreign visitors paid their calls. For some reason this underwent a change and Kissinger came himself to Blair House, where the two men, with no one else present, had a half-hour tete-a-tete. Later on I asked the Vice-Premier whether Kissinger had brought any important messages from Nixon. He smiled and said nothing. My guess was that Kissinger had made him agree not to reveal anything of their conversation. It wasn't until several years later that I learned Kissinger had actually asked Chiang Ching-kuo for his reaction should the U.S. Government decide to move from Warsaw to either Washington or Peking the ambassador-level talks with the Chinese Communists. Then and there Chiang Ching-kuo must have voiced strong opposition to the idea.

During the pre-dinner conversation with President Nixon, which lasted for more than an hour, the Vice-Premier conveyed the *Gimo's* perception of the situation in East Asia as well as his endorsement of the new U.S. Asian policy, the "Nixon Doctrine." Though at the time the world's attention was riveted on Indochina and the Korean Peninsula, Taiwan remained the center of the Asian problem; any developments in the Taiwan Straits would inevitably affect the security of both the Republic of China and the United States. After all, the Chinese Communists had never given up their intention of seizing Taiwan by force. The only way to ensure peace and security in the Western Pacific was to turn the 700 million people on the Chinese mainland into friends of the United States. The Vice-Premier stopped short of asking President Nixon to back up the *Gimo's* "recover the mainland" campaign, but he did point out that it was imperative for the Republic of China, the Republic of Vietnam, the Republic of Korea, and Thailand to work out a system of collective defense against Communist aggression. He stressed that the effectiveness of such an alliance was dependent on American support and guidance.

Nixon was polite but noncommittal. The "Nixon Doctrine," he said, did not mean American withdrawal from Asia. It merely signalled a change in the way the United States would be dealing with problems in the Asian region. The real emphasis was on enabling Asian nations to help themselves.

Turning to bilateral relations, Nixon said the Warsaw talks, just resumed, between U.S. and Peking representatives were exploratory in nature and would not affect America's friendship with the Republic of China. The United States never would forsake its allies and friends—"I can assure you that the United States will always honor its treaty obligations and, to use a colloquial expression, I will never sell you down the river."

As the conversation continued Chiang Ching-kuo moved to other points, including the Republic of China's urgent need for more sophisticated weapons for defense. He didn't go into the matter at any length because he would have an opportunity to see Secretary of Defense Laird and other Pentagon officials before he left Washington.

Nixon was very curious about developments on the Chinese mainland. He particularly wanted to know whether the Vice-Premier saw any possibility of Peking and Moscow patching up their feud in the foreseeable future. Chiang-Ching-kuo answered in the negative.

What with time consumed by two-way translations, which it was my privilege to provide, the hour before dinner went quickly enough. When other dinner guests began to arrive, the conversation in the Oval Office ended.

In his dinner toast President Nixon welcomed the Vice-Premier as a friend from a great country that has made immense contributions to world civilization; as a representative of an allied nation that fought shoulder to shoulder with the United States in two world wars; as the son of the great Chinese national leader; and as someone who has earned respect and admiration for his own achievements in the service of his country.

Nixon reiterated the U.S. Government's determination to stand firm with the Republic of China in international affairs. He recalled with pleasure his six visits to Taiwan over a period of more than ten years, during the time he was Vice-President and in a period when he held no official post. Whatever his status, he said, he had been warmly received by President and Madame Chiang Kai-shek and other Chinese leaders.

In his return toast Chiang Ching-kuo referred to the "unbroken record of friendship and alliance" between the two countries and to the important implications of this record for the Asian situation. "In assessing the future of Asia," continued the Vice-Premier, "let us not overlook the fact that the Republic of China, Korea, and Vietnam can marshal more than two million troops. This suggests that the Nixon Doctrine of free Asian manpower for free Asia's defense is attainable in a united regional effort back by the United States."

The Vice-Premier described the Republic of China as not only an obstacle to Communist aggression, but an alternative to communism. He went on to say that if the Chinese Communists were permitted to enslave the Chinese people on the mainland in perpetuity, there could be no peace or security in

Asia—or, for that matter, in the rest of the world—for a long, long time.

Chiang Ching-kuo ended his toast by expressing the hope that "President Nixon, whom we saw so often before his election, will return to Taiwan soon to pay us an official visit." This was a hope never realized in fact.

On Friday, April 24, Chiang Ching-kuo went on to New York to keep several engagements, including a luncheon in his honor by the Far East–American Council of Commerce and Industry; a reception by the Council on Foreign Relations, the citadel of the so-called Eastern Establishment; and a dinner by Chinese community leaders in Chinatown.

At noon, accompanied by a few aides and U.S. secret service men, the Vice-Premier left the Hotel Pierre, where he was staying, and crossed Park Avenue to the Hotel Plaza for the luncheon. On the sidewalk that faces Park Avenue there were a dozen or so Formosans for Independence holding a shouting demonstration. Just as Chiang was entering the Plaza, someone fired a shot at him. Luckily he made it safely into the lobby and the bullet simply pierced the glass of the revolving door. No one was hurt.

I and several others, all members of the entourage, were only a few feet behind the Vice-Premier. In the ensuing scuffle policemen disarmed a Chinese youth—one of two, it later turned out, whom the Formosans for Independence organization had assigned to assassinate Chiang Ching-kuo.

When I went upstairs to the Grand Ball Room, I found the Vice-Premier already in the receiving line, greeting other guests as they came in. He was as calm and cool as if nothing untoward had occurred. For the rest of the day—and, for that matter, for the rest of the ten-day drip—he kept all his scheduled engagements without the slightest change or deviation, including the restful stopover at the King Ranch in Denver, Colorado, where he met Richard V. Allen, later President Reagan's National Security Advisor, for the first time.

On the Northwest airlines plane that carried us across the Pacific, Chiang Ching-kuo sat by himself most of the time, deep in thought for hours on end. Our Chinese Airline plane, to which we changed in Tokyo, landed in Taipei's International Airport just before noon on April 30. A huge crowd was waiting to give the Vice-Premier a warm welcome home. As everybody rushed up to shake hands with him it occurred to me that April 24, 1970, the day of the shooting, would be remembered by the free Chinese in the same way an earlier generation of Chinese remembered December 24, 1936—the day the *Gimo* returned safely from Sian after his horrifying experience at the hands of the erstwhile Young Marshal Chang Hsueh-liang and other commanders who had been unhappy with the Government's continuing military campaigns against Communist remnants in Northwest China.

It was almost exactly a year later that I returned to Washington to take up my post as Ambassador. (My wife stayed behind for a month to wait for our son Carl's graduation from high school.) At the Dulles International Airport to meet me were members of the embassy staff, personal friends, and our second daughter, Cynthia, a graduate student in biochemistry at the State University of New York at Stony Brook. The State Department was represented by Ambassador Winthrop Brown, Deputy Assistant Secretary of State for East Asian and Pacific Affairs, and Thomas Shoesmith, Director of Republic of China Affairs.

I remember telling the U.S. news media representatives how happy I was to have this important assignment. "The United States is our most important ally. Our two countries fought World War II together, and today we are engaged in a collective security effort to keep peace and stability in the Western Pacific," I told them.

Asked whether in view of Washington's ongoing review of its China policy I was still optimistic about the future of Sino-American relations, I answered in the affirmative, pointing out that the Republic of China was a time-tested friend and ally of the United States: "Our two countries have important common interests, and there is something permanent about our relationship."

I presented my credentials to President Nixon on the afternoon of May 18, 1971, in a spacious room in the White House reserved for such occasions. Unlike the elaborate ceremony I had gone through earlier in Canberra, Australia, in August, 1966, this was a simple one lasting less than twenty minutes. The Presidet entered from one side and I from the other, meeting in the center of the room. Both of us were clad in dark business suits. I presented two Chinese letters personally signed by President Chiang Kai-shek and accompanied by English translations. One was the official recall of my predecessor, S.K. Chow; the other appointed me the new Ambassador. Nixon took the letters but gave their contents not even a glance. He quickly passed them to an aide and then posed with me for official pictures. I later received two autographed copies; one I kept and the other I sent back to the Foreign Office in Taipei for its files.

The ceremony over, Nixon asked me to join him in a smaller room, where we sat down. He first inquired about the health of President and Madame Chiang and then welcomed me as the new Ambassador from the Republic of China. I reminded him that I had had the honor of being his interpreter during his numerous visits to Taipei and assured him that I would be most happy now to serve as the official link between the two presidents. Nixon said he remembered me very well and that in my new capacity I had a bigger job than two-way translating: I had to interpret the views and policies of two governments. I said I would do my best.

Nixon then complimented the Republic of China on its progress in economic, cultural, and scientific development. He went on to say that the relations between the United States and the Republic of China had been not only friendly but of long standing; he hoped that these relations would be maintained *and* strengthened. He said he realized that the Republic of China was having some difficulties and that these could be overcome if our two countries worked together closely. He compared the question of our representation in the United Nations with his own difficulties in the U.S. Congress. According to the President, the question really boiled down to one of how many votes could be mustered to support the Republic of China's position in the world organization. He emphasized that the United States alone no longer could control the situation.

At this point I conveyed to him President Chiang's warm greetings. I told him of the great importance President Chiang attached to Sino–American official relations as well as to their personal friendship. I assured Nixon that President Chiang was confident that, given full cooperation between our two governments, there was no problem too difficult to solve.

Here Nixon picked up the conversation. He made vague mention of difficulties that might arise between our countries but stated his feeling that they could be settled amicably. He didn't elaborate, but assuredly he knew we were opposed to his overtures to Peking.

The most important of his statements during our fifteen-minute tête-a-tête was his assurance to me that the U.S. policy of supporting the Republic of China both in and outside the United Nations remained unchanged, to which he added that the U.S. would continue to honor its obligations under the Mutual Defense Treaty.

In my remarks I emphasized the traditional relations between our two countries as allies. This friendship, I said, had grown in importance because of our common opposition to Communist subversion and oppression in Southeast Asia. I thanked Nixon on behalf of the Government and people of the Republic of China for the generous economic assistance the United States had given us, as well as for the moral support that helped us maintain our position in various international organizations, including the United Nations, over a period of many years. I expressed my sincere belief that the United States would continue to lead the free world in the maintenance of peace and human freedom. I assured him that the Republic of China would, without hesitation, make any sacrifices necessary to the attainment of these common goals. I concluded by saying that I was assuming the ambassadorship at a time when "winds of appeasement are blowing over many parts of the free world, but I believe that our American friends will not bow before these winds."

I was the second of three new ambassadors to present credentials to Nixon that day. The Brazilian Ambassador had preceded me, and the Togolese Ambassador was awaiting his turn. When the time came for me to leave, Nixon asked me to convey his greetings to President and Madame Chiang and to stay in close touch with both the White House and the Department of State. I had a feeling at the time that he would wish to talk with me again at some near-future date, but I didn't see him until after his dramatic visit to Peking in February, 1972. By that time the Republic of China had already been expelled from the United Nations.

On July 1, 1971, I called on National Security Advisor Kissinger for the first time since taking up my post. It was largely a courtesy call, and also intended to renew an acquaintanceship formed during Chiang Ching-kuo's visit in 1970. Though I did broach our membership/representation in the U.N., there were no detailed discussions; this was a matter about which we had been in touch all along, and almost exclusively, with the Department of State.

My appointment to the ambassadorial post had become official on April 12, 1971, a month previous to my arrival in the States. As I was making preparations for my departure from Taipei word came from Washington that Nixon was sending to Taipei a former Under-Secretary of State, Robert Murphy, to talk about our membership in the United Nations. I was asked to wait so that I could sit in on the discussions.

The message Murphy brought was this: Since it was no longer possible to bar the Chinese Communists from the world organization, Washington wanted to know our reaction if it should propose the admission of Peking to the U.N. General Assembly and request that the Republic of China be permitted to retain its membership in the same body. As to our seat in the U.N. Security Council, where our delegate had the veto power—this, Murphy said, would be a separate matter, because the Security Council had its own rules and regulations; whatever might happen in the General Assembly would not affect our seat in the Security Council. Thus, while we might have to share our General Assembly membership with the Chinese Communists, we would be able to remain in the Security Council as one of the "Big Five." Murphy offered no iron-clad assurances that the U.S. Government's plan could be carried out successfully.

President Chiang wasn't satisfied but said he would go along. He insisted, however, that the United States refrain from being one of the nations to sponsor Peking's admission. He said the Republic of China would vote against such a proposal if it actually came up, but we would not ask that all the Republic's friends vote the same way. This was the extent of our cooperation with the United States on this issue, the *Gimo* stated.

On my way to Washington I stopped over for a few days in Tokyo to brief *Gaimushu* officials on the question. I saw Mr.

Aichi Kiichi, Japan's Foreign Minister, and told him that an earlier U.S. administration had promised to use its veto power, if necessary and effective, to keep the Chinese Communist out of the world organization.

The question of our membership/representation in the United Nations began with the withdrawal of our government from the Chinese mainland in 1949 and had persisted for twenty years. Year after year we were submitted to the humiliation of a debate about our membership. Those favoring our replacement by the Chinese Communists maintained that it was a matter of *which government* should represent China in the world body; we argued that it was a matter of *membership*. Inasmuch as the Republic of China was a founding member, its official designation mentioned specifically in the U.S. Charter, and in view of the fact that our government still exercised its sovereign rights on a part, though only a smaller part, of our territory, we should occupy China's seat in both branches of the United Nations.

For the first ten years, with the help of the United States and many other friendly nations, the Republic of China was able to maintain its position in the U.N. through moratorium, a device which postponed any serious discussion of the issue everytime Peking's friends brought it up. For the next ten years our position was safeguarded by another device, that of dubbing the issue an "Important Question" under Article 18, paragraph 2 of the U.N. Charter, which requires the approval of two-thirds of the members present and voting in the General Assembly before effecting any change in any nation's membership/representation.

These two devices proved effective in deferring the issue at a time when the number of nations in the world organization was within manageable limits and when the United States stuck to its policy of recognizing the Republic of China as "China" and its government as China's sole legitimate government.

After Canada broke away and recognized Peking in October,

1970, the U.S. felt its policy on China's membership/representation becoming less and less tenable. In its search for a solution it hit upon this idea of "Dual Representation:" admitting Peking **into the United Nations while safeguarding the Republic of China's seat in the General Assembly.**

I must say that my government's leaders vacillated, when a quick decision was called for. One of my first tasks in Washington was to persuade American officials to use the "Important Question" formula at least once more. With considerable reluctance the latter agreed, but insisted that this be coupled with another resolution on "Dual Representation," to be sponsored by nations other than the United States.

The U.S. Government's reversal of its China policy was announced officially by Secretary of State Rogers on August 2, 1971, two weeks after the revelation of Kissinger's secret trip to Peking. In his statement Rogers said in part:

> No question of Asian policy has so perplexed the world in the last twenty years as the China question—and the related question is the fact that each of the two governments claims to be the sole government of China and representative of all the people of china.
>
> Representation in an international organization need not prejudice the claims or views of either government. Participation of both in the United Nations need not require that result. Rather it would provide governments with increased opportunities for contact and communication. It would also help promote cooperation on common problems which affect all of the member nations regardless of political differences.
>
> The United States accordingly will support action at the General Assembly this fall calling for seating the People's Republic of China. At the same time the United States will oppose any action to expel the Republic of China or otherwise deprive it of representation in the United Nations.
>
> Our consultations, which began several months ago, have indicated that the question of China's seat in the

Security Council is a matter which many nations will wish to address.

In the final analysis, of course, under the Charter provisions, the Security Council will make this decision.

We, for our part, are prepared to have this question resolved on the basis of a decision of members of the United Nations. Our consultations have also shown that any action to deprive the Republic of China of its representation would meet with strong opposition in the General Assembly. Certainly, as I have said, the United States will oppose it.

The Republic of China has played a loyal and conscientious role in the United Nations since the organization was founded. It has lived up to all of its Charter obligations. Having made remarkable progress in developing its own economy, it has cooperated internationally by providing valuable technical assistance to a number of less developed countries, particularly in Africa.

The position of the United States is that if the United Nations is to succeed in its peace-keeping role, it must deal with the realities of the world in which we live. Thus, the United States will cooperate with those who, whatever their views on the status of the relationship of the two governments, wish to continue to have the Republic of China represented in the United Nations.

The outcome, of course, will be decided by the 127 members of the United Nations. For our part, we believe that the decision we have taken is fully in accord with President Nixon's desire to normalize relations with the People's Republic of China, in the interest of world peace and in accord with our conviction that the continued representation in the United Nations of the Republic of China will contribute to peace and stability in the world.

Roger's policy statement did not stake out the position on which of the two Chinese governments should hold the permanent seat in the Security Council that carried with it the veto power. He said the United States was "prepared to have this question resolved on the basis of a decision by members of the United Nations," declining to discuss the technical or tactical points that might be involved in deciding the question of the Security Council seat. He indicated that the United States intended to preserve the Republic of China's representation through the continued use of the "Important Question" formula.

This put our government in a dilemma. Obviously we could not support any move to seat the Chinese Communists in the General Assembly, despite the fact that the resolution would also call for retention of the Republic of China's seat in the same body. When asked by governments friendly to us how we would wish their representatives to vote, we did not know what to say. Instead, we could only explain our dilemma and ask them to be guided by their own judgment in the balloting. As a result, many of our friends were in a quandary. In the end this proved to be our undoing because they did not know what we really wanted them to do.

By arrangement, the preliminary resolution to determine whether the issue was an "Important Question" was put to vote first. When it failed to receive a simple majority, the door to entry in the United Nations was thrown wide open to the Chinese Communists. Our Foreign Minister and Chief Delegate, S.K. Chow, walked out of the General Assembly before the Chinese Communists were actually voted in under a resolution offered by Albania. So ended our twenty-year-long battle to remain in the United Nations.

Our seat in the Security Council? Well, we were simply ejected without additional formality. And within a matter of weeks we were expelled from practically all of the U.N.'s subordinate or affiliated organizations except the International Monetary Fund and the World Bank. Within a matter of months more than twenty countries had established diplomatic relations with the Peking regime and de-recognized the Republic of China.

It should be recalled that our expulsion from the United Nations in October, 1971, was preceded by a secret trip by Kissinger to Peking in July. The National Security Advisor was in Peking this second time when the question of Chinese membership/representation came up for discussion in the General Assembly. Worried lest Kissinger do or say something while in Peking to add to our difficulty in New York, three of us—S.K. Chow, I, and Liu Chieh, our Permanent Delegate to the U.N.— called on Secretary of State Rogers to suggest Kissinger be requested to keep quiet or exercise caution in his utterances.

There is no way of knowing whether Rogers acted on our suggestion. What actually happened is that Kissinger prolonged his stay in Peking and was still there when the "Important Question" resolution was defeated.

Years later I called on George Bush, who had been the Chief Delegate of the United States to the U.N. at the time, at his office at National Republican Committee headquarters in Washington. I thanked him for his efforts to save our seat in the U.N. and aksed him what, in his opinion, had been the decisive factor in our defeat. He answered my question with a question of his own: "What was Kissinger doing in Peking?"

Almost from the U.N.'s very beginnings in 1945 we had kept a separate mission in New York to look after our interests in the world organization. Every September our Foreign Minister, whoever he happened to be at the time, would journey to New York to head our delegation. Our Ambassador to the United States rarely took part—the reason I was not a member of our delegation to the U.N. General Assembly in 1971. As a matter of fact, on the very day of our expulsion I was up in New Haven, Connecticut, fulfilling a speaking engagement before a group of Yale University students. Ironically, the topic of my talk was "Why the Chinese Communists Must Not Be Permitted to

Replace Us in the United Nations." It the middle of the night I was awakened by a telephone call from a *New York Times* reporter who had somehow tracked me down to the campus hostel where I was spending the night. He asked whether I had heard the result of the vote in the General Assembly. I said no, because there was neither a TV set nor a radio in my room. Of course I was greatly shocked by the news, and instead of flying back to Washington directly the following morning, I went to New York. I arrived at our U.N. Mission just in time to catch the tail-end of Minister Chow's address to members of our delegation, telling everybody to remain calm and carry on while waiting for instructions from Taipei. After all, he said, this wasn't the end of the world!.

To this day I am still in the dark as to why Nixon sent Murphy to Taipei in April, 1971, to tell us we could keep our seat in the Security Council whatever might happen to our membership/ representation in the General Assembly. Did Murphy know that Nixon had asked him to sell us a bill of goods? At any rate, when I discussed the matter with Alexis Johnson, who was then Under-Secretary of State for Political Affairs, and officials in the Bureau of International Organizations, none of them warmed up to the subject at all.

Murphy was a first-class diplomat and a gentleman for whom I later developed a great admiration and affection. He lived in New York, where he was the Board Chairman of the Corning Glass Company, but kept a house in the Washington area and would come down every now and then. We played golf together several times at the Chevy Chase Country Club, and each time I was about to ask him what his role had been in "misinforming" President Chiang about our seat in the Security Council I desisted. I hadn't wanted to hurt his feelings, for in later years he was getting visibly weaker and I didn't have the heart to upset him. When he died in January, 1978, I went to his funeral. My chance of clarifying this point was buried with him.

Richard M. Nixon came to the presidency prepared to reopen contacts with Communist China. In his inaugural speech on January 20, 1969, he hinted at his desire for reconciliation with Peking by letting the world know that during his administration lines of communication would be kept open; no nation, large or small, need live in indignity or isolation. He followed this up by announcing at his first press conference on January 27 that he remained opposed to the admission of Communist China to the United Nations but hoped that Peking would agree to resume the bilateral ambassadorial talks at Warsaw.

Peking responded favorably, and a session was scheduled for February 20. A few days before the meeting a Chinese Communist diplomat, a Third Secretary in the embassy in the Netherlands named Liao Ho-shu, defected. He sought and was quickly granted political asylum by the U.S. Government. Peking, accusing Washington of having engineered Liao's defection, cancelled the meeting. Secretary of State Rogers made a statement on February 18 expressing his disappointment at Peking's action. Of course he denied Peking's charges.

But Rogers did not stop there. He went on to say: "We especially regret this action inasmuch as our representative had been instructed to make or renew constructive suggestions." These suggestions, he later revealed, included consideration of an agreement on peaceful coexistence consistent with U.S. treaty obligations in the area; the issue of an exchange of reporters, scholars, scientists and scientific information; and the regularization of postal and telecommunications matters.

The Secretary of State's statement showed how eager the Nixon administration was to establish contact with Peking—though, as a result of the Liao case, the ambassadorial talks were delayed for almost a year. On January 20, 1970, the two sides again met in Warsaw, and exactly a month later there was another meeting, during which there was discussion of concluding an agreement on peaceful coexistence that had been proposed by Peking. It seemed that the U.S. Government was about ready to join Peking in issuing a statement that endorsed Peking's so-called Five Principles of Peaceful Coexistence. A month later there was yet another meeting in Warsaw.

For me and my colleagues in the Foreign Office the two talks were most alarming. For one thing, we had hoped that Nixon, in view of his well-known opposition to communism, would not resume the talks. After all, the earlier meetings largely had achieved their original purpose: securing the release of Americans imprisoned on the Chinese mainland. Second, if, for political reasons, the new administration should find it necessary to continue these talks, we had hoped they would stop at relaxing the restrictions on trade and travel and refrain from concluding an agreement on the Five Principles or from discussing the "Taiwan Question"—both highly political and sensitive matters to us. From the very beginning our government had been opposed in principle to the U.S. ambassadorial-level talks with the Chinese Communists, and we had lodged a number of protests with Washington over a period of many years. Even before the Nixon administration came in there had been no fewer than 134 such meetings, first in Geneva and later on in Warsaw. Each time, in order to keep the record straight, our government reiterated its opposition in the form of a diplomatic protest or a statement by the Foreign Office spokesman.

What was particularly disturbing to us this time was the fact that the Nixon administration, unlike its predecessors, had failed to inform us in advance of what the U.S. side had in mind to bring up at the two meetings, and American officials were vague and evasive when we asked them for a briefing on what had actually transpired. This raised serious doubts about whether the U.S. Government could be expected to stand by the assurances it had given us at the beginning of these talks many years before: that it would not discuss with the Chinese Communists behind our back anything affecting the rights and interests of the Republic of China on Taiwan.

Another unsettling fact was the mere one-month gap between the 135th and 136th sessions. Could it mean that in the future such meetings would take place more often? Besides, what was Secretary of State Rogers thinking of when he said in a TV interview on November 18, 1969, that such talks would not necessarily have to be held in Warsaw? Was he thinking of moving them to someplace in the United States, or even to Peking, as Kissinger subsequently indicated to Chiang Ching-kuo in 1970?

The Nixon administration did not leave us long in doubt before taking a number of steps that signaled to Peking its wish to reestablish contacts and relax tensions in the area. Among them:

- the Department of State announcement on July 21, 1969, that six categories of Americans might visit the Chinese mainland as tourists and that American citizens returning from overseas trips might bring back US$100 in goods made in Communist China;

- the Department of State announcement on December 19, 1969, that American firms overseas may trade with the Chinese Communists in nonstrategic goods and that the earlier rule limiting the value of made-in-mainland China goods an American citizen may bring back from an overseas trip was forthwith suspended;

- the Department of State acknowledgement on December 25, 1969, that the patrol of the Taiwan Straits by the U.S. Seventh Fleet was being made at irregular rather than regular intervals;

- the White House announcement on the same day that it opposed making available to the Republic of China a squadron of F4-Ds;

- the vote by both houses of Congress on January 26 and 28, 1970, to delete from the Foreign Military

Assistance bill the sum of US $54,500,000, originally earmarked for our purchase of the F4–D squadron mentioned above;

- Secretary of State Roger's letter to Senator William Fulbright, Chairman of the Senate Foreign Relations Committee, on May 11, 1970, to the effect that the Department had no definite view to offer on the proposal to abrogate the Formosa Resolution and three other resolutions;

- the extension by the Department of State on March 16, 1970, for the third time after a six-month interval, of existing restrictions on travel to mainland China and three other countries, with the addendum that the U.S. Government had no objection to travel to the Chinese mainland by anyone with a legitimate reason for doing so, nor would it prosecute those who did so;

- the Departments of State and Commerce announcement on April 6, 1970, that certain goods manufactured outside U.S. territory but containing American products or technology could be exported to Communist China.

Nixon defended all these measures as being necessary for safeguarding American interests and world peace.

Chapter IV

Dropping the First Shoe

At 6:40 P.M. on Thursday, July 15, 1971, the phone rang at Twin Oaks, my official residence in Washington, D.C. Joe Hsu, my butler, told me that the White House was on the wire. When I picked up the receiver, I found Secretary of State Rogers on the line. He was calling from San Clemente, Nixon's resort in California.

Rogers said that the President had asked him to inform me that within twenty minutes the President would go on TV to break the news that Kissinger had visited Peking on July 9–11 to see Chou En-lai and that the President had accepted Chou's invitation to visit Peking at an appropriate date before May, 1972.

Rogers explained that the purpose of this move was to increase contacts and improve relations with the Chinese Communists, hoping thereby to promote world peace. He added that the move was designed only to relax tensions in the area and was not directed at any third party. He asked me to report to President Chiang Kai-shek that the United States would never forsake her friends but would stand by the Mutual Defense

Treaty. He said, finally, that he looked forward to meeting me in person as soon as he returned to Washington on the following Monday, July 19.

The Secretary sounded quite agitated and I did not interrupt him. When he had finished, I told him that this came as a great shock and that I would report to my government immediately. Rogers replied that he could well imagine my government's first reaction but hoped it would not affect adversely our bilateral relations. He stressed again that Nixon had done this for the sake of world peace. Then he rang off.

For a couple of minutes I was simply dumbfounded. I could hardly believe my own ears. Then I tried to phone Taipei, but it so happened that operators at the U.S. end of the transoceanic switchboard were on strike that day. While I was trying to dictate a message, the phone rang again. This time the Foreign Office in Taipei was on the line asking me what I had heard from U.S. Government sources about Kissinger's secret trip to Peking. People in Taipei had just heard a news flash and wanted me to confirm that they had heard right the very first time. Like mine, Taipei's first reaction was one of utter disbelief. Putting down the phone, I turned on the TV just in time to see Nixon come on with his message.

The following day I checked with Sir James Plimsoll, the Australian Ambassador, and Nobukiko Ushiba, the Japanese Ambassador. Both said that Rogers called them long-distance from San Clemente about half an hour before Nixon made the announcement the previous evening. Needless to say, neither of them was very happy at having been kept in the dark until the last minute.

For almost two months the U.S. Government had been postponing its decision on how to handle our U.N. membership/representation question. Now, suddenly this bombshell! All this stalling had only one purpose apparently: to gain time for Kissinger's secret mission to Peking.

Yes, Rogers had sounded earnest and sincere in his assurances of U.S. determination to maintain friendly relations with the Republic of China and to honor its treaty obligations. But could we take these assurances seriously anymore? Since Nixon had accepted Chou's invitation to visit Peking, was it really inconceivable that one day he might decide to recognize the Chinese Communist regime? Though the State Department ostensibly was working on the so-called "Dual Representation" formula with regard to our seat in the U.N., could it be counted on to make an all-out effort for our sake? Now that Nixon had changed course, relations between the United States and the Republic of China could never be the same again.

These were the thoughts rushing through my mind that evening as I watched Nixon's prize TV performance announcing his dramatic breakthrough—a breakthrough for which he has not stopped claiming full credit ever since.

In Taipei, because of the thirteen-hour time difference, it was already morning—Friday, July 16. In Foreign Minister S.K. Chow's absence in Manila, Vice-Minister H.K. Yang hurriedly sent for U.S. Ambassador Walter McConaughy and lodged a strong protest. He called Nixon's move "a most unfriendly act" that was bound to have serious consequences. It turned out that McConaughy was also taken by surprise. He was embarrassed beyond words. All he could finally offer under the circumstances was a promise to transmit our protest to Washington right away.

In a parallel action I was instructed to protest to the Department of State. This I did by calling on Marshall Green, Assistant Secretary for East Asian and Pacific Affairs. He gave me the administration's line that Nixon's move was aimed at relaxing tensions in Southeast Asia. When I asked him what he knew of the circumstances under which Kissinger had made his trip, Green professed complete ignorance. And it actually seemed there was no one in Washington at the moment who could shed any light on the subject until the Secretary of State returned from San Clemente. Green told me that Rogers would receive me on Monday, July 19. He practically suggested that I withhold any further questions until I saw the Secretary himself.

But I went on telling Green how indignant everybody in Taipei was, how bewildered and shocked by this sudden development. I pointed out the great irony of the situation: While the U.S. Government was assuring us of its friendship and continued support, it was secretly dealing with the Chinese Communist regime. Now Nixon had even accepted an invitation from Chou En-lai to visit Peking. Where was all this going to end?

Green's answer was that people everywhere in the world had become tired of war; there could be no world peace without Communist China's participation. This was why the U.S. Government had decided to contact the Peking regime. Of course it was too early to say what would come out of this attempt. At any rate, he claimed, the initial reaction of people in various countries to Nixon's move seemed quite favorable. Henceforth, the pressure would be on Peking to show a similar desire for relaxation of tensions as a way toward world peace. Green ended by reassuring me that the U.S. in her history of foreign relations had never sacrificed any of her friends and she wasn't about to start now.

When I saw Secretary Rogers on Monday morning, he offered no apology. Instead he said that in view of the delicate nature of Kissinger's trip no foreign government had been informed beforehand, lest a premature leak spoil everything; and for the same reason, only a handful of people in the U.S. Government itself had any foreknowledge of what was going on. He realized the shock the trip must have caused the Chinese Government. Under the circumstances it was regrettable, but unavoidable. The move was aimed at improving relations with the Chinese Communists and not directly against any other country.

He went on to assure me that aside from Chou En-lai's invitation to Nixon, Kissinger had not reached any secret agreement with the Chinese Communists. Yes, Kissinger had exchanged views with Chou regarding the world situation and other matters of mutual concern to the two sides, but he had not discussed any concrete issues with his host. It was clear from Rogers's remarks that insofar as the United States was concerned, the time had come to consider dealings with Peking as none of the Republic of China's business—this despite his reassurance that the Sino–American Mutual Defense Treaty was still valid and would remain so. But for how much longer? He didn't say.

The Secretary then changed the subject. He wanted to know what we had decided to do about our membership/representation in the U.N. I reminded him that the ball had been in the American court for more than two months. What had the U.S. decided? He agreed that Nixon's announcement on July 15 would affect the situation somewhat. As a matter of fact, he said, initial inquiries with NATO countries indicated that unless the Republic of China agreed to yield her seat in the Security Council to the Chinese Communists, the "Dual Representation" formula the U.S. Government was then considering would have no chance whatsoever of being adopted in the General Assembly. He ventured to say that we might even fail to receive a simple majority on the "Important Question" resolution. Unless we agreed to yield our Security Council seat, he said, it was probably already too late for the U.S. to come up with another proposal. In short, we were being asked to give up our seat in the Security Council to the Chinese Communists in return for an American promise to do what it could to enable us to retain our seat in the General Assembly—without any guarantee, however, that this would work. Was this the kind of decision we had been awaiting from our ally for almost two months?

I called on Kissinger on July 27, two weeks after his return from Peking. He was in a good mood, very pleased with himself for having pulled off one of the most sensational diplomatic surprises of recent years. He began by saying that because of his friendship with the Republic of China, he felt very bad in having had to undertake the secret mission to Peking. He believed that was also how Nixon felt. But due to changes in the international situation and the mounting pressure at home, steps had to be taken to establish contact with Peking. However, they—Nixon and Kissinger—would never betray their friends.

I asked Kissinger what he and Chou En-lai talked about. He said Chou spoke heatedly on two questions, namely, Taiwan and the China seat in the United Nations. Chou claimed that Taiwan is "a province of China"—the People's Republic of China, that is—and should be reunited with the mainland. As to the China seat in the U.N., Chou called the Republic of China on Taiwan a usurper, who should be thrown out forthwith so that the Chinese people could resume their rightful membership in the world organization.

Kissinger said he lost no time in informing Chou of Nixon's position on the question of Taiwan: It must be settled by peaceful means. He also emphasized for Chou's benefit that the United States had a Mutual Defense Treaty with the Republic of China and had no intention of turning its back on the Republic of China, an ally and friend.

As to the U.N. matter, Kissinger said he hadn't discussed it with Chou at any length, nor did he touch upon the Republic of China's permanent membership in the Security Council. But he came away with the impression that the Chinese Communists would insist on our expulsion before they would agree to enter the world organization.

Kissinger assured me that he had not concluded any secret deals with Chou. Regarding Nixon's forthcoming visit to the Chinese mainland, Kissinger said that both sides had already begun preparations and that the United States most likely would propose a date for the visit. The earliest possible date was sometime in December.

What were some of Kissinger's personal impressions during this visit to Peking? I didn't have a chance to find out until he came to Twin Oaks for dinner on September 30. Then he revealed that he had been struck by the graciousness and courtesy of his Chinese hosts in Peking. He attributed this to China's long history and her old culture rather than to his hosts' communism. His experience in other Communist countries had not been quite the same. He also spoke glowingly of Mao Tse-tung and Chou En-lai as two of the most brilliant men he had ever met in his life. The inference he'd artfully arranged for me to draw was that it took a man of his caliber to stand up to these two "intellectual giants."

Kissinger told me that Nixon knew the Chinese Communists well and, therefore, harbored no illusions about what the future might have in store for his administration in its quest for a dialogue with Peking. But, Kissinger emphasized, Nixon would never sell any friends down the river.

This was two weeks after the so-called Lin Piao affair of September 13, 1971, in which Mao Tse-tung's heir-apparent was reported to have died in a mysterious plane crash in Outer Mongolia. I asked Kissinger whether Nixon would now cancel or delay his trip to Peking. He said the trip was still on because the two sides had many things to discuss.

On October 15, the day before he left for his second trip to Peking to prepare for Nixon's visit, I saw Kissinger again. I asked him whether the Taiwan question would be on the agenda. He said no but that this didn't mean the other side wouldn't bring it up. As a matter of fact, he sort of expected Chou En-lai to try to engage him in an exchange of views on "normalization of relations." He would not rise to the bait, though, since his boss was planning to go to the mainland himself shortly. Nixon would then be discussing the establishment of diplomatic relations when *he* went to Peking? Kissinger said Nixon would not initiate such a discussion, but if Chou En-lai should insist on a discussion, Nixon would preface his remarks by saying that the existing U.S. relations with the Republic of China were "nonnegotiable."

Kissinger was tremendously curious about Lin Piao's disappearance. He said he had received three different reports from three different U.S. intelligence sources. One said Lin was still alive and in good health. Another said he was seriously ill. A third said he had died in that plane crash. He didn't know which one to believe. What was *my* guess? I said Lin was probably involved in an attempted coup d'etat but had been discovered before he could pull it off. Most likely Lin had been placed under arrest to be disposed of summarily after a secret trial, if not disposed of already. At any rate, there had been a power struggle in Peking's hierarchy. The Lin Piao incident was quite likely touched off by his fear of serious consequences in Peking's relations with Moscow should Nixon succeed in his attempt to establish contacts with Peking.

Lin Piao, "Conqueror of Manchuria" in China's Civil War and Commander of the Chinese Communist "volunteers" who fought the Americans in the Korean War, had emerged as the most powerful military leader in the early phase of the Cultural Revolution. It was only with his backing that Mao had managed to dislodge Liu Shao-chi and Teng Hsiao-ping from their respective positions as the Communist regime's Chief of State and the Chinese Communist Party's Secretary-General. Lin's power finally became so great that Mao, much against his will and better judgment, agreed in the revised party constitution of April, 1969, to name Lin as the sole Vice-Chairman and, therefore, his successor. That Lin had sought this designation actively was to Mao certain proof of Lin's intentions of overthrowing him someday.

Judging by Kissinger's question, he was greatly puzzled by the Lin Piao affair and what it might portend for the United States. He didn't seem to think much of the U.S. intelligence community and its reporting on the Chinese mainland situation. It was largely a case of graded ignorance, he implied.

I turned to the question of our membership/representation in the U.N. General Assembly, which would soon meet in New York for its annual session. He was reasonably optimistic and thought we could survive again that year. He didn't think Peking would come in even if the "Dual Representation" resolution should be passed awarding Peking membership in the General Assembly and a seat in the Security Council while allowing the Republic of China to remain in the General Assembly. His reasoning was that Peking was really more interested in getting us out than in getting itself in. He advised us to keep quiet and let the Chinese Communists be the first to say "no" when the time came. This would improve our image as the more reasonable of the two parties to the dispute. What would happen in 1972? Kissinger didn't venture a guess, saying merely that it would indeed create a most interesting situation in the world organization.

I was about to leave when Kissinger put in what I thought was a most extraordinary performance. He said he had many friends in the Republic of China and, therefore, found going to Peking exceedingly painful. He really didn't care for the assignment but, with the situation being what it was, he had no choice but to go again, this time to make detailed arrangements for Nixon's official visit. According to his tentative schedule, he would be returning on October 25 and would see me again then.

John Holdridge, a China expert on Kissinger's staff who sat in during this conversation, saw me and my aide Henry Chen to the door. He added his own expression of the painfulness of having to go to Peking again so soon after the first trip. On the way back to the Chinese embassy Henry Chen and I exchanged glances. Neither of us said a word, but we were both wondering what had made Kissinger and Holdridge say such things to us. Could they be sincere in their professions of friendship for us, or was this a case of the crocodile shedding tears before devouring its helpless victim?

At any rate, it was during Kissinger's second visit to Peking that the U.N. General Assembly debated the question of Chinese membership/representation and then voted against the Republic of China, a founding member of the world organization and a permanent member of its Security Council. No doubt Kissinger's untimely presence in Peking was taken as an indication of America's change of policy from one of opposition to the Chinese Communist regime's admission to one of welcome. No country took seriously the argument of George Bush, the U.S. Ambassador to the U.N., that Washington wanted the Republic of China to remain in the General Assembly as an ordinary member. When the preliminary resolution to determine whether the issue was an "Important Question" was defeated, Communist China was quickly voted in. The "Dual Representation" resolution, concocted by the Americans, hadn't even had the chance to be brought up.

Sometime later I asked Kissinger what had gone wrong. Nothing had, he replied with a straight face—except that Bush had failed to delay the debate until after his return from Peking. Bush himself, it is clear, thought Kissinger was at the wrong place at the wrong time. Yet here was Kissinger suggesting that, had he been in charge, he would have found some excuse to hold off the debate/decision—even to the extent of declaring the U.N. building off limits for a week because of an outbreak of bubonic plague or some such disaster.

To the free Chinese this mutual recrimination between Bush and Kissinger gave little cause for comfort; by then it was just so much water over the dam.

By all criteria Nixon's week-long trip to mainland China in February, 1972, was an unprecedented event, and one of great historical importance. It was stage-managed with a view to achieving the maximum effect in worldwide publicity. Nixon said of his trip: "this was the week that changed the world." Of course he didn't mention whether the change was for the better or for the worse. To be kind, let us say that only the future will tell.

Watching Nixon's arrival in Peking on TV in Washington, I noticed the shock on his face as he and Mrs. Nixon emerged from the *Spirit of '76* to find only Chou En-lai and a few Chinese Communist officials waiting at the foot of the ramp to greet them. There was an honor guard but no crowds. Nixon looked sheepish and visibly ill at ease. He grinned nervously as he shook hands all around. Then he and Mrs. Nixon were quickly ushered into limousines with drawn curtains and driven away.

Another unforgettable scene is how painfully obeisant Nixon was when he met Mao Tse-tung in the latter's book-lined study. Yes, Mao was the undisputed ruler of the most populous nation in the world, but he had never been elected to the position. Why should the popularly elected President of the world's leading democracy appear so humble and respectful? True, for centuries Chinese emperors called themselves "Sons of Heaven" and expected all barbarians to kowtow to them. Nixon didn't kowtow physically, but psychologically he was on his knees paying homage to Mao.

A third indelible picture is that of Nixon going the rounds of the banquet tables that night to drink with everybody present whoever they were and whatever their rank. This was something no Oriental guest of honor with any sense of personal dignity would have done. Nixon demeaned himself on that occasion. He was too anxious to please the Chinese Communists, and this unfortunately set the tone for all of Washington's subsequent dealings with Peking.

In the first place, Nixon's trip to the mainland was unnecessary. He could have asked Chou En-lai to meet him at least halfway—say, in Honolulu. Instead, he chose to go to Peking himself, thereby confirming Chou and his colleagues in their belief that the Americans were prepared to make a deal.

Nixon might have imagined himself a China expert, having

visited the Republic of China a number of times before he became president. But Kissinger, his chief foreign affairs advisor, ought to have consulted some experts—not necessarily Harvard professors, but people who had lived in China for a number of years and were familiar with the traditional Chinese way of conducting business. If so, some of the laughable episodes of Nixon's visit to Peking could have been avoided.

Another thing which I found disconcerting was the fact that Nixon and Kissinger in their conversations with Mao and Chou had to rely on interpreters provided by the Chinese Communists. Surely someone in their own entourage could have handled two-way interpretation during high-level conversations. Instead, the Americans were at a disadvantage in that the Communist interpreters could slip in nuances or change the shades of meaning of what was being said. True, there were American officials who understand Chinese sitting in on these conversations to check on the accuracy of the translations, but did they have enough self-confidence to interrupt the flow of discussion and ask for corrections?

In my own experience as an official interpreter for our late President Chiang Kai-shek and our late Vice-President Chen Cheng, and also in my numerous trips to the United States as an aide to the incumbent President, I met a number of U.S. officials who were sufficiently bilingual to do a good two-way interpreting job. A few of them are descendants of American missionaries and were born or raised in China.

Apparently realizing the need for more such people, the U.S. Government has maintained Chinese-language training centers. There used to be one in Taichung, Taiwan! But it takes time. Two or three years are hardly enough time to learn any language well. It could enlist the services of Chinese–American scholars, of whom there are many nowadays, but it has not done so. This is probably because of the extremely sensitive nature of this kind of work, especially when the other side is Peking.

To back up a bit. I had gotten together with Kissinger again in mid-November, 1971, after his second trip to Peking. I had asked him what he had found out about Lin Piao's mysterious disappearance. Had he noticed any military activities around Peking? Did he think Chou En-lai was still very much in control?

In reply he said he hadn't found out anything about the Lin Piao case because, as a visitor, it would have been most inappropriate to be too inquisitive about his host's "family affair"...! No, there were no visible military movements around Peking. Of course, he added, he had no way of knowing what was going on elsewhere in the country. Yes, Chou seemed to be more in control than when he had seen him in July.

At the time, the Nixon administration was still speaking glibly of its determination to maintain friendly relations with the Republic of China on Taiwan while actively seeking to establish contacts with the Chinese Communists. I asked Kissinger whether there wasn't an inherent inconsistency here. How long did he think this could go on without causing irreparable harm to Washington–Taipei relations? He proferred no answer to my question. Instead, he confined himself to a reiteration of his earlier assurance that the U.S. Government would "absolutely not" sell us out or terminate the Mutual Defense Treaty. He was asking us literally "to take it easy." How could we, I asked, when our vital interests as a nation were at stake? He said he realized it was difficult for us but that it was U.S. policy to see to it that Taiwan remained a viable entity, regardless of what might come out of the U.S. attempt to reopen contacts with Peking.

How long would this U.S. policy last—five years, ten years? Kissinger said it would not change for at least five years and maybe even longer, depending on the world situation. Besides, in the meantime there were bound to be changes on the Chinese mainland now that Lin Piao had dropped out of sight. The question of succession after Mao's death, he said, would create a new crisis for an already shaky regime. As to the possibility of collective leadership in Peking after Mao's death, apparently Kissinger didn't think it would work, certainly not for long.

By then Kissinger and I had had three or four meetings and had come to know each other reasonably well. He understood that I was reporting on important conversations directly to the highest authorities in Taipei. He wanted us to remain calm while he worked out his scheme of "having the China cake and eating it too." He admitted that his primary concern, as that of Nixon, was the Soviet Union.

Probing a little deeper with him, I asked Kissinger what he saw in store for the Republic of China in the future. There were three possibilities, he said: (1) Talk with Peking and work out a peaceful settlement; (2) declare ourselves independent and thereby split China into two states; (3) wait for a big upheaval on the mainland and then ally ourselves with one of the Communist factions, perhaps reestablishing our rule in some of the mainland provinces. For the time being, however, his advice to us was "work hard and sit tight."

In this conversation, as in many others that followed it, Kissinger knew he wasn't "negotiating" with a foreign envoy. He was therefore relaxed and expansive and didn't have to watch every word he said.

The next time I saw Kissinger was on February 16, 1972, only a little over a week before he was to accompany Nixon to Peking. I had scarcely time to sit down before Kissinger said that as soon as the President left China he would send Marshall Green, Assistant Secretary of State for East Asian and Pacific Affairs, to Taipei to brief my government. He wanted my government to withhold all official comments on the Nixon trip until he'd had a chance to talk to me in person. He said nothing would please Peking more than to see Washington and Taipei exchange unfriendly remarks. He assured me that the U.S. Government would not make any concessions to Peking on matters of principle. In fact, no one expected anything concrete to come out of the trip. I asked Kissinger which side would be the first to raise the Taiwan question. Peking undoubtedly, he said, but the U.S. side would not accept the Communist regime's claim to being the sole legal government of China. He expected it to understand that the U.S. position on Taiwan wasn't going to change in a single encounter. Nor did the U.S. Government want *us* to negotiate with Peking: "We will never urge you to do anything against your will."

Moving further afield, I asked Kissinger what Nixon would have to talk about if he should be received by Mao Tse-tung. Taiwan and the Soviet Union, in that order, Kissinger replied. How far would Nixon be prepared to go to accommodate Mao? Not far, Kissinger allowed, except that the meeting would enhance Mao's prestige. I myself happened to think it would work the other way around, but I said nothing.

Kissinger stressed that as both Mao and Chou were getting on in years, the identity of his successors was a matter of great concern to everybody. What Nixon was doing was to ease the world tension, expecially the free world's relations with the Soviet Union. I asked him what effect Nixon's proposed trip would have on Japan. Kissinger said Japan had complained bitterly of the Nixon "shock," though her leaders knew very well the great importance the U.S. Government has always placed on maintaining close relations with Japan. Time and again Kissinger spoke of the deteriorating relations between Moscow and Peking. He predicted that this would dominate the world situation for a long time to come. He said a Soviet military attack on mainland China "cannot be ruled out even now."

And again Kissinger assured me that insofar as Washington–

Taipei relations were concerned, "nothing is going to change" as a result of Nixon's trip to Peking. The U.S. Government would not urge us to seek any "peaceful settlement" with Peking. It certainly would not bring any pressure to bear on us on this matter. This decision would not change. For Taiwan he could see no threat of a Chinese Communist attack for at least two or three years, unless the U.S. should terminate the Mutual Defense Treaty; and as far as he knew, the U.S. Government had no intention of doing so.

Kissinger was obviously doing his best to allay our government's growing apprehension in connection with Nixon's forthcoming trip to Peking.

The Shanghai Communique, which Nixon and Chou En-lai signed in Shanghai on February 28, 1972, at the end of Nixon's visit, was a most unusual document. It preceded by about seven years the establishment of formal relations between the United States and the Peking regime. Strictly speaking, the communique did not have the force of even an executive agreement because Nixon simply could not sign any such agreement with the head of a foreign government his own government had not recognized. Yet judging by all the official statements made by both parties to the communique and the outpourings of writers and commentators advocating close Washington–Peking ties during the interval, the communique came to assume an importance far greater than that of a formal treaty. Such was the effect of the communique signed by the two politicians—one subsequently disgraced and forced to resign because of the Watergate scandal; the other dead, but not forgotten—that it eventually superceded the Mutual Defense Treaty of 1954 which had bound the United States and the Republic of China as allies in the West Pacific for twenty-four years. Could this have been in Nixon's mind when he signed that piece of paper in Shanghai on that day?

The Shanghai Communique made strange reading indeed. Each side stated its position on various questions of special concern or vital interest to itself. Neither side denied the essential differences between them in their social systems and foreign policies. Both sides, however, agreed that the two countries, regardless of their different social systems, should conduct their relations in accordance with the so-called Five Principles of Peaceful Coexistence, without resorting to the use or threat of force.

At the time, the United States was trying to disengage itself from the Vietnam war. Its "constant primary objective" was a negotiated settlement of that conflict. It supported the Republic of Korea's efforts "to seek a relaxation of tension and increased communications" in the Korean Peninsula. It pledged to "continue to develop the existing close bonds" with Japan. Between India and Pakistan the U.S. favored the confirmation of the cease-fire." Conspicuously absent from the communique was any mention of U.S. relations with the Republic of China on Taiwan and the U.S. commitment under the Mutual Defense Treaty of 1954. The omission was, of course, deliberate.

The Chinese Communist side said: "China will never be a super-power and it opposes hegemony and power politics of any kind." It expressed firm support for "the struggles of all the oppressed people and nations for freedom and liberation" and for their right "to choose their social systems according to their own wishes" and the right to safeguard their own independence. Then it went on to lend "its firm support to the peoples of Vietnam, Laos and Cambodia in their efforts for the attainment of their goal" and to the eight-point program for "the peaceful unification of Korea" put forward by the Government of the Democratic People's Republic of Korea on April 12, 1971; and it took a stand for the abolition of the U.N. Commission for the Unification and Rehabilitation of Korea. It also noted its "firm opposition to" the revival and outward expansion of Japanese militarism and its support of Pakistan in the latter's dispute with India over the question of Jammu and Kashmir.

Subsequent developments, especially Communist China's border war with Vietnam of February–March, 1979, surely must have made Peking's current leadership wish Chou had not been so firm in his support for "the peoples of Vietnam, Laos and Cambodia."

So much for their respective positions. The two parties to the communique really got down to business when they stated their mutual goals, to wit:

1. Progress toward "normalization of relations" between China and the United States is in the interest of all countries.

2. Both wish to reduce the danger of international military conflict.

3. Neither should seek hegemony in the Asia–Pacific region and each is opposed to efforts by any other country or group of countries to establish such hegemony.

4. Neither is prepared to negotiate on behalf of any third party or to enter into agreements or understandings with the other directed at other states.

The expression "normalization of relations" appears no fewer than four time in the communique. But nowhere in the document is there a definition of what this really means. Whether the omission was intentional or otherwise on the U.S. side, this was quickly seized upon by the Chinese Communists as the basis for their demand that, as the price for "normalization of relations," Washington must sever diplomatic relations with the Republic of China, abrogate the Mutual Defense Treaty of 1954, and withdraw all U.S. military forces and installations from Taiwan.

It was on the question of Taiwan that Chou En-lai showed his diplomatic skill. He claimed that the Government of the People's Republic of China is the sole legal government of China; that Taiwan is a province of China that has long been returned to the mainland; that the liberation of Taiwan is China's internal affair, in which no other country has the right to interfere; and that all U.S. forces and military installations must be withdrawn from Taiwan.

In one masterful stroke Chou left open only one option to the United States on the matter of Taiwan, when he had the following sentence inscribed in the communique:

> The Chinese Government firmly opposes any activities which aim at the creation of "one China, one Taiwan," "one China, two governments," "two Chinas," and "independent Taiwan" or advocate that "the status of Taiwan remains to be determined."

All five of those formulas probably had received American consideration at one time or another during the thirty-year span between the Communist seizure of power on the Chinese mainland in 1949 and Carter's recognition of the Peking regime as the sole legitimate government of China at the end of 1978.

In acknowledging in the communique that "all Chinese on either side of the Taiwan Straits maintain there is but one China and that Taiwan is a part of China," Nixon (or, rather, Kissinger) thought he was being clever, since this was also the position of the Republic of China—though for a reason that is diametrically opposite the Communist regime's. But Nixon's greatest mistake was to have said that "The United States does not challenge that position"—especially when the words "not challenge" were translated by the Chinese Communists to mean "approve" in the Chinese text.

The U.S. side reaffirmed "its interest in a peaceful settlement of the Taiwan question by the Chinese themselves." What a feeble counterproposal to the Chinese Communist demand that "the liberation of Taiwan is China's internal affair in which no other country has the right to interfere."

It appeared on the surface that the only commitment Nixon made in the communique was the withdrawal of U.S. forces and military installations from Taiwan. He thought he was being very prudent by prefacing this pledge with the qualifying phrase, "with this prospect in mind." He no doubt believed that a peaceful settlement of the Taiwan question would take a long, long time. All he had to do in the meantime was "progressively reduce" U.S. forces and military installations on Taiwan "as the tension in the area diminishes."

At the time of the signing of the Shanghai Communique, there were close to ten thousand U.S. troops on Taiwan, stationed at Republic of China bases to support U.S. military operations in Vietnam. As the United States began to disengage itself from Vietnam, naturally the need for keeping U.S. forces in Taiwan was proportionately reduced. While Nixon anticipated no difficulty in this connection, his counterpart, Chou En-lai, saw in this an opening wedge to prod the United States military forces to leave Taiwan as a prelude to the termination of the Mutual Defense Treaty.

It should be pointed out, though hardly necessary at this late date, that nowhere in the communique did Nixon promise to sever diplomatic relations with the Republic of China on Taiwan or to abrogate the Mutual Defense Treaty. As a matter of fact, immediately after the signing of this mongrel document, Kissinger called a news conference in Shanghai at which he emphasized that there had been no change in U.S. relations with the Republic of China and in U.S. determination to honor its commitment under the Mutual Defense Treaty. Someone later asked him why, if this was the case, it hadn't been put in the Shanghai Communique. His bland reply was to the effect that the Nixon party were guests on the Chinese mainland and it would have been inappropriate to include such a passage in the communique—especially in view of the fact that the Mutual Defense Treaty was directed at their host. Besides, he said, the Chinese Communists did not mention the Mutual Defense Treaty anywhere in their presentation in the communique. However, if anyone had taken this as evidence of the Chinese

Communists' lack of concern over the continued existence of this treaty, he was sadly mistaken, as later developments would prove.

Chapter V

A Round of Calls

On the morning of February 28, 1972, General Alexander Haig, Kissinger's deputy in the National Security Council, asked me to drop in at his office. He said Kissinger had just called from Anchorage, Alaska, where the *Spirit of '76,* carrying the Nixon party back to Washington, had stopped for refueling. Kissinger was worried because American news media reports on the Shanghai Communique all tended to play up the part concerning Taiwan. He wanted Haig to tell me that the section on Taiwan was the result of a careful study by the President, the Secretary of State, and himself. The U.S. position on Taiwan remained unchanged. As to the American pledge to withdraw military forces and installations from Taiwan, Kissinger wanted him to tell me that this was not unilateral but based on the principle of reciprocity, as evidenced by such quali- fying phrases as "with this prospect in mind" and "as the tension in the area diminishes." The whole idea was to let the Chinese Communists know that they must not attack Taiwan.

Haig made a point of reminding me of what Kissinger had told the news media following the signing of the communique in Shanghai: that the United States would continue to abide by its Mutual Defense Treaty with the Republic of China on Taiwan. But why wasn't this stated in the communique itself? I asked Haig. The latter replied that probably it had been considered unnecessary, since President Nixon had already noted in his foreign policy report to Congress on February 25, only three days earlier, that the United States would continue to honor her treaty commitments to the security of her Asian allies, and had mentioned the Republic of China by name as one of these allies. Now that the American news media had singled out for special attention the section of the communique concerning Taiwan, the question clearly had become an issue in American domestic politics. Kissinger hoped that Taiwan's news media would not be going off on the same tangent, because to do so would yield results that were not to our own benefit. He had asked Haig to tell me that he, Kissinger, would suggest that the President reiterate his determination to honor the U.S. commitment for the defense of Taiwan in case of a Chinese Communist attack.

The Spirit of '76 landed at Andrews Air Force Base outside of Washington, D.C., on the evening of the 28th. Vice-President Spiro Agnew, members of the Congress, members of the Cabinet, and members of the diplomatic corps were on hand in great numbers to give Nixon an enthusiastic welcome. I was not there but home at Twin Oaks hosting a dinner for some American friends. NBC, probably considering the dinner a made-up excuse, asked permission to send a camera crew to my residence to film the occasion. At the appropriate hour I had the dining room TV set turned on so everybody could watch the presidential party's return. And our dinner too was on TV that night.

Why wasn't I there at Andrews Air Force Base that evening? It is true that according to protocol, whenever an ambassador has been notified that he ought to be on hand to see off or welcome home the chief of state of the country to which he is accredited, he is expected to be on hand, especially if the chief of state is going to or returning from the ambassador's own country. But in the case of Nixon's visit to mainland China there was an important difference. Of course China is still my country, but no one can deny the fact that since 1949 the mainland portion has been under Communist control. Nixon was now returning from meetings with Communist leaders, who, in the eyes of the laws of the Republic of China, are rebels, their government a rebel regime. As the Ambassador of the Republic of China, I simply could not go out to Andrews Airbase that evening. But I needed an excuse. I could have left Washington to visit with some outlying Chinese community or fulfill a long-standing speaking engagement or host a dinner myself. As it happened, a dinner originally set for February 27 had been moved back a day at the guests' request. At the time this change was made there had been as yet no definite word from the White House regarding the exact date and hour of Nixon's return. I would have been in a tough spot had the *Spirit of '76* landed at Andrews Air Force Base early in the afternoon. In that case I would have pleaded a sudden indisposition and cancelled the dinner as well; nothing would make me do what I had been forbidden to do. The U.S. protocol people showed good sense in not asking me for an explanation.

In his homecoming speech President Nixon said that "the primary goal of this trip was to re-establish communication with the People's Republic of China after a generation of hostility. We achieved that goal." Then he ticked off various agreements reached with Peking to expand cultural, educational, and journalistic contacts; to broaden trade; and to strengthen future communication. "Most important," he added, "we have agreed on some rules of international conduct which will reduce the risk of confrontation and war in Asia and in the Pacific. We agreed that we are opposed to domination of the Pacific area by any one power." This was the closest he came in that speech to stating the real purpose of his trip to Peking—a warning to the

Soviet Union not to establish hegemony in the Asia–Pacific region, for to do so would be to risk the joint opposition of the Chinese Communists and the United States.

Of particular interest to the Republic of China were the following short paragraphs in Nixon's speech:

> With respect to Taiwan, we stated our established policy that our forces overseas will be reduced gradually as tensions ease, and that our ultimate objective is to withdraw our forces as a peaceful settlement is achieved.
>
> We've agreed that we will not negotiate the fate of other nations behind their back and we did not do so in Peking. There were no secret deals of any kind.
>
> We have done all this without giving up any United States commitment to any country.

These three short paragraphs merit the closest study by students of diplomacy. In the first one Nixon was talking about Taiwan, and yet he said "our forces overseas" would be reduced gradually as tensions eased. Why hadn't he said "our forces in Taiwan?" He was vague again in the next clause in stating that "our ultimate objective is to withdraw our forces as a peaceful settlement is achieved." Withdrawn from where? From Taiwan? If so, what "peaceful settlement" did he have in mind?

In the second paragraph Nixon proclaimed "There were no secret deals of any kind." Nixon was said to have given Chou En-lai privately an understanding that he would establish diplomatic relations with Peking should he win a second term. Nixon denied this, but few doubted that this was the impression he had left with Chou!

In the third paragraph Nixon claimed to have reached all these agreements "without giving up any United States commitment to any country." He probably hadn't, at least not right away. But can anyone deny that Nixon paved the way for Jimmy Carter to renege on the U.S. commitment to the defense of Taiwan and the Pescadores when, in December, 1978, he gave the Republic of China a year's notice of the abrogation of the Mutual Defense Treaty of 1954? (The fact that Nixon accepted Carter's invitation to attend the White House dinner in honor of Chinese Communist Vice-Premier Teng Hsiao-ping on January 29, 1979, was his way of reminding everybody that it was he who had taken the first step toward reopening to mainland China; that if there was credit to apportion, he should be awarded his share.)

Kissinger did keep his word and received me the very first day after his return to Washington. He was anxious to explain that although the Mutual Defense Treaty of 1954 had not been mentioned in the Shanghai Communique, he had lost no time in making up for this omission by announcing to the U.S. news media accompanying them that the United States was determined to abide by its commitment to the Republic of China under that treaty. He said the President had also stressed this point when he briefed congressional leaders and a group of selected journalists.

According to Kissinger, the Mutual Defense Treaty was not mentioned in the communique because the treaty was directed at the Chinese Communists; the U.S. side felt it could not very well refer to its existence "while on their soil." However, the Chinese Communists had been told in no uncertain terms that the United States would continue to honor this treaty.

Continuing, Kissinger said that he realized the importance of this treaty to Taiwan's security and that he understood the difficult position in which the recent turn of events had placed us. But the United States had said nothing about its possible abrogation. Why, then, he asked, were people in the Republic of China speculating on its future? Certainly this could only be harmful to our own interests.

Kissinger then drew my attention to such wordings in the communique concerning the Taiwan question as "It affirms its interest in a peaceful settlement" and "with this prospect in mind"—adding that they showed that the United States had not made any concrete concessions to the Chinese Communists. The latter certainly knew of the existence of the Mutual Defense Treaty. Since they neither demanded its abrogation nor referred to it in the communique, why should the United States?

I asked Kisinger what was meant by the sentence, "The United States Government does not challenge that position." His explanation was that this was because Chinese on both sides of the Taiwan Straits maintain there is but one China and that Taiwan is a part of China. I pointed out that the "China" referred to here would be taken to mean Communist China and not free China. He said that such an interpretation would be most unwise.

The next question I put to Kissinger was why throughout the communique were we referred to as "Taiwan," the name of the island, and never by our proper name, the "Republic of China?" His explanation was even harder to believe: There was no special significance. It was purely a case of oversight, he said with a straight face. If true, this certainly reflects on the competence of the China experts in the presidential party, though I happen to doubt the truthfulness of this explanation.

Kissinger went on to say that the Shanghai Communique was not a treaty or a secret agreement. That was why the U.S. side had made it deliberately as vague as possible. With regard to the withdrawal of American forces from Taiwan, the U.S. Government had notified Taipei already of its intention to withdraw the two squadrons of C-130s and three thousand troops in fiscal year 1973. There were no plans for more withdrawals.

On the question of a peaceful settlement of the Taiwan question, Kissinger disclosed that Chou En-lai would like to talk with President Chiang Kai-shek face-to-face and had wondered whether the U.S. could help bring this about. Kissinger's reply had been: "This is your business." The U.S. position was neither to encourage nor to discourage direct talks between Peking and Taipei. The U.S., Kissinger added, would never pressure the Republic of China in this connection. Then what were we expected to do? "Nothing. Just sit tight!" he said.

I hazarded the remark, "I suppose Chou En-lai must have been very pleased with what he got out of the communique." Not quite, Kissinger said. Chou had at first asked that the "Chinese side" in the communique be referred to simply as "China." The American side, however, insisted that the full name, "People's Republic of China," be used so as to avoid any ambiguity. He further revealed that Chou wanted Nixon to agree to an immediate withdrawal of American forces in Taiwan, with no condition attached as to time-frame and the circumstances under which this was to take place. The American side, according to Kissinger, could not accept this and insisted that some qualifying phrase be inserted. Hence such expressions as "with this prospect in mind" and "as the tension in the area diminishes."

Remembering what General Haig had told me the previous morning, I asked Kissinger regarding the likelihood of the Shanghai Communique kicking up an internal political dispute. Not unless men like Senators Goldwater and James Buckley and former California Governor Ronald Reagan, all Republicans, should use the communique to attack their own President, he ventured.

Quickly changing the subject, Kissinger observed that Mao and Chou would most likely pass away within the next five years, and by then there were bound to be upheavals on the Chinese mainland. In the meantime Taiwan must be kept alive. He didn't think the Chinese Communists would try to take Taiwan by force before 1976. Here Kissinger was probably thinking of the end of Nixon's second term.

Throughout this meeting Kissinger looked uncomfortable

and was on the defensive. Before I stood up I made two requests: First, that Nixon reassure us of continued U.S. friendship and support and issue a definite statement on U.S. determination to honor its commitment to us under the Mutual Defense Treaty in order to offset the apprehension in my country aroused by the failure to mention the treaty in the Shanghai Communique; second, that having received instructions to return shortly to Taipei for consultations, I would very much like to see Nixon before I left. Kissinger said he would see what could be done. As it turned out, he failed on the first matter but delivered on the second.

As Kissinger had promised, Marshall Green, Assistant Secretary of State for East Asian and Pacific Affairs, made a visit to Taipei on March 3, 1972, to brief my government on the Nixon visit to Peking. Earlier he had been in Tokyo and Seoul on similar missions.

Marshall was received by Foreign Minister S.K. Chou, Vice-Premier Chiang Ching-kuo, and Vice-President/Premier C.K. Yen. But he didn't see President Chiang Kai-shek. Emerging from these meetings, Green told the press corps in Taipei that he had assured our officials that "faithfully honoring all of our commitments remains a cornerstone of U.S. policy." These commitments were understood to include mutual defense and other ties with Taiwan. Green also stressed that Washington would encourage continued investment in Taiwan by American firms.

A week or so after his return to Washington I met Green in person. He told me that when he'd heard I was not at Andrews Air Force Base the night of Nixon's return, he knew that he would not be received by President Chiang.

As soon as I arrived in Taipei on March 8, I was shown minutes of Green's talks with our government leaders. He had covered more or less the same ground, stating U.S. determination to honor its treaty obligations to the Republic of China, stressing the absence of any secret agreements, and explaining why the United States had felt it necessary to reestablish contacts with the Chinese Communists, etc.

Green, I thought, did a good job of detailing the mechanics of the two-tier discussions that were held first in Peking and later moved to Hangchow and finally to Shanghai, where the communique was signed and released. Kissinger attended the Nixon–Chou talks, while Green was present at the conversations between Secretary of State Rogers and Peking's Foreign Minister Chi Peng-fei. Green stayed in constant touch with Kissinger so that American participants of one group would know what was being discussed by the other group.

According to Green, Nixon and Chou spent most of their time exchanging views on philosophical and historical questions and covered a wide range of subjects. Each stated his ideas on various international problems. Because of the great dissimilarity in their ideological concepts and in the national interests of the two countries, naturally there were differences and disagreements. The two men had taken note of the differences and agreed to move on to the next topic.

Problems concerning third parties, such as Japan, Korea, and countries in Southeast Asia, were taken up only marginally. The Chinese Communist side reiterated its continued support of North Korea and North Vietnam. This was Peking's way of letting its friends in Pyongyang and Hanoi know that it was not negotiating their interests behind their backs. The American side used the same approach while discussing international problems. It would not negotiate on behalf of any third party but confined itself to stating and explaining its own positions and policies.

At the Rogers–Chi meetings, despite Peking's dissatisfaction with the then existing world situation and its earlier grievance against the United States, the atmosphere was on the whole congenial. The emphasis was on finding ways and means to increase contacts in trade, cultural exchange, science, and technology. The American side had no illusions and therefore would seek only gradual improvement and on a limited scale, according to Green.

The drafting of the Shanghai Communique was a most time-consuming and frustrating exercise, Green revealed. John Holdridge, who took notes at the Nixon–Chou talks, had the unenviable task of working on the draft on the U.S. side. Several times he had to work till early in the morning. The Rogers–Chi talks touched upon topics in the communique, and then it was left to staffers on both sides to battle over the wordings. Significantly, the Chinese Communist side never asked the United States to get out of Asia or to discontinue its friendly relations with the Republic of China, Japan, Korea, and countries in Southeast Asia. The American side took this as an indication that Peking was prepared to accept the status quo.

Did acceptance of the status quo also apply to the Republic of China? The communique was silent on this point. Three of Peking's subsequent demands for "normalization of relations" with the United States—severance of diplomatic relations, abrogation of the Mutual Defense Treaty, and withdrawal of all American military forces and installations from Taiwan—showed how sadly mistaken the Americans were.

The American side, except for stating its position on its relations with the Republic of China, didn't insist on mentioning the Mutual Defense Treaty lest Peking refuse to sign the communique. Peking, for that matter, hadn't condemned the treaty either in the communique. Nor had it asked for the immediate and unconditional withdrawal of American forces from Taiwan. According to Green and Holdridge, this in a way was Peking's concession.

Green maintained, as President Nixon had indicated before he went to Peking, that there was no previously agreed agenda.

The communique came as the result of preliminary discussions between Rogers and Chi, with each side stating its positions on various matters. There were long and heated exchanges before the final draft was agreed upon.

Secretary of State William P. Rogers—the Attorney-General in the Eisenhower administration—was an old acquaintance of mine. He had been a successful corporation lawyer and was smooth and gentlemanly. For the Nixon party's Peking visit it was arranged that the President, accompanied by Kissinger, would meet with Mao Tse-tung and Chou En-lai; Rogers was shunted aside to spend hours on end discussing matters of secondary importance with Foreign Minister Chi Peng-fei, who was nothing but a bureaucrat. Kissinger got all the publicity and Rogers received very little credit for his effort. But to members of the Washington diplomatic corps Rogers was the head of the foreign affairs establishment in the U.S. Government. To be perfectly correct, I also asked to see him when arrangements were being made for me to meet with Kissinger.

My meeting with Rogers took place at the Department of State on March 2. He knew I had been received by Kissinger the previous day and that at that very moment (already March 3 in Taipei) Marshall Green was in Taipei briefing our government officials. Rogers wanted to make sure that no misunderstanding whatsoever had arisen between our two governments as a result of Nixon's trip. He said he would be happy to answer any questions.

Continuing, Rogers said the Nixon trip had gone off according to plan; there were no surprises. Although the Taiwan question was an important one, each side merely stated its own position in the Shanghai Communique without trying to reach any agreement. The wording was carefully chosen to avoid any unnecessary offense or irritation to the other side. This showed that the Chinese Communists "wished to get along with us," Rogers said. Taiwan was a minor problem to them. Their main concern, he said, was the presence of large Soviet military forces on their border. But for domestic political reasons the Chinese Communists had to list the Taiwan question as an important item on the agenda. The American side had its own reason to emphasize its relations with the Republic of China, including the commitment under the Mutual Defense Treaty to Taiwan's security. It was on the basis of this understanding that the Shanghai Communique was drafted and finally agreed upon. As the Chinese Communists hadn't demanded the abrogation of the treaty in the communique, so too the American side hadn't insisted on mentioning its treaty commitment to the Republic of China. To avoid any wrong impression, Kissinger then announced the U.S. Government's determination to honor its treaty commitment and Nixon made a similar statement in his homecoming speech at Andrews Air Force Base. Rogers wanted me and my government to stop worrying on this score. "We are going to live up to our commitment" was how the Secretary of State summed it up.

Asked what the U.S. side meant when it said that "it does not challenge this position," Rogers declared this could also be interpreted to mean that the U.S. side had not accepted this position either, since both Peking and Taipei maintained there is but one China. The U.S. purpose was to improve relations with the Chinese Communists but not to extend diplomatic recognition; after all, the United States had diplomatic relations with the Republic of China. What the two sides in the communique had agreed to were cultural, scientific, journalistic, and trade contacts and consultations that would further the normalization of relations, to which end a senior U.S. representative would be sent to Peking from time to time. Peking would not send anyone to Washington so long as there was a Republic of China embassy there. Later on the two sides might establish a regular point of contact in another country close to the United States. Rogers didn't say exactly which country that would be, but I got the distinct impression the choice was Canada, where Peking already had an embassy. As it turned out later on, Paris was selected.

No country need derive any fear from Nixon's trip to Peking, Rogers went on. There were no secret agreements and no under-the-counter deals. The U.S. side expressed the hope of easing tensions and the Chinese Communist side agreed not to resort to the use or threat of force in settling international disputes. Moreover, the U.S. side pointed out its interest in a peaceful settlement where Taiwan was concerned. The ultimate American goal was peace. The expression "as the tension in the area diminishes" did not apply to the Taiwan area alone. It was put in the communique because the Chinese Communists objected to any specific mention of Vietnam in this context. Besides, the few thousand American forces were in Taiwan to support U.S. military operations in Vietnam and would be withdrawn as part of the American disengagement from the Vietnam war. The Americans had nothing to hide, Rogers emphasized.

Why was the communique completely silent on U.S. relations with the Republic of China? I asked. Only the previous October the U.S. Government had taken the position in the United Nations that there was one China but two governments. Yet in the Shanghai Communique the Republic of China was reduced to a mere island, Taiwan. "Don't you people also maintain there is but one China?" Rogers retorted. Yes, I asserted; that was because the Government of the Republic of China, having been elected by the Chinese people as a whole in accordance with our constitution, was the only legitimate government of our country. The so-called People's Republic of China was nothing but a rebel regime.

Under my persistent questioning the Secretary of State was getting noticeably snappy in his replies. Finally he said: "We do not challenge your position either."

Moving to another part of the communique, I asked why the U.S. side had accepted, this time, Peking's so-called Five Principles of Peaceful Co-Existence, including "non-interference in the internal affairs of other states." Since the Chinese Communists claimed that Taiwan is "a province of China"—meaning *their* China—wouldn't they interpret the maintenance of the Mutual Defense Treaty as U.S. interference in their China's internal affairs? Rogers's reply was that these so-called Five Principles did not differ much from the principles on which the United Nations had been founded and the United States found it difficult not to agree to them. Of course, he added quickly, he knew very well that Chou En-lai had Taiwan in mind when he talked about noninterference in the internal affairs of other states. "But from your country's point of view," Rogers said, "this wouldn't have any effect whatsoever, nor would it cause your country any problem. Others, however, might take this as an impairment to your country's international status." That's why, Rogers explained, Marshall Green would also be visiting and briefing the leaders of several other countries in the area on the Peking conversations.

I thanked the Secretary for his kindness and patience in explaining things to me. "I believe I am correct in my understanding that the Mutual Defense Treaty is still very much alive and that your country will continue to supply us with needed defense weapons." "Yes," he answered, "but I do not have all the details at my fingertips." Here an aide to Rogers interjected, remarking that the established U.S. procedure for considering our requests for military assistance would remain unchanged despite the Nixon trip, but the general trend was toward further reductions.

One last question. "Is it true that the U.S. Government has already, as a matter of policy, decided that henceforth we would be referred to only as Taiwan instead of by our proper name, the Republic of China?" Rogers's answer was that the U.S. Government would continue to address us as the Republic of China, except when it was negotiating with the Chinese Communists. And why was that? "Well," he explained, "since it is our avowed purpose to improve relations with them, we mustn't irritate them unnecessarily." "But then why did President Nixon refer to us as Taiwan in his homecoming speech? He wasn't negotiating with anybody then!" I hated to embarrass the Secretary of State, a man for whom I had developed great admiration and respect. He was obviously defending a foreign policy in whose formulation he had played only a nominal role. He was quick-witted, however, and came up with the plausible-sounding explanation that the President, having used the term "Taiwan" so many times in Peking for the last few days, hadn't had time to readjust himself mentally to the Washington parlance.

Rogers is one of the finest men I met during my tour of duty in Washington, a warm and charming man and a man of known integrity. We invariably greeted each other as "Mr. Secretary" and "Mr. Ambassador" and then quickly switched to "Bill" and "Jimmy." Whenever I was with him I felt at ease. We got along very well.

Rogers left the Department of State in September, 1973, before the Watergate scandal had implicated Nixon and some of his principal White House aides. He couldn't have picked a better time to return to private life and all his friends were happy for him. Bill Rogers simply cleaned his desk and moved back to his old law firm, Rogers and Wells. He came through all this untarnished, as clean as a hound's tooth.

Looking through my notes to refresh my memory, I find that a year after the Peking trip, 1973, I had two more interesting visits with Rogers—one while he was still the Secretary of State and another some three months after he had returned to law practice.

The first of these took place on June 19, two months after my return from another round of consultations in Taipei. I had asked for an earlier appointment but the Secretary was out of the country much of the time. I conveyed to him greetings from Premier Chiang Ching-kuo and also briefed Rogers on our basic policy of not having anything to do with either the Peking regime or the Soviet Union. He agreed it was a right policy.

"On our part," Rogers said, "we do not intend to sever our diplomatic relations or abrogate our Mutual Defense Treaty with your country. We are not just saying this to your government but are saying the same thing to other governments for their information."

Rogers admitted that the U.S. Government would continue to seek improved relations with the Chinese Communists, but the latter had not tried to bring pressure to bear on the United States for diplomatic recognition. Nor, he revealed, had Chou En-lai expressed any such wish in his talks with visitors from other foreign countries. On the contrary, Chou had told a Danish diplomat that he was quite satisfied with the newly established relations.

Rogers assured me that he anticipated no changes in Washington–Taipei relations. The United States would continue to help the Republic of China in every way possible. He was most pleased with our economic progress. As far as he knew, no one in the Nixon administration had even suggested that the existing bilateral relations be changed.

"Despite rumors to the contrary," Rogers emphasized, "we have repeatedly announced that our China policy is working."

The timing of my visit had double significance: First, it came only a month after Washington and Peking had exchanged liaison offices headed by an officer with the rank of ambassador; second, although Leonid Brezhnev was visiting in Washington, Rogers took time out of a busy schedule to be with me.

On December 6, 1973, I called on Rogers again, this time in the Washington office of his law firm. He received me cordially. Now that he no longer was the Secretary of State, I said, he might find it possible to talk more freely about Chinese–American relations. First of all, what did he think of this latest visit of Kissinger's to Peking, and how would he interpret the joint communique? Rogers replied that there was nothing new in this communique. He saw no special implications in its wording.

Did the U.S. Government have any timetable for normalization of relations with Peking? Rogers said Nixon had never mentioned one to him. If there was such a timetable, it could only exist in Kissinger's head. He certainly was not aware of one. As far as the U.S. Government was concerned, all it wanted was to establish contacts with the Peking regime in order to facilitate trade, cultural, and other substantive relations. Having achieved these objectives, the U.S. Government ought to feel satisfied. The title each other's representative would carry was not a matter of great concern to the U.S. side. Furthermore, the U.S. Government was not about to sacrifice an old friend, the Republic of China, just to please Peking. Rogers could not see any advantage to the United States doing so.

He expressed serious doubts about political stability on the Chinese mainland. He recalled that when he accompanied Nixon to Peking in February, 1972, he had been struck by Mao's decrepitude and Chou's failing health. What would happen on the mainland when the two old men left the scene was anybody's guess. For these reasons and more, Rogers said, there was no need from the U.S. standpoint to change the liaison offices into something else.

President Nixon received me in the Oval Office on the afternoon of March 6, 1972, shortly after his return from a vacation in Florida. In accordance with Kissinger's suggestion, I was unaccompanied by any of my embassy aides. The only third party present at the meeting was Kissinger himself.

I began by thanking Nixon for his kindness in receiving me. As I would be leaving for Taipei the following day to report to my government on recent developments, were there any messages he would like me to relay to President Chiang Kai-shek?

"Please convey to both your President and Madame Chiang my warmest personal regards, as well as my best wishes for their continued good health," Nixon said. He also wanted me to assure our President of his personal friendship and the friendship of the United States for my country.

"Between our two countries we have a Mutual Defense Treaty. Please tell your government that the United States is determined to abide by its commitments to the Republic of China."

I thanked him for this reassurance, which, I said, I felt certain would be greatly appreciated by President Chiang.

I followed this up by asking Nixon whether, aside from what Kissinger and Rogers had told me in Washington and what Green had told our government leaders in Taipei, there was anything about his recent trip to Peking he might want me to report to my President in person. He said he regretted very much that Green had not been able to see President Chiang Kaishek; apparently our government officials felt that Green, not having been present at the Nixon–Mao and Nixon–Chou conversations, was therefore not completely privy to what had transpired at those top-level meetings. Actually, Green knew everything about these discussions, and what Kissinger had told me in Washington and what Green had told our officials in Taipei "was the whole truth."

Nixon said that while it was true that nothing was said in the Shanghai Communique about the Mutual Defense Treaty, Kissinger had clarified this point at his news conference in Shanghai by reiterating the U.S. Government's determination to honor the treaty, and that he himself, in his homecoming speech, had emphasized that there were no secret deals of any kind. He didn't negotiate the fate of other countries behind their backs.

Speaking of the Shanghai Communique as a whole, Nixon said it was a joint statement in which each side stated its positions on various subjects without trying to reach an agreement.

In other words, as he put it, the two sides merely "agreed to disagree."

"Besides, the communique is not a treaty," Nixon asserted, but he didn't elaborate the point. Could he have meant that since it was not a treaty, the communique was not binding on the two parties concerned? Obviously the Chinese Communists thought differently, and Carter's action of December 15, 1978, showed how he felt about it too.

Nixon confirmed that the Chinese Communists at first demanded that throughout the communique Taiwan be referred to as "a province of China." He said he had demurred, insisting that the U.S. side could refer to Taiwan only as "a part of China." Nixon's reasoning was that being dubbed "a province of China" would place Taiwan immediately in a subordinate position vis-a-vis the People's Republic of China; whereas being labeled "a part of China" would give Taiwan, despite its smaller size, a higher status vis-a-vis the mainland. I could tell by listening to Nixon that he was very pleased with himself on this matter.

Further on the Taiwan question, Nixon said that it had been the U.S. Government's position that this should be settled by peaceful means. The United States had no intention of interfering, nor would it urge either side to negotiate or offer any suggestion or formula. How should the question be settled? That was something for the two parties directly concerned to study and work out by themselves. The United States, Nixon stressed, wanted no part of it.

What sort of time-frame was he considering when he used the phrase "with this prospect in mind?" Nixon's answer was "Maybe two years, three years or five years. Anyway, the United States will not try to rush things."

Kissinger, who had sat quietly facing Nixon all this time, spoke up at this point. He said the U.S. Government wanted to give the Republic of China time. Within a matter of three to five years both Mao and Chou would most likely pass away and the entire mainland might be thrown into chaos. The Republic of China would in the meantime be well advised to pursue a steady course and "do nothing to rock the boat." He didn't amplify this bit of unsolicited advice, but obviously he didn't want us to do anything that might spoil the American plans.

Picking up the thread of conversation again, Nixon asked us not to question the U.S. Government's determination to honor its treaty commitments to the Republic of China. Any expression of doubt in our news media could be used by isolationist elements in the United States to start a big controversy over American commitments to countries in Southeast Asia. In the end this would be counterproductive to both the Republic of China and the United States.

Pointing to Kissinger, Nixon said that what his National Security Advisor had told me fully represented the President's own thoughts; he would not permit Kissinger to receive any foreign ambassador at random. He asked me to give Kissinger's words the same weight I would give to those from his own lips. He hoped I would carry this message back to Taipei.

Kissinger wanted to know how long I would be away. I said it would be two to three weeks at most. Nixon added: "Be sure you see Henry when you come back."

Before the meeting ended Nixon said he realized that his trip to Peking had upset many of his friends in Taiwan. He hoped they would all understand that if the United States and the Chinese Communists should keep on being hostile to each other and suspect each other's motives, tensions were bound to increase, and this would be harmful not only to the United States but to all the countries of Asia.

I directed a last question at President Nixon: "Did Chou En-lai promise not to use force against Taiwan?" "No, we didn't discuss this question at any length in our meeting," he replied.

Throughout the twenty-minute audience Nixon was in control. His body was relaxed and his voice was even. At one point he actually put his right leg on his desk. He grinned but never really smiled. Yet I could tell that he felt very pleased with what he had pulled off. The trip to Peking was a major "breakthrough" in his foreign policy and he was now basking in the glow of a great diplomatic feat.

Nixon was sincere, I believe, in expressing sorrow that his trip to Peking had upset many of his friends in Taiwan. Earlier, Rogers had indicated to me that Nixon felt very bad about the pain and anguish he had caused in Taiwan but had rationalized to his own satisfaction "that the trip was necessary for the sake of world peace."

The reader will have noticed that in these three meetings with Kissinger, Rogers, and Nixon, I had asked the same questions, though each time I tried a somewhat different wording. I had learned in my days as a working journalist that the same question, if put to different participants in an event, sometimes yields different answers about that event; the truth usually lies somewhere among them. I didn't relish being repetitious. I was just interested in ferreting out the truth!

So, I returned to Taipei for consultations. Ten months earlier, before taking up my new post as Ambassador, I had been received by President Chiang Kai-shek at his Shihlin residence. Nixon, then in his third year in the White House, had already taken a number of steps to establish contacts with the Communist regime in Peking. President Chiang had been the first to see these as precursors to even more important changes and issued his now-famous warning to the nation: "Don't be upset in time of adversity but remain firm with dignity and strive to be self-reliant with vigor."

The President, serene as ever, had been dressed in his Chinese long gown. He was very courteous and bade me sit down, inquiring about my travel plans. When I reported that I planned to spend two or three days in Tokyo for consultation with Japanese government officials on our membership/representation problem in the United Nations, he thought the matter over for a minute or so before nodding his approval.

The prestigious ambassadorial appointment, one of three top posts in our Foreign Service, had come as a surprise to me. I now voiced my personal trepidation at the heavy responsibility that would soon be mine and beseeched President Chiang for instructions. He knew that I asked this not as a formality but earnestly. The instructions were: "No matter what happens, always maintain dignity and act on principles!"

On March 9, 1972, I was again received by the President at his residence and was bade to sit in the same chair. In the interval the Republic of China had been expelled from the United Nations and from many of its subsidiary or affiliated organizations. More important, Nixon had just visited Peking.

The President looked serious but not grave. Through decades of self-discipline, the *Gimo* was generally able to hide from his visitors and subordinates much of his inner feelings. This time too he was wearing his dark-blue Chinese long gown.

On this occasion he was carrying in his right hand a copy of the English–language *China News,* an odd touch because the President did not read English. The moment I sat down beside him he asked whether I had read Foreign Minister S.K. Chow's interview. I said I had only glanced at the headlines. President Chiang gave me the paper and I quickly read the story, which had been written by Joseph Kingsbury Smith and Robert E. Thompson of the Hearst Headline Service. Its opening paragraph reported the Foreign Minister to have told them that the Republic of China was prepared to explore the possibility of establishing friendlier relations with the Soviet Union and other Communist nations in the wake of President Nixon's visit to Peking.

The President asked me what I thought of the news story. This immediately put me on the spot. I qualified my reply by saying that I had not been present at the interview and so had no way of knowing whether the Foreign Minister had been quoted correctly by the two American journalists. The subject matter was most delicate and, in my opinion, should have been sidestepped. The Republic of China, like any other sovereign nation, has the right of self-defense. If and when our national survival was in danger, our government would be fully justified in taking any action it deemed necessary to ensure our continued existence as an independent nation. The question that one must ask was whether such a crisis actually had arisen. At any rate, in view of the grave nature of such a policy statement, great care should have been taken. It was not something that any government official should feel free to say to visiting journalists, since it was bound to create confusion at home and arouse speculation abroad.

The President heard me out and said nothing. He put aside the *China News* and began to ask me about Nixon's trip to Peking and its implications. I could tell by his questions that he had read all my dispatches on the subject. Tea and refreshments were brought in.

Summing up, the President said the Republic of China would soon be faced with a serious challenge but that he was optimistic about the future. "Henceforth," he stated, "we must rely on ourselves more than ever before and we must work harder than ever before.

After leaving the President, I stopped by the nearest newsstand to pick up a copy of the *China News* and reread the whole story. I found it well written, coherent, to the point. The two journalists could not have made it up out of whole cloth, though they probably could be accused of playing up the angle about the Soviet Union. Foreign Minister Chow, my predecessor in the Washington post, ought to have known that was the way the American press operated.

In this column-long story the Foreign Minister was purported to have said that he did not foresee the possibility of diplomatic relations between Moscow and Taipei, but had added: "Of course, diplomatic practice in recent years has changed a good deal. You can deal with countries with whom you do not maintain conventional diplomatic relations. What I have in mind is to break the ice first—to have some exchange of personnel."

Chow said that as the world changes so do alignments. We, on our part, have to adjust to the new situation without shifting our basic position. "We are anti-Communist. Without affecting our fundamental policy, our philosophy, we will have to explore what we could do with countries which are not hostile to us," Chow was reported to have said.

In rereading the story, I thought the most mischievous paragraph was this one:

> He [Chow] envisioned Moscow and Taipei entering into
> secret discussions similar to the Warsaw talks between
> Washington and Peking that preceded Mr. Nixon's visit
> by many years. Chow said his country would be ready
> to study the possibilities and feasibilities of such talks if
> the opportunity presented itself.

Minister Chow's interview immediately revived rumors that the Republic of China was contemplating a major change in its foreign policy vis-a-vis Communist countries, including the Soviet Union. There was even speculation that Taipei already had been in contact with Moscow through Victor Louis, a Soviet citizen who had visited Taipei in 1967 as a correspondent of the *London Evening News*.

"We are all realists," Chow was reported to have said. "If the Soviets have any use for us, they would make the approach. Otherwise, it would be useless for us to approach them."

One thing was clear. He had failed to clear his remarks with the higher authorities before uttering them. Maybe he was only thinking aloud. Chow was replaced in a cabinet reshuffle shortly after this incident.

March 9 was the last time I saw the *Gimo* alive. In 1973, when I came back again for consultations, he had grown weak and was not up to seeing anybody but members of his family. He passed away on April 5, 1975.

Chapter VI

The Japan Breakaway

In late March, 1972, the month following Nixon's visit to mainland China, American and Chinese Communist ambassadors held their first meeting in Paris. We were not sure whether this was something new or a continuation of the ambassadorial talks that had been held in Geneva and later on in Warsaw. We asked the U.S. Government to brief us afterwards, as it had on all previous occasions. The latter declined, however, saying that only inconsequential matters had been discussed. This aroused our suspicion; in the case of the Geneva and Warsaw meetings, where trivial matters were sometimes discussed, the U.S. Government stood by its pledge never to negotiate with Peking behind our back and to brief us each time. I was therefore instructed to find out from Kissinger the real reason for failure to brief us on the Paris meeting. I was unable to arrange an appointment with him until May 3, at which time he said that what the Department of State had told us was correct. Only matters pertaining to the exchange of medical and scientific personnel, but no political problems, had been discussed. After Hwang Chen, the Chinese Communist Ambassador in Paris, left for Peking, volunteered Kissinger, the American and the

Chinese Communist embassies in the French capital had maintained contact at only the first secretary level.

There had been press reports about a Kissinger visit to Japan. He had informed the American news media that no date had been set and that, when he was able to go—most likely after Nixon's projected trip to Moscow—he would stay for a mere seventy-two hours, exchanging views on political matters only; he was not, he admitted uncharacteristically, an expert in economic matters. It may be recalled that Japan, which had been upset by the Nixon "shock" on China policy, was now coming under increasing American criticism for piling up a huge surplus in its trade with the United States. To show Japan's "independence" in foreign policy, the Japanese Cabinet had been giving serious thought to moving ahead of the United States in formally recognizing China.

Nixon went to Moscow the last week of May, but he failed to reach an accord with the Soviet Union on the second phase of a strategic arms control agreement. Kissinger didn't make the Japan trip until early June. I saw him on June 13 to receive a fill-in about it. His principal impression, Kissinger told me, was that the Liberal–Democratic administration was about to take a major step. He had repeatedly assured Japanese government officials that in its policy toward Peking the United States would not exceed the limits set by the Shanghai Communique and would, at the same time, maintain its diplomatic and Mutual Defense Treaty ties with the Republic of China on Taiwan. He urged Japan to coordinate its steps with the United States. Kissinger reported agreement by Tanaka, Japan's Minister of Finance, and a non-committal response from Fukuda, Minister of Foreign Affairs.

Kissinger also told me that at Peking's urgent request he would soon go to Peking again to brief the Chinese Communists on Nixon's abortive discussions in Moscow. Of course he would also probe Peking's thoughts on the early termination of the Vietnam war. Peking's mild reaction to the U.S. naval blockade of North Vietnam's sea ports and the massive bombing of Hanoi and its immediate environs might indicate a readiness to be of some help in this connection. But, he stressed, he would not discuss the Taiwan question, since it had been dealt with already in the Shanghai Communique.

Kissinger had to leave for his next appointment and asked his aide John Holdridge to stay behind to carry on the conversation. Holdridge said that Prime Minister Sato had decided to retire as soon as the Japanese Diet went into recess on June 16. The two principal contenders for the premiership would be Fukuda and Tanaka. As history records, Tanaka emerged the victor.

Kissinger returned from Peking on June 23. On June 30 he telephoned to apologize for having failed to keep his promise to see me as soon as he was back. He just wanted to assure me that he hadn't discussed the Taiwan question with the Chinese Communists. He and his hosts spent most of their time talking about the situation in Southeast Asia.

Did he reach any agreements with the Chinese Communists on such specific matters as trade and credit loans? "If I were you," Kissinger answered, "I would not worry over what the United States might do next, but really worry about Japan, because the Japanese Government is seriously thinking of moving on the Chinese question."

Kissinger said he wouldn't be surprised if the next Japanese government should succumb to Peking's terms for the establishment of diplomatic relations: de-recognition of the Republic of China and termination of the ROC-Japan Peace Treaty.

What had the U.S. Government done to dissuade Japan from taking such a step? Kissinger said the U.S. Government was doing all it could to discourage Japan, but he wasn't sure the Japanese would listen this time.

In retrospect, the American effort—if it actually had been made—was doomed to failure. The Japanese Government was still smarting under Nixon's failure to inform it, let alone consult with it, before sending Kissinger on the first mission to Peking in 1971. Japan felt it no longer could trust Kissinger or any other American official on matters it considered of vital importance to Japan's national interests.

Had Peking promised to cooperate with the United States in bringing the Vietnam war to an early end? Kissinger said he wouldn't know for at least a month. Sometime later I met William Sullivan, Deputy Assistant Secretary of State for Asian and Pacific Affairs, in charge of Vietnam and other Indochina states, who indicated that "Peking was in no mood to twist any arms in Hanoi."

Early in July, when Assistant Secretary of State Marshall Green was passing through Taipei on his way back to Washington from Canberra, Australia, where he had attended the ANZUS Foreign Ministers Conference as a member of the U.S. delegation headed by Secretary Rogers, he provided our government leaders with a briefing.

In Washington, on instructions from our Foreign Office, I called on Kissinger again on July 25. There were ominous signs from Tokyo that Tanaka, by now Prime Minister, was about to recognize Peking.

I conveyed to Kissinger my government's serious concern and requested that the U.S. Government urge the Japanese Government to go slow and exercise great caution. Kissinger was sympathetic, saying that the U.S. Government fully realized the seriousness of the question and the possibility of a chain reaction. "We are establishing relations with Peking largely for tactical reasons," Kissinger asserted, "but the Japanese are doing it with a vengeance."

According to *Webster's New International Dictionary* "vengeance" means "the return of an injury for an injury." And it is true that Nixon and Kissinger "shocked" Japan with their secret diplomatic move toward Peking in July, 1971. The United States had spoiled its own case by trucking secretly with Peking; it couldn't very well ask Japan not to do the same thing. The Japanese had reason to doubt Kissinger was speaking the truth when he told them—if indeed he told them—that the U.S. Government had no intention of recognizing the Peking regime in the foreseeable future. U.S. credibility had been damaged seriously.

Kissinger repeated what he had told me after his return from Tokyo in June: that he had asked Japanese political leaders to "stay in step" with the U.S. Government on this matter. Fukuda had demurred but Tanaka had said he would do so. Once in the saddle, Kissinger complained, Tanaka took a different position. This was most disturbing. Nixon had decided therefore to invite Tanaka to meet him in Honolulu at the end of August; the President would use "very strong terms" to urge Tanaka "to go slow." But Kissinger felt there was no assurance Nixon would succeed.

Kissinger went on to say that the communique to be issued at the end of the Honolulu summit conference would contain no expression of American support for, understanding or endorsement of Japan's contemplated move toward Peking at the expense of its relations with Taipei. Furthermore, if Japan should propose to revise the Taiwan clause in the U.S.-Japanese Security Pact, the United States would resolutely refuse to consider it and would warn Japan of the serious consequences.

Kissinger also disclosed that the U.S. Government had already informed the governments of Australia, New Zealand, South Vietnam, and South Korea of its stand. Now, at the ROC's request, he said, the governments of the Philippines, Thailand, Indonesia, Singapore, and Malaysia would be similarly notified so that they would all know where the U.S. Government stood on this issue.

Kissinger advised our government to be "tough" in dealing with the Tanaka administration and to give no indication that Taiwan would continue to trade with and welcome investments from Japan in the event of Japan establishing diplomatic relations with Peking. Of course if the Tanaka government should decide to go ahead with its plan anyway, the U.S. Government, aware of Taiwan's dependence on Japan as a market and also as a source of capital and supplies, would not wish us to sever all economic and trade relations with Japan.

I asked whether there would be a chance for me to see Nixon before he left for Honolulu. Kissinger did not think so, because for the next few weeks Nixon would be preoccupied with the presidential election, then only ten weeks away. I never did see Nixon again before he left the White House in disgrace in August, 1974.

To the Republic of China the maintenance of full diplomatic relations with postwar Japan was a matter of great importance. The reasons were simple:

Politically, both Japan and the Republic of China are members of the free world. Militarily, both are vital links in the chain of collective defense built by free nations off the eastern coast of the Asian continent after the Korean War, with the United States their common defender. Economically, Japan for many years has been the Republic of China's No. 1 supplier and No. 2 buyer and investor, second only to the United States. Culturally, Japan and China are closer to each other than to any other country in the area. Japanese scholars freely acknowledge Japan's cultural indebtedness to China in the past.

Yet during the last century Japan and China fought two wars—in 1894–95 and in 1937–45—and in both cases Japan was the aggressor and China the victim. The first war resulted in the ceding of Taiwan and the Pescadores to Japan; the second one ended in Japan's defeat and the return of these islands to China.

After Japan's surrender President Chiang waived China's legitimate claim to indemnities; allowed more than two-and-a-half million Japanese soldiers and civilians on Chinese territory to return unharmed to their homeland; and declined to take part in the joint occupation of the Japanese home islands, thereby denying the Soviets a chance to occupy Hokkaido,

Japan's northernmost island. Earlier, meeting with Roosevelt and Churchill at the Cairo Conference in 1944, President Chiang had spoken in favor of letting the Japanese people decide for themselves whether to retain the institution of the emperor as a symbol of national unity and purpose.

The fact that President Chiang's policy of "returning magnanimity for malice" was proclaimed even before the Republic of China Government was forced to withdraw from the mainland because of the Chinese Communist insurrection shows what a great statesman the *Gimo* really was. He wanted the two peoples to forget the unhappy past and to forge a happy future together.

Even today there are many people on Taiwan and elsewhere—most of them sixty or older—who blame the Japanese, certainly the Japanese militarists, for what befell the Republic of China. Had it not been for the Japanese militarists' attack on Manchuria in September, 1931, and the subsequent invasion of North China, which led to the outbreak of major hostilities in July, 1937, the Chinese government forces would have cleaned up in no time at all the Communist remnants in and around Yenan in Shensi Province. And there would have been no second Sino-Japanese War for the Communists to take advantage of, even had their hard core survived the government's military pressure. In the eyes of those people Japan was not only the aggressor, but also the spoiler of China's chance to build up the country in keeping with its new status as a major force for peace in Asia.

Owing to British and Soviet objections, the Republic of China, though a major ally in the Pacific war, was not a party to the Japanese Peace Treaty signed in San Francisco in July, 1951. The following year it signed a separate treaty with Japan to conclude the war.

After moving its seat of government to Taiwan in 1949, the Republic of China spared no effort in rebuilding its relations with Japan. For years, despite occasional difficulties caused by

Tokyo's ambivalent policies, the two countries were successful in maintaining reasonably satisfactory relations. In the meantime Japan pursued a policy of "separation of political ties from economic relations": Many Japanese industrialists, riding the coattails of their politicians, went to the Chinese mainland to conclude lucrative business deals, even in the absence of political ties with the Communist regime; another set of industrialists, on the coattails of *their* political front men, went to Taiwan to promote profitable trade with the Republic of China, with which the Japanese Government maintained full diplomatic relations.

Thus, in the summer of 1972, when the Tanaka faction of the Liberal-Democratic Party came to power, some Japanese business groups were already in on the ground floor of profitable commerce with the Chinese mainland. How much more of an advantage they would have if Japan were to establish political ties as well? This necessitated a reversal of the then existing policy—breaking political ties with the Republic of China and confining all future relations with Taiwan to the economic and cultural spheres. Their main argument—though not stated in so many words—was that the United States, following Nixon's visit to Peking, could be expected to recognize the Chinese Communists sometime soon; Japan had better move quickly on the question of recognition in order to secure its own economic advantages in mainland China and also to show Japan's displeasure at Nixon's failure to take Japan into his confidence before making his secret approaches to Peking.

Establishing diplomatic relations with Peking was therefore Tanaka's way of thumbing his nose at the United States. But he was extremely clever in withholding action until after he had met with Nixon in Honolulu at the end of August, leading some people to believe that he had obtained Nixon's endorsement for what he was going to do on the China question. As a matter of fact, Tanaka had told a Liberal–Democratic Party caucus as early as July 24 that, in his opinion, the time was finally ripe for normalizing relations with Peking. He said he fully understood the "three principles" which Chou En-lai had laid down as conditions of Peking's agreement to establish diplomatic relations with Japan:

1. Japan's recognition of the Peking regime as the sole legal government of China;

2. Japan's agreement that Taiwan is a part of the People's Republic of China; and

3. Japan's agreement to annul its Peace Treaty with the Republic of China.

With such an attitude there was really nothing Tanaka had to negotiate with Chou En-lai on the question of recognition when he visited Peking in September, 1972. In their joint statement of September 29, Chou and Tanaka made the following points:

1. The abnormal state of affairs which has hitherto existed between the two countries is declared terminated.

2. Japan recognizes the Government of the People's Republic of China as the sole legal government of China.

3. The PRC reaffirms that Taiwan is an inalienable part of its territory, and Japan fully understands and respects this stand of the Government of China and adheres to its stand of complying with Article 8 of the Potsdam Proclamation.

4. The two governments have decided upon the establishment of diplomatic relations as of September 29, 1972.

5. The PRC declares that, in the interest of the friendship between the peoples of China and Japan, it renounces its demand for indemnities from Japan.

6. The two governments agree to establish durable relations of peace and friendship between the two countries on the basis of the Five Principles of Peaceful Co-

Existence. They affirm that in their mutual relations all disputes shall be settled by peaceful means without resorting to the use or threat of force.

7. The normalization of relations between China and Japan is not directed against third countries. Neither of the two countries should seek hegemony in the Asia-Pacific region, and each country is opposed to efforts by any other country or group of countries to establish such hegemony.

8. The two governments agree to hold negotiations aimed at the conclusion of a treaty of peace and friendship.

9. The two governments agree to hold negotiations aimed at the conclusion of agreements on trade, navigation, aviation, fishing, etc.

It may be noted that in their joint statement Chou and Tanaka spoke only of the "abnormal state of affairs" between the two countries; the "state of war" had been terminated already in Japan's peace treaty with the Republic of China. The same war needn't be terminated twice.

On the question of Taiwan, the joint statement repeated Peking's claim that the island is an "inalienable part" of its territory and expressed Japan's understanding of and respect for Peking's stand. But by referring to Article 8 of the Potsdam Proclamation, which required Japan to return all stolen territories to their original owners, Tanaka stopped short of "signing over" Taiwan to Peking.

The joint statement declared that the normalization of relations between Japan and the PRC was not directed against third countries. Disclaiming any intention to seek hegemony in the Asia–Pacific region themselves, the two signatories also voiced opposition to "efforts by any other country or group of countries to establish such hegemony." This section was lifted almost word for word from the Shanghai Communique. At the time, Tanaka had no idea that Peking would later insist on the inclusion of an anti-hegemony clause in the "new" peace treaty, which was not concluded until six years later.

At any rate, Peking came out of this round a big winner, leaving Tanaka with nothing but an empty bag.

The joint statement didn't say what was going to happen to Japan's relations with the Republic of China on Taiwan. This was left to the Japanese Foreign Minister, Masayoshi Ohira, who announced on the same day that Japan's Peace Treaty of 1952 and diplomatic relations with the Republic of China were thenceforth terminated.

On that very day Minister of Foreign Affairs Shen Chang-huan of the Republic of China issued a strong statement condemning the Japanese Government "for its perfidious action . . . in total disregard of treaty obligations" and declared "its decision to sever diplomatic relations" with Japan, which "shall assume full responsibility for the rupture."

Shen went on to say that "any action or situation arising out of or created by the Tanaka government's unilateral abrogation of the Sino–Japanese Peace Treaty and its fraternization with the Chinese Communists that is damaging to the lawful position, territorial right and all lawful rights and interests of the Government of the Republic of China, shall be illegal and null and void. Whatever consequences that may result therefrom, the Japanese Government shall also be held totally responsible."

Japan's switch of recognition from Taipei to Peking in September, 1972, was a most traumatic experience for the government and people of the Republic of China. They felt terribly hurt by Tanaka's action. Despite President Chiang Kai-shek's magnanimous policy after the war, the Tanaka government had repaid kindness with ingratitude.

But it must be said for Tanaka that he and his government at no time kept their moves a secret from us. In fact, before he went to Peking to conclude the deal, he had sent a former Foreign Minister, Etsusaburo Shiina, to Taipei to discuss ways and means of maintaining substantive relations with the Republic of China once the recognition switch had taken place.

It was Shiina's talks with our government leaders that led to the creation in December of the Interchange Association in Japan and the East Asia Relations Association in Taiwan, both composed of nonofficials who would provide informal channels of contact and communication between the two countries. The Japanese body later set up a representative organ in Taipei, while the Chinese group set up an office in Tokyo, each headed by a fairly senior official—a retired ambassador in Japan's case and a legislator in ours.

My role in the whole matter was a supportive one only. My instructions were to urge the U.S. Government to dissuade Tanaka from making the switch and, failing that, to ask him to go slow. Whether or not Nixon talked seriously to Tanaka at Honolulu was anybody's guess. Anyway, it would have been difficult for Nixon to be convincing, since it was he who broke the logjam by going to Peking himself earlier in the year.

The Japanese handling of the China question later became known as the "Japanese formula." It has two parts—recognition of Peking as the sole legal government of China, which led automatically to the de-recognition of the Republic of China and termination of the Sino–Japanese Peace Treaty of 1952; and the establishment of unofficial organs in both Tokyo and Taipei to maintain substantive commercial and cultural relations between the two countries.

The Carter administration used the "Japanese formula," with some modifications, when it recognized Peking and de-recognized Taipei in December, 1978.

Chapter VII

Halfway House

Early in February, 1973, the White House announced that Kissinger would be visiting Peking again. I received instructions from Taipei to see both Secretary of State Rogers and National Security Advisor Kissinger to express our serious concern and also to ask for a reiteration of U.S. determination to maintain diplomatic relations with and defense commitments to the Republic of China.

On February 6, before he left Washington, Kissinger asked one of his aides to phone me to express his regret at not being able to see me right away. He would arrange a meeting with me soon after his return from Peking. The aide was also authorized to assure me that the question of recognition would not be discussed on this trip, scheduled for February 15-19.

I called on Rogers on February 9. The Vietnam cease-fire agreement had just been signed, and I began by expressing my government's pleasure at the successful conclusion of American efforts to wind up the war. Being very much a self-effacing man, Rogers gave Nixon full credit for this happy turn of events.

Coming to the purpose of my visit, I told Rogers my government was perturbed to learn that Kissinger was about to go to Peking again, and we wondered what would be discussed this time. While our government leaders trusted Kissinger would not do anything to hurt our national interests, this feeling of confidence was not shared by my fellow citizens, especially in view of what Kissinger had done on his previous visits to the Chinese mainland.

Rogers's explanation was a simple one. He said that because of the absence of diplomatic relations between Washington and Peking, it had been agreed in the Shanghai Communique that the United States would send a senior representative to Peking from time to time "to further the normalization of relations between the two countries and continue to exchange views on issues of common interest." Kissinger's trip was therefore a routine one, and no special significance need or should be attached to it.

But was it really going to be that simple? What sort of agenda would Kissinger have for his discussion in Peking? No agenda, said Rogers, but it would be wide-ranging enough to cover developments subsequent to the Vietnam cease-fire, the situation in neighboring Laos, the question of reconstruction in the three Indochina countries, and matters pertaining to trade, travel, and exchange of visits with the Peking regime. But he assured me—as Kissinger had done through his aide—that the National Security Advisor would under no circumstances discuss with his hosts anything detrimental to the interests of the Republic of China. He, Rogers, therefore wanted me to report what he had just said to my government. "Don't worry" was his advice.

Then he tried to change the subject by complimenting my government on Taiwan's economic progress—by then a favorite tactic of American government officials in their conversations with us. He gave me the impression that he did not wish me to pursue the subject of Taiwan any further. Not easily daunted, I pressed on. Would the U.S. Government propose or consider the exchange of a kind of resident missions with Peking? Rogers's reply was that the American side would not bring up this matter formally for discussion but that he would not rule out such a possibility completely.

This was a harking back to Nixon's visit to Peking a year earlier. Rogers, in his conversations there with Chi Peng-fei, his Chinese Communist counterpart, apparently had broached the subject of exchanging trade missions. Chi, on Chou En-lai's instructions, poured cold water on the idea, saying that this could not and would not be considered so long as the Republic of China had its embassy in Washington.

Rogers assured me that the American side would not take the initiative in proposing the exchange of trade missions but would not oppose its being brought up. And indeed, as it turned out, the Chinese Communists *did* remind Kissinger of Rogers's 1972 suggestion. The idea of setting up trade missions in Washington and Peking quickly led to the agreement on an exchange of liaison offices.

During my talk with Secretary Rogers he asked me a question I considered rhetorical: "Why does your government think that normalization of relations will necessarily mean diplomatic recognition? The U.S. Government does not share this view, because relations between many countries remain abnormal despite the existence of diplomatic ties." I said I did not know the answer.

Would the White House or the Department of State consider reiterating the U.S. position vis-a-vis the Republic of China following Kissinger's return from Peking? Rogers smiled and said: "If we have to reiterate our assurance to your country every time we have had some contact with the Chinese Communists, it would give people the impression that your country does not have much faith in us."

When I explained to him that in announcing Kissinger's trip,

Ron Ziegler, Nixon's Press Secretary, had precluded Vietnam as a topic for discussion in Peking and that naturally this had aroused a great deal of uneasiness in my country, Rogers relented somewhat. He promised to take care of my request in a forthcoming news conference either at the White House or at the Department of State. Actually, however, nothing came out of it—certainly not in the way or language we had hoped for. The reason for this was not hard to find: The Washington-Peking courtship was still on.

According to the communique issued at the end of Kissinger's visit to the mainland, the two sides reviewed the development of relations between the two countries in the year that had passed since Nixon's trip to Peking and other issues of mutual concern. They reaffirmed the principles of the Shanghai Communique and pledged a joint commitment to bringing about "normalization of relations." They both felt that the progress made during this period had been beneficial to the people of their two countries. And more:

> The two sides agreed on a concrete program of expanding trade as well as scientific, cultural and other exchanges.
> To facilitate this process and to improve communications, it was agreed that in the near future each side will establish a liaison office in the capital of the other. Details will be worked out through existing channels.
> The two sides agreed that normalization of relations between the United States and the People's Republic of China will contribute to the relaxation of tension in Asia and in the world.

Kissinger had the courtesy to hand me an advance copy of this communique when I called on him on February 21, the day after his return from Peking.

The very first question I put to him was about the status of the liaison office he had agreed to exchange with Peking. What would be the scope of its functions?

Kissinger replied that it would have absolutely no diplomatic status. Its functions would be limited to matters concerning trade and cultural and scientific exchanges. Peking's liaison office in Washington would not display outside the flag of the People's Republic of China and its personnel would not be included in the Department of State's diplomatic list, nor would the latter be invited to any of the diplomatic functions such as official receptions and dinners. As to contacts of a really diplomatic character, they would be maintained in Paris as before.

What of the relations then existing between the United States and the Republic of China? In answer to my question Kissinger said they would remain unchanged—Mutual Defense Treaty and all.

I asked Kissinger why he thought the Chinese Communists agreed this time to exchange liaison offices, when only a year before they had turned down a similar American proposal. His answer was Peking's mounting fear of the Soviet Union.

Kissinger said that details remained to be worked out, but he expected the two liaison offices to be set up within two to three months, each with five to ten people, who would not be accorded diplomatic privileges and immunities.

I asked him whether he had discussed the Taiwan question with the Chinese Communists on this trip and, if so, what they'd had to say. Kissinger reported that he had spent twenty hours talking to the Chinese Communists, chiefly on post-Vietnam war problems in Southeast Asia, and that out of the twenty, less than thirty minutes were expended on the Taiwan question. The Chinese Communists had wanted to know more about the withdrawal of American troops from Taiwan. As this was a unilateral decision to be made by the United States, Kissinger saw little point in discussing the subject. At any rate, he had assured Peking that, as the U.S. side had indicated in the Shanghai Communique, they would be withdrawn "as the tension in the area diminishes." The word "area" in this context really meant Vietnam, Kissinger explained.

What did he think the Chinese Communists had in mind with regard to Taiwan? Kissinger disclosed that both Mao and Chou commended President Chiang Kai-shek for his consistency on the question of national unity. They wanted to negotiate and, in the meantime, would refrain from using force. How the two Chinese Communist leaders would feel about exercising such restraint five or ten years thence was something else. Anyhow, said Kissinger, the Chinese Communist leaders had not asked the U.S. Government to pressure Taiwan, nor had they asked for American mediation.

It was Kissinger's personal observation that Mao and Chou had changed little since he had met them a year earlier. But like everybody else, they were not getting any younger. When they disappeared from the scene, anything could happen on the Chinese mainland. There were signs already that some of the military commanders were not carrying out orders as promptly as before. The succession problem would raise its ugly head sooner or later to plague the leadership. No new potential leaders had come up. The people he had met on this trip were the same as in his earlier visits.

Kissinger concluded by saying that the U.S. Government still had vivid memories of some of the things the Chinese Communists had done since coming into power in the late '40s and, therefore, harbored absolutely no illusions about future relations with Peking. What the U.S. Government was now seeking was nothing but "mutual self-interest."

As Kissinger looked at it, relations between the United States and the Republic of China would not change "in the foreseeable future." How long was the "foreseeable future"? Till the end of 1974. This did not mean there necessarily would be changes after that, he added quickly.

What could Kissinger have had in mind when he proffered

that time-frame? By the end of 1974, Nixon would have completed the first half of his second term in the White House. Wouldn't he be thinking then of finishing what he had started, lest someone else come around to claim credit on the China question?

Peking opened its liaison office in Washington in May in an old building on Connecticut Avenue that had once been a hotel. Its first director was Hwang Chen, with Han Hsu as his deputy. Both carried the rank of ambassador. The first American representative in Peking was David Bruce, a veteran diplomat already in his seventies who had served as ambassador in the three major Western European countries—Britain, France, and Germany. One of the reasons why he, and not a younger man, was chosen for the post was said to be the fact that both Mao Tse-tung and Chou En-lai were also in their seventies; a younger man would be at a disadvantage in dealing with them. This shows how knowledgeable and profound were some of the China experts in the U.S. Government!

Before Mr. Bruce left for Peking I asked to see him. To my pleasant surprise he agreed. But instead of receiving me in his own office, which was part of the People's Republic of China and Outer Mongolia section of the Department of State, he met me in the Republic of China section. A diplomat of the old school, he was most courteous to me and was a delightful conversationalist. In a way I felt sorry that of all the places where one might top off a long and illustrious career, his had to be Peking, where diplomatic niceties were largely unknown, much less practiced.

I saw George Bush, Mr. Bruce's successor, under false pretenses in 1975—due not to anything I had done but to ignorance and overeagerness on the part of his secretarial staff at the Republican National Committee, of which Bush was Chairman before being given the Peking assignment. The morning I went to his office to keep the appointment, the female receptionist on the ground floor surprised me with a big smile. "What a

wonderful morning, Mr. Ambassador!" I had been in that building on several occasions and couldn't remember ever having
been greeted before with so much warmth. When the elevator
stopped at Mr. Bush's floor, he was standing there to meet me. I
sensed instantly that something was wrong. As the smile on his
face began to fade I hazarded a guess: "Mr. Bush, are you by any
chance expecting somebody else? Hwang Chen, for instance?"
Bush's jaw dropped. Quickly regaining his composure, he admitted frankly that his secretary must have misunderstood
when my secretary phoned to set up an appointment for "the
Chinese Ambassador."

As to Leonard Woodcock, who succeeded Mr. Bush in Peking
in 1977, I have never laid eyes on him. When his appointment
was announced, I asked to see him too, but he declined. A man
who has grown up in the rough and tumble American labor
movement has very little in common in training or in tempera-
ment with either the late Mr. Bruce or Mr. Bush. Would a
professional diplomat or a politician have performed differently
in Peking in the last months of 1978 before Carter's decision to
"normalize relations" with Peking? One can't help wondering!

A liaison office was something totally unprecedented in the
history of international diplomacy—a halfway house between
full diplomatic relations and no diplomatic relations. Whoever
invented this setup as a vehicle of representation between
Washington and Peking deserves a medal for ingenuity. Either
side could interpret a liaison office as a forward move or a
holding pattern, depending on its point of view. Quite likely the
Americans at one time or other hoped the Chinese Communists
would accept it as a forward move toward normalization of relations, whereas the Chinese Communists at one time or other
suspected it was Kissinger's device to stave off the final outcome as long as possible—like an engagement with no date set
for the wedding. Nixon may have intended to formalize relations with Peking before the end of 1974, but Watergate intervened. Ford might have done it had he been elected in his own

right in November, 1976. It was left for Jimmy Carter to consummate the love-hate relationship by a formal declaration on December 15, 1978.

Why did the Chinese Communists suddenly yield on what they had previously rejected as a matter of principle? I spent the next few days in Washington getting "answers" from various sources, official and otherwise. These replies, and my response to them, can be summed up as follows:

1. *There was a serious food shortage on the Chinese mainland and the Communists needed to buy American grain.* This was not a very satisfactory explanation, because it was available from other grain-producing countries such as Canada and Australia—and, if necessary, also from the United States, without setting up a liaison office in Washington.

2. *The Chinese Communists were so backward in science and technology that they needed large transfusions from the U.S., and the process could be speeded up once there was some sort of a mission in the United States in addition to their delegation to the United Nations in New York.* This explanation, however, failed to take account of the fact that the exchange of scientific and technological personnel was stipulated in the Shanghai Communique; there really was no need to have a liaison office to do it.

3. *Now that the Vietnam war had ended, the military threat to South China formerly posed by the presence of large American forces in Vietnam and neighboring areas would soon disappear. It was therefore time for Peking to relent a little bit in its attitude toward Washington. What a better way to express this than letting the Americans have what they had asked for in February, 1972?* This explanation made some sense, but this could not have been the only reason.

4. *Chou En-lai had become convinced by then that the U.S. would not sever its diplomatic relations and abrogate its Mutual Defense Treaty with the Republic of China anytime soon merely because of*

Peking's insistence that "there is only one China and Taiwan is a part of China." Considerable time must be permitted to elapse before the United States could be pressured or seduced into weakening its ties with the Republic of China on Taiwan. In the meantime, Chou must have felt Peking could do worse than agree with the Americans on setting up an intermediate machinery to carry on the new relations with Washington. Chou was a wily old fox in diplomacy, and this explanation came close enough to the truth but still was probably not the whole truth.

The real truth must lie in Chou's realization of how serious was the Soviet military threat, how important was the United States to Peking's continued survival, and how urgent it was to have Mao committed to exchanging some sort of an official mission with Washington before he changed his mind—something that had happened not once, but many times in his political career. It is noteworthy that Chou arranged for Kissinger to call on Mao everytime the latter went to Peking. Obviously Chou was letting everybody know that "the reopening to the United States" was a policy decision of Mao himself; thus he would have little difficulty defending this policy against another Lin Piao or any other challenger, even after Mao was dead and gone.

The agreement to exchange liaison offices came as a great surprise to many people in Washington's diplomatic circles. No one was more surprised than Mr. Ushiba, the Japanese Ambassador, with whom I was in frequent contact to exchange information and compare notes on matters of mutual interest to Japan and to us. I saw him the day after the communique was released.

"What has happened, Jimmy-*san*?" "It's very simple," I said. "Tanaka has overpaid for what he got out of Chou En-lai. It goes to show that one is apt to make a bad bargain if he is too anxious." Many people believed that if Tanaka had held out longer, he could have come away with something better—

establishing a new relationship with Peking without terminating an old one wih Taipei. He threw in his hand in the diplomatic poker game much too soon. It also proved that Tanaka was no match for Chou En-lai.

The Foreign Office in Taipei issued a strong statement as soon as Washington released the new communique. It began by reminding the U.S. Government of the Republic of China's solemn declarations that it would consider null and void any agreement which had been reached between the United States and the Chinese Communist regime, because the regime now occupying the Chinese mainland was a rebel group, having no right whatsoever to represent the Chinese people:

> The present U.S. announcement that so-called "liaison offices" will be established in Washington and Peking contravenes the wishes of the Chinese people. The Government of the Republic of China hereby reiterates its firm and resolute position set forth in the statements of February 17 and 28, 1973
>
> Being the legitimate government elected by the people of China in accordance with the constitution, the Government of the Republic of China has spared and shall spare no efforts in persistent struggle in pursuing its sacred mission of upholding freedom and democracy and maintaining world peace. Any move taken by the United States and the Chinese Communist regime shall under no circumstances affect the firm stand and the national policy of the Government of the Republic of China to fight against Communism and to recover the Chinese mainland.

Like all previous statements issued by my government, this one was largely ignored by the U.S. news media. Nor was there any response from the Department of State, where it was presumably noted and filed away for the record.

But with so much at stake, my government could not simply let the matter rest. I soon received instructions to seek clarifications and reassurances from the U.S. Government. I therefore started another round of visits to the Department of State.

Secretary of State Rogers was traveling in Europe. I was instructed to ask for an appointment to see him as soon as he returned to Washington and, in the meantime, not to see anybody else in order to show how seriously our government viewed the recent development. The idea was always to see the top man and then work one's way down to his important aides and assistants. I had to wait for a week before Rogers came back. I saw him on March 8. He was his affable self again, but I was solemn in both manner and tone.

I began by conveying to him my government's serious concern as a result of the U.S. Government's decision to exchange liaison offices with the Chinese Communist regime. In my government's considered view this had greatly injured our national interests and, at the same time, damaged ROC–USA friendship. The news had shocked our people, and there were strong reactions in our representative assemblies and in our news media.

In regional terms, I continued, this would encourage a number of countries in Southeast Asia also to establish contacts with the Chinese Communists. This necessarily would cause greater disunity among the free nations of Asia, thereby upsetting the balance of power in the region.

On Capitol Hill a number of senators and congressmen were echoing the views favoring early recognition of the Peking regime expressed by certain sectors of the U.S. news media. This I pointed out, was already having an adverse effect on our existing bilateral relations.

I reminded Rogers of Kissinger's assurance that the liaison offices to be exchanged would have no diplomatic status. Yet, according to press reports, their personnel are now to be accorded privileges and immunities usually reserved for diplomatic representatives. My government still hoped that the U.S.

Government would remain firm and not extend such privileges and immunities to Chinese Communists staffing the liaison office in Washington.

I then reiterated my government's consistent stand that it would consider null and void any agreement the Chinese Communist regime might enter into with any foreign government. It was our government's hope that henceforth the U.S. Government would give adequate consideration to our position as well as to the traditional ties and defense treaty relations between our two countries.

Now that harm had been done to our position and interests, our government hoped that President Nixon would stress in his forthcoming State of the World message the U.S. Government's respect for our national position and interests and the importrance the U.S. attached to maintaining the traditional ROC-USA friendship.

It was about the longest presentation I had been instructed to deliver to the Secretary of State in my entire tour of duty. He sat through it all quietly. Apparently he was surprised by our vehement reaction. He said he would have to study the various points I had raised before he could give me a reply. As to the last point, he said, he would try to ask President Nixon to say something about the U.S. Government's friendship and treaty commitment in his State of the World speech.

If the Secretary of State thought I had finished, he was mistaken, for I was under instructions to make three more points. The first one had to do with his own assurance to me that Kissinger would do nothing detrimental to our national interests while in Peking. It had turned out to be quite to the contrary.

Then there was the Secretary of State's private meeting with Peking's Foreign Minister Chi Peng-fei during a recent visit to Paris. This had aroused great apprehension in Taipei about still other meetings in the offing. Our government hoped that in order to still our apprehensions, the U.S. Government would agree to brief us each time on what was discussed.

According to news reports, the Secretary of State had discussed with Chi, among other things, the question of frozen assets in the U.S. and on the Chinese mainland. With regard to Chinese assets frozen in the United States, some of them belonged to public enterprises that were left behind when our government moved to Taiwan. To these assets our government had full claim; the Chinese Communists had no right to them. There was also the matter of the assets of private Chinese citizens who were entrapped on the Chinese mainland; certainly no third party had a right to dispose of these. Our government therefore had the legal right to raise objections in the future. The Secretary of State's talks with Chi in Paris inevitably would have a great effect on the future security and welfare of all countries in Southeast Asia, and our government was asking to be informed of what had transpired during those talks.

Rogers gave a very short and what must be considered inadequate answer to all three points by saying that he would arrange for someone to brief us. Regarding the frozen assets, he confirmed that a tentative agreement had been reached in Paris, whereby Chinese assets seized by the U.S. Government on American territory at the time the Chinese mainland fell to the Communists would be used to compensate American firms and individuals for properties seized by the Communists on the Chinese mainland in the same period. The Secretary of State estimated that the Americans would receive about 40 cents to the dollar.

At the conclusion of what was largely a monologue on my part, I repeated our government's position about reserving the right to raise objections in the future. The Secretary assented. Then and only then did we exchange such pleasantries as "How is your golf?" and "How is the family?" just to make sure that we both understood it was all official business and there was absolutely nothing personal involved.

As a bit of side news Rogers told me that Andre Gromyko and Chi did not call on each other, though both had been in Paris at the same time. Both men were invited to Roger's reception, but they never met or mixed. Instead, the Soviet Communists and the Chinese Communists remained apart from one another throughout the affair, as if a wall stood between them.

On March 13, I called on Kenneth Rush, who had just replaced Elliot Richardson as the Deputy Secretary of State. Rush was a successful businessman and had risen to the position of Board Chairman of Union Carbide, the big petrochemical manufacturing company in the United States. Aside from his other qualifications, it was his managerial ability and experience that had recommended him to Rogers, who was known to be looking for someone to help him run the Department of State.

I found Rush very personable. He was quite sympathetic when I told him that since Nixon's trip to Peking in February, 1972, the number of countries that were maintaining diplomatic relations with the Republic of China had dropped from sixty to fewer than forty. Now that Kissinger had arranged to exchange liaison offices with the Chinese Communists, the latter could be expected to step up their diplomatic offensive until we were completely cut off from the international community. Yes, we had made some progress in our economic development, but economic strength alone would hardly be enough to safeguard our international status. I was therefore expressing to him the same hope I had expressed to Rogers himself on March 8: that the U.S. Government would kindly bear in mind our position, our interests, and the traditional ROC–USA friendship and our treaty commitments to each other for the maintenance of peace and security in the Western Pacific.

Rush said in reply that he did not have the slightest doubt regarding the U.S. Government giving continuous support to our position in the international community. He had heard a great deal about our economic achievements, which confirm the high caliber of our political leadership. President Nixon's policy of substituting negotiations for confrontation was aimed at preserving world peace. Only through negotiations could the danger of a nuclear war be averted and the freedom of humanity protected. There are 850 million people on the Chinese mainland, and the United States simply could not close its eyes to their existence. In dealing with the Chinese Communists, however, the U.S. would under no circumstances sacrifice the national interests of the Republic of China, nor those of any other country in the world. He used as an example American relations with the Soviet Union. At one time, he said, some of the Western European countries felt that they stood to lose if negotiations ever replaced confrontation in U.S.–Soviet relations. But subsequent devlopments showed that such apprehensions were unwarranted. Rush felt certain that people in the Republic of China soon would come to the same realization.

Turning to the various points I had raised with the Secretary of State on March 8, Mr. Rush said he would answer them on Rogers's behalf.

The exchange of liaison offices, he asserted, was primarily to improve contacts and communications between Washington and Peking. It would not affect the existing U.S. diplomatic relations with the Republic of China on Taiwan. The United States had not recognized the Chinese Communist regime and was not going to give diplomatic status to Peking's liaison office in Washington.

With regard to the possible effect of the new arrangement on the situation in Asia as a whole, Rush voiced the U.S. Government's belief that normalization of relations between Washington and Peking would be conducive to the maintenance of peace in the region. This would also rebound to the benefit of the Republic of China.

True, some congressmen were advocating early recognition of the Peking regime, but Rush said the U.S. Government had no control over them. At any rate, unless authorized to do so, congressmen could not speak for the Nixon administration when it came to matters of foreign policy; just look at the congressmen who had been advocating for years immediate and unilateral withdrawal of U.S. forces from Vietnam!

Here Rush repeated an earlier U.S. reassurance that the liaison offices would have no diplomatic status. He also said he could well understand our government's position in considering null and void any agreement a foreign government might enter into with the Chinese Communists.

As to our request that President Nixon be asked to say something in his next State of the World message to Congress, Rush said the Secretary of State had already indicated his willingness to try. He felt certain that this would be taken care of without too much trouble. At any rate, he assured me, the message would not say anything harmful to our country.

About the Rogers–Chi discussions in Paris, Rush referred me to William Porter, a career diplomat who only recently had succeeded Alexis Johnson as Under Secretary of State for Political Affairs, the third-ranking position in the Department of State. Porter, he said, was present at the Rogers–Chi talks and would, therefore, be able to give me a fill-in on what was actually discussed.

According to Porter, on whom I called shortly afterwards, most of the Rogers–Chi meetings was taken up by questions related to the cease-fire agreement in Vietnam and the twelve-nation Paris peace conference that would take place later in the year to formalize the withdrawal of American forces from the Indochina Peninsula. There had been no discussion of the American forces on Taiwan that, as mentioned in the Shanghai Communique, would be withdrawn gradually "as tension in the area diminishes."

The only topic Rogers discussed with Chi that was of possible interest to us, Porter said, was the question of frozen assets.

The American side had already sent a proposal to the Chinese Communists, but the latter had yet to respond. In fact, this question was not solved until Michael Blumenthal, Carter's Treasury Secretary, went to Peking in February, 1979, fully six years after Rogers thought he had the agreement in his pocket.

That was the first of my several meetings with Porter, for whom I have retained a great deal of respect for his professional ability and with whom I have a personal friendship. After a stint as Ambassador to Canada he retired in 1977 to write a weekly column on international politics.

The agreement to exchange liaison offices between Washington and Peking had created a new situation. Before many days had transpired I was called back to Taipei for consultations.

Returning to Taipei before the end of March, 1973, I had three busy weeks calling on government leaders and attending conferences as well as taking part in discussions at the Foreign Office itself. Chiang Ching-kuo, who had assumed the premiership less than a year earlier, even summoned the cabinet ministers concerned to a meeting in his own office to discuss the new situation. Never before had the Chinese Communists consented to station any official representatives in a foreign capital in which there was a Republic of China embassy. Now all of a sudden and for reasons not immediately clear, they had agreed to set up a so-called liaison office in Washington, D.C., in exchange for a similar American mission in Peking. No one really knew how to interpret this unprecedented development, let alone deal with it. The consensus was that our embassy in Washington would now be competing with the Chinese Communist liaison office for attention—not only from the executive branch of the U.S. Government, but also on Capitol Hill, where Peking certainly did not lack for sympathizers. It was also felt that a number of pro-Peking academic or pseudo-academic organizations would soon come into being and that those already in existence would step up their activities. There was also concern that the Chinese Communists, with their liaison office as a command post, would infiltrate Chinese communities in various parts of the United States that had hitherto been supportive of our government.

One or two officials at the meeting even suggested that the Communist liaison office might resort to subversive action or violence against our diplomatic personnel in Washington and elsewhere in the country.

I disagreed with the last observation, not because I thought the Chinese Communists had reformed overnight, but because I believed they were out to create a new image for themselves in America. They wanted to appear as the good guys. Of course they could stir up trouble to embarrass us, but they would remain behind the scenes; if anything went wrong, they would not have to bear the responsibility. Subsequent events proved that this analysis was substantially correct. Especially was this true on various Eastern seaboard college campuses, where pro-Peking Chinese students sought to whip up anti-ROC sentiment in mass rallies and what passed for forums and discussions. Several times they clashed with other Chinese students who were loyal to our government. But not once were any of their liaison office people caught red-handed. They were clever.

By comparison a few of our embassy staff and their children were less circumspect in their conduct. So outraged were they by the arrival of Chinese Communist officials for the liaison office that they took part in a demonstration organized by pro-ROC students in the Washington metropolitan area early in May, 1973. Understandably they were all so carried away by their patriotism that they ignored my specific warning that all with diplomatic status must refrain from such activities. In the end I had to apologize to the Department of State for this transgression of diplomatic propriety. Numerous anti-Peking demonstrations were held in Washington after that, but none of our embassy staff or their families was ever again involved.

The appearance in Washington of Peking's liaison office

created a new situation for us and for the U.S. Government as well. The Department of State's protocol people devised a dual set of rules to make certain that our embassy people and the liaison office staffers would not be invited to the same parties. If it was a formal diplomatic function, I, as the Chinese Ambassador officially accredited to the U.S. Government, was the one invited. Even in the case of the annual dinner given by the Secretary of State to celebrate the founding of the United Nations the Ambassador of the Republic of China was the one invited and not the head of Peking's liaison office—this despite the fact that Peking had gained admission to the world organization as far back as October, 1971.

As to functions at various embassies in town, those having diplomatic relations with the Republic of China would only invite us; others having relations with Peking would invite only the liaison office people. From May, 1973, till the end of 1978, this rule was meticulously observed by all embassies, except once. In 1977 the embassy of an oil-rich Arab country broke this rule. At the time, that country had diplomatic relations neither with us nor with the Chinese Communists. In all previous years, however, when I went to their national day reception, there was no one from Peking's liaison office. This time I almost met Han Hsu, its Deputy Director, face to face. Later on I asked the inviting embassy's ambassador what had happened. He apologized for any embarrassment caused me but, he said, he had done it on specific instruction from his Foreign Office. Shortly afterwards Oman, the said Arab country, established diplomatic relations with the Chinese Communists.

Following that incident, in all dubious cases I made it a practice to remind my social secretary to contact her counterpart at the host embassy to make sure there was no mistake. In other cases no such inquiry was necessary. Once, for instance, I received an invitation from a West European embassy. Just as I suspected, a new girl was on the job. To save her embarrassment, my secretary was instructed to return the invitation to the young woman in a sealed envelope.

Many times letters meant for the Communist liaison office came to our embassy. Those that bore the sender's address were returned. There were occasions on which U.S. senators mistook our embassy for the liaison office. One such senator, a member of the Foreign Relations Committee, phoned me one day about his daughter, who had applied for a visa to visit the Chinese mainland several months earlier and was still waiting for a reply. He wanted an explanation. Apparently he had asked his secretary to call the Chinese Ambassador. The secretary looked up the diplomatic Blue Book and called me instead. I told the senator he had the wrong party.

And there were people active in the Washington cocktail circuit who were do-gooders at heart. They proposed to invite both me and the Chinese Communist representative to their homes so that we could meet casually without attracting public attention. I have no idea what the liaison office chief told such would-be matchmakers, but my invariable answer was that I could not accept invitations to functions to which Communist China's man was also invited.

Upon their arrival in May the liaison office people proceeded rather cautiously. They took up an entire floor of the Hotel Mayflower in downtown Washington, rarely venturing forth from their rooms. Whenever they did, it was never singly but in groups. They engaged a pro-Peking Chinese restaurant as caterer for their daily meals. Sometimes they would travel by bus to eat at the restaurant, which is only a few blocks away. American plainclothes security people would accompany them as they moved between the hotel and the restaurant. This went on for several months until they moved finally to a hotel on Connecticut Avenue and had their own cooks to prepare meals for them.

One big change in the hotel was noticed immediately by

passersby: At night all lights in the building were turned off, except in a few rooms, where thick curtains were drawn to shut out the street lights. From the outside it began to look like a haunted house, much to the dissatisfaction of people living in the neighborhood.

About two weeks before the first liaison office celebration of the PRC's national day on October 1, 1973, several workmen in gray uniforms were seen erecting a flagpole in front of the building. Sure enough on the celebration day they ran up their five-star flag. I went to the Department of State to complain, because I had been given to understand that the liaison office would not fly Peking's flag on the outside, though they might display it inside. My complaint elicited only a perfunctory reply.

Another "breach" of our understanding occurred when the liaison office people were all accorded privileges and immunities normally reserved for accredited foreign diplomats. This was definitely contrary to Kissinger's assurance to me that Peking's representatives would have no diplomatic status. As a matter of fact, the two top men in the liaison office were permitted to carry the rank of ambassador and were addressed as such by the U.S. government officials whose job it was to deal with them on day-to-day matters.

A third "departure" came to light when the Department of State discussed diplomatic problems with the liaison office instead of only nondiplomatic questions such as trade, travel, and exchange of scientific and technological personnel. This did not quite square with Rogers's assurance to me that diplomatic issues would be taken up by their respective embassies in a third country.

Shortly after the liaison office exchange was announced, Senator Edward Kennedy, who had favored recognizing the Peking regime all along, proposed in the U.S. Senate that Chinese Communist representatives in Washington be accorded diplomatic privileges and immunities. He had blundered in adding that, when the time came for the United States to set up an embassy in Peking, Taipei should be permitted to retain a liaison office in Washington, with its personnel accorded similar privileges and immunities. This statement immediately aroused Peking's ire and protest. Subsequently, the second part of the senator's proposal was deleted from the resolution.

Chapter VIII

Two Hats and
One China

In September, 1973, the United States had a new Secretary of State. As generally expected, it was none other than Kissinger who replaced William P. Rogers as the top man in the Department. The U.S. Senate passed the nomination with only a perfunctory hearing. In fact, statements made by some of the senators were so commendatory that they would have served equally well at testimonial dinners two-and-a-half years later.

Two months earlier Kissinger had been planning yet another visit to Peking—his sixth. He had to postpone the trip because Nixon's way of prosecuting the Indochina war was being challenged by the U.S. Congress, which, in mid-August, succeeded in passing a resolution that called on the administration to discontinue the bombing of Cambodia. Though Cambodia was nominally neutral under Prince Norodom Sihanouk, a strip of its eastern territory was being used by the North Vietnamese as a segment of the Ho Chih-min trail, down which Hanoi had been pouring a steady stream of soldiers and supplies to support its war against South Vietnam.

Another reason for postponement of Kissinger's trip to

Peking was that the Tenth National Congress of the Chinese Communist Party was also scheduled for August. Then, too, Nixon must have told Kissinger about the timing of the Secretary of State switch, requesting that he stick around Washington until it had come through. As for Kissinger himself, presumably nothing would have pleased him more than to go to Peking in the capacity of Secretary of State rather than of merely the President's Advisor on National Security Affairs.

Anxious, like everybody else in Washington, to find out what was about to happen, I found an excuse to see Kissinger on August 6. He seemed to be in a happy frame of mind. When I reminded him that it had been more than four months since my last visit with him, he laughed. "This shows," he said, "that our bilateral relations must have been satisfactory and there are no pending problems between our two countries that need my attention."

When I had briefed him about my trip back to Taipei for consultations in March–April and relayed to him our government's firm decision not to negotiate with Peking and not to have anything to do with the Soviets, he asked half-jokingly: "What did I hear about the Soviets having asked your government for the use of the Pescadores by their navy?"

The Pescadores—known to the Chinese as the Penghu Islands—lie midway in the Taiwan Straits between Taiwan and the Chinese mainland and, because of the deep water around them, are considered of great strategic importance in the Western Pacific.

"This is news to me," I replied. "Knowing our government's attitude toward the Soviet Union, I can deny the report as completely groundless. Even if the Soviets should seek our permission for their navy to use the Pescadores, our government definitely would not grant it."

I could tell that the U.S. intelligence community had picked up this mischievous report somewhere, otherwise Kissinger would not have brought it up. It showed how sensitive the U.S. Government was about the possibility of Taipei having contacts with Moscow as an antidote to Washington's own reopening to Peking. It also showed how closely the U.S. Government, especially the Pentagon people, must have been watching developments in the Taiwan Straits; a Soviet fleet in the Pescadores would upset the balance of power in the Western Pacific practically overnight.

I sent a special dispatch to Taipei on Kissinger's question and included my reply. In no time at all I received a cable confirming that I was absolutely right in what I had said to Kissinger.

Having thus disposed of the Pescadores question at our meeting, I asked Kissinger about his next trip to Peking. He said he had planned to go in mid-August but later decided to postpone it because he did not wish to give the Chinese Communists the satisfaction of learning, while he was still in Peking, that the U.S. Government had been ordered by Congress to stop bombing Cambodia. The trip, however, was still on.

What did the U.S. Government have in mind when it talked about "normalization of relations" with Peking? Now that both sides had exchanged liaison offices, weren't relations between Washington and Peking normal enough? Or would there be further movement or movements?

In reply Kissinger said there were no plans to move further ahead in the near future. The two liaison offices were already serving as useful channels of communication. He claimed that two months had gone by since he himself had talked to anyone in the Chinese Communists' liaison office.

Without openly contradicting him, I asked him about Hwang Chen's recent flight to San Clemente in a presidential plane to see Nixon. The privilege and honor accorded Hwang were rarely extended to other diplomats. According to news reports, the Department of State had even arranged for Hwang to meet with some Hollywood stars. Poking Kissinger in the ribs, I said jokingly that I had been accredited to the U.S. Government as a full-fledged ambassador for more than two years. I, too, would like to ride in a presidential plane and meet some movie stars. Could the Department of State arrange it for me?

To the first part of my question, Kissinger had a plausible, but unconvincing, answer. Following Nixon's meeting with Brezhnev in Moscow, he said, it was thought necessary for the sake of balance that Nixon give Hwang a personal briefing. As Nixon was still resting in California from his long and tiring trip, Hwang was offered a seat on a courier plane which shuttled between Washington and San Clemente whenever Nixon was staying in California. It was certainly not a special plane, Kissinger emphasized. But he didn't take up the second part of my complaint about movie stars. My pointed remarks, however, must have appeared in official records of my conversation with him, for before long some of my contacts in the Department of State were teasing me about my wish to meet American movie stars.

At any rate, I told Kissinger that the impression was growing that the Nixon administration was putting greater distance between Washington and Taipei as part of its preparations to recognize the Chinese Communist regime. I cited as an instance Secretary Rogers's failure to visit Taiwan during his recent trip to Tokyo and Seoul.

Kissinger assured me, however, that the United States would not recognize Peking presently. He asked me whether I still remembered what he had said to me in 1972. At that time he had assured me that the United States would not change its policy before the end of 1974. He had expressed the hope that in the meantime we of the Republic of China would take all necessary measures "to symbolize your permanence." Insofar as the U.S. Government was concerned, it would "not tolerate" an armed invasion of Taiwan by the Chinese Communists.

But in the event of Washington's recognizing Peking and de-recognizing us one day, wouldn't that lead to the abrogation of U.S. defense commitments to us? "That's an interesting question," Kissinger observed, "but we haven't even begun to think about it." There was neither a blueprint nor a timetable. He felt certain that Nixon, a great friend of the Republic of China, would, when the time came, devise a special arrangement to safeguard our country's security and well-being.

Coming back to his proposed trip to Peking, I asked Kissinger what he had to discuss with the Chinese Communists this time. "Absolutely not about recognition," he told me. I suggested that Chou En-lai might offer to help the United States in Cambodia in return for U.S. diplomatic recognition. Kissinger predicted U.S. efforts in Cambodia were doomed to failure now that Congress had banned any further military pressure, and he didn't see how Chou could be of any help.

Kissinger was interested in the possibility of peace talks between Peking and Taipei. He wanted to know, for instance, whether Lee Kuan Yew, Singapore's Prime Minister, had offered himself as a go-between in his recent trip to Taipei. I assured him that as far as I knew, Lee's visit had nothing whatsoever to do with peace talks.

Nixon's National Security Advisor was also thirsty for reliable news from the Chinese mainland. According to one U.S. source of information, the Tenth National Congress of the Chinese Communist Party and the National People's Congress, after repeated postponements, would soon be held.

Three months after this meeting with Kissinger, he went to Peking, and he was wearing two hats: one as Nixon's Advisor on National Security Affairs and the other as the Secretary of State of the United States.

Kissinger and members of his party were in Peking from November 10 to November 14, 1973. He was received by Mao Tse-tung, and the two men "held a wide-ranging and far-sighted conversation in a friendly atmosphere." Kissinger and his colleagues also held "frank and serious talks" with Chou En-lai, Chi Peng-fei, Chiao Kwang-hwa, and the others. Officials of the two sides "conducted counterpart talks on bilateral issues of mutual concern and made good progress."

On the morning of November 14, as I was listening to the seven o'clock news, the phone in my residence rang. Kenneth Rush, the Acting Secretary of State, was on the line. He told me that in exactly an hour's time the Department of State would release a communique to mark the end of Kissinger's visit to Peking. He would be glad to rush me a copy before it went on the air. I thanked him and hung up.

When the copy came, I took a quick look. There were only twelve short paragraphs, the longest of which had only eleven-and-a-half lines in it. But there were hidden meanings in the communique that would take time to study.

The first thing that caught my eye was the expansion of the area "where both Washington and Peking would be opposed to the establishement of hegemony by any other country or group of countries from the Asia–Pacific region as mentioned in the Shanghai Communique to any other part of the world." This was a matter of great significance. The United States and the Chinese Communist regime now considered it in their common interest to oppose Soviet expansion not only in the Asia–Pacific region, but in other parts of the world as well—the Middle East and Africa, for example.

Up to this point, by popular estimate, Peking's influence was confined to the Asia–Pacific region. Now all of a sudden it was being accepted as a major power with global responsibilities. Had Kissinger agreed to this expansion merely as a matter of courtesy? Or did he really think that the Chinese Communist regime had what it takes to play an important role on the global scene as America's partner on the anti-hegemony issue? Had the United States really become so weak over the years that it had to enlist the help of a Communist government against the

Soviet Union in matters that went beyond the Asia–Pacific region? Worse still, could there have been further deterioration in USA–USSR relations, especially in the strategic weapons area, such as to make Washington so accommodating to Peking? To all these questions, and more, there were no immediate answers. In the meantime, one could only speculate.

Another noteworthy point in the communique was that "the two sides agreed that in present circumstances it is of particular importance to maintain frequent contact at authoritative levels in order to exchange views and, while not negotiating on behalf of third parties, to engage in concrete consultations on issues of mutual concern."

It would require no stretch of the imagination to include the Republic of China among the so-called "third parties." Washington's reopening to mainland China had already hurt the interests of the Republic of China. What was there to prevent our future from being bartered away behind our back? Could we trust the U.S. Government to look after our security in case of a major crisis?

The most subtle statement, however, appeared in the last sentence of the seventh paragraph. Here "the Chinese side reiterated that the normalization of relations between China and the United States can be realized only on the basis of confirming the principle of one China." This was clearly Chou En-lai's handiwork; it could not have been anyone else's. Had Kissinger or any of his China experts understood what Chou En-lai was really saying, or had they accepted what *they* thought Chou was saying?

Regarding the two liaison offices which were exchanged in May, the communique said that both sides agreed to continue to expand the scope of their functions. This was an unmistakable indication that trade and exchanges of personnel could be expected to increase in the short run.

According to American news media representatives who

accompanied Kissinger to Peking, the Secretary of State and Chou haggled over the communique till 3:00 A.M. on the night of November 13–14. That gave Kissinger only six hours of sleep before his departure for Tokyo, where aides told the press that the U.S. side had tried to be as vague as possible in some of the wordings in the communique.

Reactions to the new communique in Washington's diplomatic circles and major news outlets were mixed. Some took the Chinese Communists' statement that "the normalization of relations between China and the United States can be realized only on the basis of confirming the principle of one China" as a significant concession on Peking's part, indicating that negotiations on details could be expected to begin soon. Others, however, tended to see new significance in Peking's insistence on "normalization of relations between China and the United States on the basis of the Shanghai Communique," as reiterated in the penultimate paragraph of the communique. In other words, Washington would have to forsake its relations with the Republic of China before Peking would agree to establish diplomatic ties with the United States. The general consensus, however, was that as a result of Kissinger's latest trip to Peking, the U.S. Government had moved its timetable forward.

Some American newspapers pointed to the stepped-up withdrawal of U.S. military forces from Taiwan, which lacked any reference to "with this prospect in mind" or "as the tension in the area diminishes," as evidence that things would begin to move faster now. The *Washington Post*, for instance, saw special significance in the failure of the U.S. side to affirm "its interest in a peaceful settlement of the Taiwan question by the Chinese themselves" in this communique, when it had done so in the Shanghai Communique. Could this mean the U.S. Government was now backing down from its earlier position?

Kissinger tried to assure his hosts in Peking that, regardless of any changes in the U.S. Government, the latter's long-term policy of friendship for the Chinese regime would remain unchanged. This he implied in his toast at dinner on the eve of his departure from Peking. Of course everybody there knew that the Secretary of State was making reference to the Watergate case, which was then consuming much of the American nation's attention. Chou En-lai must have asked him what would happen to Washington–Peking relations should Nixon be impeached or forced to resign. The Chinese Communists had been having doubts that Nixon's successor would pursue exactly the same foreign policy insofar as the relationship with Peking was concerned. Kissinger's reassurances, therefore, must be taken as his way of allaying Chou's growing apprehensiveness as he witnessed Washington's bewildering political scene from thousands of miles away.

Kissinger's sixth trip to Peking and the resultant communique were the subject of countless news stories and analyses, many of which were highly speculative in nature. Much of this was due to the way the Department of State handled the event.

At first the Department's spokesman declined to answer all questions relating to the communique on the ground that Kissinger was giving a news conference in Tokyo that day and he did not want to second-guess his boss. But later that day— this was November 14—it became known that what the Secretary of State had given in Tokyo was not a news conference at all but a background briefing—and for understanding only, not for attribution. The Department spokesman apologized for the misinformation he had supplied earlier. Nevertheless, he declined questions concerning the communique for lack of guidance and adequate information on the subject matter.

By and large Washington observers saw the new communique as an advance over the Shanghai Communique of February, 1972. They paid particular attention to the sentence about confirming "the principle of one China," although no one was sufficiently clairvoyant to know what the Chinese Communists really meant by it.

Murray Marder of the *Washington Post*, who traveled with Kissinger, reported acknowledgement by U.S. officials that it was now up to Washington to make the next move in furthering relations with Peking, in recognition of the Chinese Communists' "flexibility" on the question of Taiwan. Marder said that Kissinger and his advisors viewed Peking's new approach toward the question of normalization of relations "as a potentially important moderation of its earlier position on diplomatic recognition because it could leave the U.S.–Taiwan relationship undisturbed, while setting the stage for enlarging relations between Washington and Peking, in effect ignoring Taiwan."

Frank Starr of the *Chicago Tribune*, also a member of the press corps accompanying Kissinger, proclaimed the trip to Peking a success and asserted that Kissinger felt certain of an expansion of U.S. relations with the Maoist regime.

James Keat of the *Baltimore Sun* reported that Kissinger would now try to solve the last issue—the political future of Taiwan. He quoted American officials as saying that the apparent modification of Chinese Communist insistence on U.S. abandonment of the Republic of China on Taiwan came at Peking's own initiative and not as a result of bargaining. (One recalls that on Kissinger's fifth trip to Peking, in March of that very year, it was also the Chinese Communists who took the initiative in broaching the subject of exchanging liaison offices, having turned down an earlier U.S. proposal during Nixon's official visit in 1972.)

According to Keat, Chou En-lai took an American draft communique and wrote in the thought-provoking 29-word sentence himself. The new language seemed to signal Peking's willingness to make it less painful for the Nixon administration to recognize it as "the sole legitimate Chinese Government."

What did Kissinger actually tell the press corps in his background briefing in Tokyo? No transcript was made available to the media people back in Washington. But soon afterwards stories began to appear both in the print press and on the tubes about what "a senior U.S. official" or "a senior official traveling with the Kissinger party" had to say on the subject. Such an official was probably none other than Kissinger himself.

Now this "official," according to some of the inspired stories, regarded the Chinese Communists' statement as a "softening" of their position on the question of Taiwan; and such a "subtle advance" could lead to a breakthrough in the push for the establishment of diplomatic relations between Washington and Peking.

In private conversation some Department of State officials reportedly concurred in the above assessment. They pointed out that the Chinese Communists *could* have said something like this: "Unless the United States breaks off its relations with Taiwan, relations between Washington and Peking cannot be fully normalized." The "softening" is in the ambiguous phrase, "confirming the principle of one China." Yet the same officials had no idea of what the U.S. Government had to do by way of "confirming" that principle. There were suggestions that Kissinger might have reached an agreement in principle with Chou En-lai on the establishment of diplomatic relations. But it would take time to work out the details, which Nixon would take back to Peking in 1974 to clinch the deal. (This was a trip which, if contemplated, never did take place when Watergate intervened.)

At his press conference in Washington on November 21, Kissinger said that, despite Washington's attempt to normalize relations with Peking, there had been no changes in the basic relationship between the Republic of China and the United States. He denied reports that he had attempted to bring about full "normalization of relations" with Peking during his recent trip. He characterized such reports as "totally incorrect."

Speaking of Washington–Peking relations, the Secretary of State said the United States always had "placed primary emphasis on the substance of communications and the substance of consultations rather than on the form in which it took place." He claimed that his trip had resulted in an expansion of the functions of the liaison offices, a continuation of the exchange programs, an expansion of trade, and a substantial expansion of the consultative process. He emphasized that "this was the maximum we have set ourselves as a goal."

As to future prospects for normalization of relations with Peking, Kissinger remarked significantly that "there are certain indications in the communique which remain to be explored as to the form that might take." Here of course he was referring to the matter of "confirming the principle of one China," which Peking had said must precede full normalization of relations.

Chinese reporters present at Kissinger's press conference reported that he studiously avoided using the name "Republic of China" in his answer to the only question concerning Taiwan, which was asked by an Associated Press correspondent. He began by saying, "With respect to our relations with . . ., then switched to "The situation on Taiwan." Clearly there had been a policy decision to refer only to "Taiwan" in the future and no longer to the "Republic of China." It was a deliberate way of down-grading us as a political entity.

It seems appropriate to reproduce the full text of an analysis of Kissinger's visit and the new communique that was sent by the United States Information Agency to all USIS posts abroad. Labeled an important item, it carried a Tokyo dateline but actually originated in Washington.

> Tokyo, Nov. 15—U.S. officials accompanying the Secretary of State on his sixth trip to Peking report that the momentum toward normalization of the Sino–American relationship was increased during his three and one-half days of talks with Chinese Communist Party Chairman Mao Tse-tung and Premier Chou En-lai.

The American officials point out, however, that a delicate period of negotiations lies ahead even though the U.S.-China joint communique of November 14 manifests a substantial identity of views over the direction as well as the pace of normalization.

The November 14 communique is an advancement over the joint communique issued at Shanghai in February, 1972, at the end of President Nixon's visit, for four reasons, according to U.S. officials.

(1) It broadens the general principles of the Shanghai Communique beyond the Asia–Pacific area to the world in general.

The Shanghai document stated that neither China nor the United States should seek hegemony in the Asia-Pacific region and each is opposed to the efforts by any other country or group of countries to establish such hegemony.

The latest communique extends this principle to any other part of the world.

(2) The new communique has a much stronger statement about the need of continuous U.S.-Chinese consultations at authoritative levels.

It states that the two sides agreed that in present circumstances it is of particular importance to maintain frequent contact at authoritative levels and to . . . engage in concrete consultations on issues of mutual concern.

(3) There is a major evolution represented in the latest document because it contains a nuance in the Chinese statement about what normalization depends upon. This will be the basis for further discussions.

(4) Also it calls for a qualitative updating of the liaison offices in each others' capitals, agrees upon a number of new people-to-people exchanges in the coming year, and states a mutual interest in increased trade. None of these factors existed at the time of the Shanghai Communique.

U.S. officials refused to speculate on what can, in fact,

be practically achieved toward formal Washington–Peking diplomatic recognition.

But they repeatedly emphasized that a nuance exists in the words of the latest communique that forms the basis for exploring the further advancement of evolution towards diplomatic recognition.

It is clear, these officials said, that Premier Chou En-lai is a man whose sense of nuance is highly developed. And, they noted, the following wording in the communique was carefully chosen:

"The U.S. side reaffirmed: The United States acknowledges that all Chinese on either side of the Taiwan Straits maintain there is but one China and that Taiwan is a part of China; the United States Government does not challenge that position.

"The Chinese side reiterated that the normalization of relations between China and the United States can be realized only on the basis of confirming the principle of one China."

The point was made by U.S. officials that the communique produced in Peking was intentionally subtle on many matters, including recognition, because it has been found more productive in negotiating with the Chinese to establish a principle first and then to work out the details.

The formal establishment of diplomatic relations, it was said, does not loom as decisively in U.S. official thinking as it does in speculation by the press, for the reason that Peking and Washington already have extensive contacts which permit deep exchange of views.

This, after all, U.S. officials emphasized, is what is desired in a relationship between the two countries.

When Secretary of State Kissinger first visited Peking in July 1971, U.S. officials noted, neither side knew exactly how fast the Sino–American relationship would go or how deep it would ultimately become.

The genius of the two sides' approach has been ever since that they do not try to spell everything out; and,

for this reason, Secretary Kissinger did not on his last
visit try to explore every detail that the Chinese
Premier had in mind.

He deliberately did not do so, U.S. officials said,
because both sides must think some more about what
complete meaning can be given to the principles already
established.

But, it was stressed, while issues are complex, the United
States expects a definite further evolution towards
normalization.

There was no way of knowing it at the time, but my meeting
with Kissinger on November 19, 1973, turned out to be my last
meaningful conversation with him during my tour of duty in
Washington. It was also the only time he received me in his new
capacity as the Secretary of State. After that he always referred
me to a deputy—Kenneth Rush at first, and later on Robert
Ingersoll, two successful businessmen brought in to handle
day-to-day operations at Foggy Bottom. To this day it is a
mystery to me why he suddenly decided to close his door on me.
Did he find it insufferably painful or embarrassing to talk to me
at this point? Did the Chinese Communists complain to him
about his frequent meetings with me? Or had Nixon changed
his mind and asked Kissinger not to see me anymore as he
moved closer to Peking? We still greeted each other warmly
whenever we happened to meet at some diplomatic function.
For instance, we were both at the South Vietnamese embassy
for the November 1 national day celebration in 1974. I remember everybody was waiting for Kissinter to arrive. As he walked
in people rushed to meet him and cameras were clicking away.
Before I knew it I was shaking hands with him. Kissinger
quipped: "You don't want to be photographed with me. It is
going to ruin you. They won't let you go back to Taipei again." I
quickly retorted: "It is you I am worried about. Now that you
have been photographed with me, they won't let you go back to
Peking again." This little exchange, coming as it did on the spur
of the moment, was widely reported in the American press.

Because our November 19 meeting was our first since he had taken on his new duties, congratulations on his new appointment were in order. He thanked me and said it was always a pleasure to see me. (He must have said this with tongue in cheek.) It was my turn to thank him for seeing me so soon after his return from trip No. 6 to Peking. "How was the trip? Were you satisfied with its outcome?"

"Everything is in the communique," Kissinger answered. "Nothing different from what is in the Shanghai Communique, except that at the last minute the other side added something at the end of the seventh paragraph."

Kissinger disclosed that as he and members of his party had to keep to their departure schedule, there had not been time to explore the significance of this new sentence. As far as the U.S. side was concerned, everything was based on the Shanghai Communique, as before.

"Why do you think the Chinese Communists added such a sentence at the last minute?" Kissinger asked. I said I couldn't answer his question but that it had an unmistakable nuance, all right.

Kissinger recalled that the Chinese Communists didn't say that the United States must sever diplomatic relations with the Republic of China as a prerequisite to "normalization of relations." Could this mean that they would be willing to normalize relations with the United States without the prerequisite?

I told him that I smelled something here. The Communists wanted the U.S. side to confirm the principle of one China first, without specifying what the United States must do later on to honor that principle. I counseled extra caution.

We have learned from experience that a favorite tactic of the Chinese Communists is to entrap an opponent in negotiations by having him agree to certain so-called principles at the outset and then bargain on details. If the Communists fail to get what they want, they can always accuse the other side of violating one or more of the principles until the latter finally yields to their blandishments.

Kissinger, an experienced negotiator himself, must have been well aware of Peking's tactics. He told me that there had been no exchange of views with Peking on this point. As a matter of fact, the U.S. side had not even begun to study it.

When I asked him why, this time, the U.S. side hadn't reiterated its interest in seeing the Taiwan question settled by peaceful means, he raised his voice noticeably as he declared: "We are absolutely firm on our defense commitment to Taiwan." I sensed right away that I had touched a very sensitive nerve and had better change the subject.

How did the Chinese Communists respond when Kissinger assured them that no matter what happened to the U.S. Government its long-term policy toward Peking would remain unchanged? They responded in a reciprocal vein, according to Kissinger—although this hadn't been mentioned in the news dispatches. He felt certain that the Chinese Communist Government was beset by many serious problems and major changes were bound to come one day. At the moment, he added, there were no signs of instability, but this would be deceptive, because Mao was already seventy-nine and Chou seventy-five. Younger leaders were not anywhere visible on the horizon.

Kissinger then assured me that there would be no dramatic development in U.S. relations with the Republic of China, including the Mutual Defense Treaty of 1954.

When I reminded him of what he had said earlier about anticipating no changes in U.S. relations with the Republic of China before the end of 1974, only a year away, he said the U.S. Government still had no timetable. He attributed to the liberal press the recent crop of speculative news articles about the U.S. normalizing its relations with Peking shortly thereupon. "We have no need to establish diplomatic relations with Peking," Kissinger avowed. "In substance, our present level of relations with Peking is quite adequate to take care of our needs. What some of the papers are saying is absolutely nonsense!"

Kissinger's theory was that the liberal press was taking its position now so that later on, if and when the U.S. Government's present policy toward Peking should come to naught, it could always accuse the administration of maladroitness and bungling.

The new communique mentioned that the scope of the function of the liaison office was to be expanded. According to Kissinger, the expansion would result only in additional trade officials, but no military attaches, for the respective staffs.

What was meant by "to maintain frequent contact at authoritative levels in order to exchange views"? Who could be expected to come from Peking? Would Chou En-lai or somebody under him come to Washington? Would the Secretary go to Peking as frequently as he had when he wore only one hat?

To all these questions Kissinger gave no direct answers. Instead he said: "You must have had experience yourself in drafting communiques. You know very well that not every word in a communique means what it says."

But Kissinger did hint that he would not visit Peking as frequently as he had in the past. "Perhaps twice a year?" I suggested. He said, "I doubt it."

At this point I asked Kissinger what place the Republic of China now occupied in U.S. foreign policy. Didn't we still merit some serious consideration in U.S. policy decisions? Here Kissinger made a most surprising remark. "Everytime I talk with you I have a dreadful feeling," he confessed. He didn't explain, but I inferred that it had to do with his discussing with the Chinese Communists and behind our back questions affecting the national interests of the Republic of China. He apparently wanted me to know that he really didn't enjoy doing it but that, because of his official position, he had no choice.

Kissinger confided in me that during his three meetings with Mao Tse-tung, all Mao wanted to talk about was Soviet Russia. On his most recent visit, he said, very little time was spent on the Taiwan question.

Here he moved away from his earlier "no change before the end of 1974" position to assure me that the United States would not establish diplomatic relations with Peking even after the end of 1974.

That being the case, why not issue an official statement openly reiterating the U.S. Government's determination to maintain diplomatic relations with the Republic of China? Kissinger didn't take up my suggestion. He contented himself with the remark: "Our policy has remained unchanged."

Ever since Nixon's trip to Peking in 1972 the U.S. Government had been ignoring our requests for a clear-cut public statement of continued support for our government. It chose to give private assurances instead, and not in writing but orally.

How was the U.S. Government going to explore the meaning of the ambiguous sentence in the new communique? Kissinger said this would take several months. But even after the study had been completed, the U.S. Government would not act on it necessarily, because it had no intention of establishing diplomatic relations with Peking.

I was glad to hear that. I told Kissinger that the Republic of China and the United States had been friends for a long time and that it would be to our mutual advantage to maintain the existing relations.

At this point Kissinger made a very significant remark. Under no circumstances, he said, would the U.S. Government abandon its treaty commitment to our defense. "But what about our diplomatic ties?" I pressed. He didn't answer.

This led to my follow-up question. In the event the U.S. Government recognized the Chinese Communist regime as the sole legal government of China, how would it propose to maintain its treaty obligations to the Republic of China?

"That is a good question," Kissinger said. Before the U.S. Government found a proper way to maintain its treaty commitment to the Republic of China it would not recognize Peking. It was that simple. He also indicated that the U.S. Government had no "compelling reason" to move precipitately on the recognition issue.

I came away from this meeting with a distinct feeling that Kissinger was not altogether happy with his most recent visit to Peking. He was dined and wined, as in his previous visits, and was again received by Mao. But somehow, listening to him on November 19, I could tell that he was somewhat disenchanted with his new friends in Peking. Perhaps their tactic of keeping him up late with endless haggling over minor points and introducing new subjects for discussion at the last minute with no time for him to think or study was beginning to tell on his patience. What he could also have found galling was the Chinese Communist's habit of often "talking down" to him. They were condescending to him to the point of hurting his self-respect. In the eyes of Chou En-lai and the others, he said, he was only above average in intelligence. It is common knowledge that Kissinger is a brilliant man—one of the most talented to have graced Washington's political scene in many years. To have been treated like an ordinary politician with no special claim to any real scholarship, diplomatic skill, and savoir faire was simply more than he could take.

Another indication which came out quite clearly was that now that he was the U.S. Secretary of State, he would not overburden himself unnecessarily by making frequent visits to Peking. Perhaps this was why he said "I doubt it," when I asked him whether he would be keeping up his two-trips-a-year schedule. He seemed not to relish anymore the attendant publicity. The glamor was gone. Kissinger is quoted as having said once that power is a powerful aphrodisiac. If so, glamor, in my opinion, must be an important ingredient in that potion.

From this meeting with Kissinger the following tentative conclusions could be drawn:

1. Due to global strategic considerations, there was no change in the Nixon administration's decision to move closer to Peking and, one day, to normalize relations with it.

2. Full normalization of relations logically meant the U.S. establishment of diplomatic relations with Peking and the de-recognition of Taipei.

3. Because of the Watergate scandal, the "end of 1974" timetable was delayed, probably by one year.

4. The Nixon administration hoped to be able to maintain the substance of the U.S. treaty commitment to Taiwan's defense, but it did not know how this could be done.

5. The sentence Chou En-lai added to the new communique at the last minute had aroused hopes in Washington that Peking, on account of its worsening relations with Moscow, might prove somewhat more flexible on the question of Taiwan and let Washington keep substantive relations with Taipei so long as the U.S. confirmed the principle of one China.

6. The Nixon administration would not move on the Washington–Peking–Taipei relationship until it found a satisfactory formula to ensure Taiwan's continued security and the well-being of its 17 million people.

Chapter IX

Green Light, Red Light

Nineteen seventy-four will be long remembered in the United States as the year of Watergate. On August 9, Nixon resigned under the threat of impeachment and Gerald Ford, who had replaced Spiro T. Agnew as the Vice-President in December, 1973, became the thirty-eighth President of the United States.

The first Nixon cabinet member Ford called and asked to stay on was Kissinger, signaling to everybody in Washington that there would be no change in U.S. foreign policy and that Kissinger would play an even more important role in the new administration.

To the Republic of China, Ford's retention of Kissinger had a special significance. It meant that the policy of normalizing relations with Peking would remain on course and that, if at all possible, the Secretary would try to adhere to the timetable that must have existed in his head, if not on paper. It may be recalled that during his November, 1973, visit to Peking, Kissinger had assured the Chinese Communists that no matter what happened to the U.S. Government, the American policy of moving toward closer relations with Peking would remain unchanged. And, indeed, in November, 1974, he went back to Peking, as if to confirm his earlier assurances.

Before Kissinger left on the trip his aides told everybody not to expect any dramatic results. That turned out to be a piece of disinformation, for Kissinger secured Peking's invitation to Ford to visit the mainland in 1975. A brief joint communique contained the invitation, which reads as follows:

> Dr. Henry A. Kissinger, U.S. Secretary of State and Assistant to the President for National Security Affairs, visited the People's Republic of China from November 25 through November 29, 1974. The U.S. and Chinese sides held frank, wide-ranging and mutually beneficial talks. The two governments agreed that President Gerald R. Ford would visit the People's Republic of China in 1975.

The communique did not give the names of any of the Chinese Communist leaders Kissinger had met during the visit, nor did it claim that further progress had been made in their discussions about "normalization of relations." It merely stated that "they reaffirmed their unchanged commitment to the principles of the Shanghai Communique."

The only thing new or "dramatic" in the communique was Ford's acceptance of Peking's invitation to visit the Chinese mainland in 1975. As it turned out, Ford didn't go to Peking until the end of 1975. What was the hurry? Why announce his visit fully a year in advance?

Perhaps more puzzling was the communique's failure to comment on the sentence Chou En-lai had inserted at the last minute in the November, 1973, communique, asserting that the normalization of relations "can be realized only on the basis of confirming the principle of one China." At the time of my meeting with Kissinger following his sixth visit to Peking, he had declined to comment on this addition, pleading lack of time to explore its meaning. Now, a year later, he had nothing to say about it in another communique at the end of another visit to Peking. Why? Hadn't he said in November, 1973, that a study would soon be made to ascertain the implications of what appeared then to be a "softening" in Peking's position on the question of Taiwan?

The really revealing development in this, Kissinger's seventh visit to Peking, was that he had *not* been received by Mao Tse-tung. Had Kissinger asked for an audience and was turned down? Or hadn't he asked for one and the Chinese Communists hadn't offered to arrange one either? In either case, was Peking trying to indicate its displeasure at the lack of momentum toward normalization of relations three years after Nixon's visit?

The same autumn Mao was known to have received foreign visitors, some of whom were much lower in rank and of less consequence than the U.S. Secretary of State. During the week of Kissinger's visit to Peking there had been no reports in the *People's Daily* or any other Chinese Communist publications on Mao's being indisposed or out of town. From the enthusiastic way Kissinger used to talk about his earlier philosophical conversations with Mao, he obviously had looked forward to meeting the "Chairman" again on this trip. Did he feel snubbed, if not rejected, when he learned that no meeting was scheduled this time?

Something else unusual occurred on Kissinger's trip. He was given only half an hour by Chou En-lai, instead of the long discussions of his previous visits. True, Chou was not well and the meeting took place in a hospital room. But was Chou really that sick? He didn't die until January, 1976, fully a year later.

The invitation to Ford was also shrouded in mystery. Which side had initiated the proposal? Aides close to Kissinger said it was the Chinese Communists who had raised first the possibility of a Ford visit. If so, why?

One thing seemed clear: The Chinese Communists were perplexed as well as disturbed by the Watergate scandal. Nixon's resignation came as a surprise to them. They had taken under advisement Kissinger's assurance during his November, 1973, visit that no matter what happened to the U.S. Government there would be no change in its policy on "normalization of relations" with Peking.

But somehow the Chinese Communists were not quite satisfied with this assurance. Another point was that they knew Ford would be in the White House at least until the end of 1976, but how much longer would Kissinger remain as the Secretary of State? After all, hadn't Kissinger threatened to resign once because of public criticism? What if one day he should walk out in a huff?

If the Chinese Communists were the ones to suggest the Ford visit, this sounded to me, also a Chinese, like Peking's way of saying to Kissinger: "Bring your new boss with you the next time so we can really talk business."

Earlier there had been reports that Chinese Communist leaders, especially Chou En-lai, had accused Nixon and Kissinger of dragging their feet on the question of normalizing relations. There were even rumors that they felt they had been sold a bill of goods by Kissinger and that he had no serious intention of delivering them. Kissinger returned frustrated from his sixth visit and had indicated to some people that most likely he would find it impossible to keep to the same two-trips-a-year schedule as in the previous three years. This explains partly at least why Kissinger went to Peking only once during 1974.

Though the invitation to Ford was the only concrete result of Kissinger's week in Peking, it was seized upon immediately by the American news media as a development of major importance.

According to Joseph Lelyveld, Hong Kong correspondent of the *New York Times*, who accompanied Kissinger, the Chinese Communists "may not have been pushing [for full diplomatic relations or American disengagement from Taiwan] but their invitation to the President raises the pressure on the United States to say it will finally declare that the one China it recognizes is governed from Peking and not Taipei." The invitation to Ford, Lelyveld contended, gave the United States almost a year to come up with something concrete to satisfy Peking's demand for normalization of relations, no longer satisfied with an annual visit or two by Kissinger.

Lelyveld quoted an American briefing official with the Kissinger party as saying that the United States had made no commitments to Peking on normalization or other issues in connection with the presidential visit. But, the official added, "it was in the nature of a Presidential visit to create incentives for reaching agreement." One may be reasonably certain that the briefing official in question was none other than Kissinger himself. According to the ground rules, he could not be identified, nor should any remarks be attributed to him.

John Burns of the *Christian Science Monitor* reported from Peking that the Ford invitation was taken by diplomats there as "a manifest of continuing momentum in the rapprochement between [Communist] China and the United States.

"Diplomats [in Peking] think it unlikely that the Chinese would have invited Mr. Ford—or that the President would have accepted—unless the two sides had already decided that the visit can be used as the occasion of the next major move forward in the normalization of relations." Burns reasoned that Ford was unlikely to want to commit himself to a China visit unless he was guaranteed something more substantial than the frank, wide-ranging, and mutually beneficial talks the official communique had spoken of in summing up Kissinger's stay.

Robert Keatley of the *Wall Street Journal*, another member of the press corps that had accompanied Kissinger's party, discounted the significance of the absence of a Kissinger–Mao meeting. He thought this could be due more to health than to politics. He contended, therefore, that the U.S. Secretary of State "leaves China today apparently satisfied that relations with Peking are good enough at present and getting better."

Personally, I believe this must be the impression that Kissinger sought to create in his anonymous briefings to the U.S. media representatives traveling with him and, through them, to the American people at large. He was reported to have gone even so far as to say "that both sides had reached a decision to let the relationship stand at its present level."

Press aides in Washington canvassed by the Central News Agency for an unofficial survey were unanimous in the view that Ford's visit to Peking in 1975 would set the stage for establishment of diplomatic relations with Peking. But in 1975 something intervened: the Vietnam debacle. Ford and Kissinger may well have wished to move on the China issue in 1975, but even some of the most cynical people in Washington political circles felt that to sell the Republic of China down the river in the same year would be more than the American people could take. When Ford did go to Peking in November, 1975, the Chinese Communists claimed, he pleaded with them for more time to tackle such a controversial issue as the "normalization of relations." Because of the presidential election, 1976 too did not seem propitious. Ford may have hinted to his hosts that when (and if) he was elected in his own right, he would move promptly on this problem. We know the election was won by someone else.

But here I am racing ahead of the story again. Two additional developments concerning Kissinger's seventh visit to Peking should be mentioned. One was the appointment of Chiao Kwan-hwa as Peking's Minister of Foreign Affairs only a few days before Kissinger's arrival. The other was Peking's offer to sign a nonaggression pact with Moscow. The offer was contained in a message of felicitations on the fifty-seventh anniversary of the Soviet Revolution. Obviously Peking was sending a signal to Washington.

After Kissinger's return to Washington I asked to see him, just as I had done after his November, 1973, visit to Peking. He declined, suggesting that I see instead Robert Ingersoll, his new Deputy Secretary of State. This confirmed my suspicion that Kissinger was avoiding me. For more than three years Kissinger had been my main contact with the administration at its policy-making level. Now he had obviously decided not to see me anymore. It enhanced my feeling that my usefulness in Washington was at its end.

When I was in Taipei for consultations in 1973, I had told Premier Chiang Ching-kuo that I had become quite weary of the burden and responsibility and asked him to recall me at a time he thought appropriate within the next six months to a year.

Toward the end of December, 1974, I got the green light and felt greatly relieved. I asked the Department of State to set up an appointment with Deputy Secretary Ingersoll. When asked the purpose of the visit, I said I was about to retire and had received instructions to seek agreement for my successor, whose identity I did not disclose. This would give Ingersoll time to report to Kissinger. Then I prepared a formal letter addressed to the Secretary of State, informing him of my government's decision to recall me and to appoint as my successor the man whom I had succeeded, S.K. Chow. The day I was ushered into Ingersoll's office he was ready for me. I told him that I had received permission to retire and handed him the written communication. Without even opening the envelope, which was unsealed, Ingersoll returned it to me and said he could not accept it. Had he accepted the letter, he would have had to respond in writing, and there would have been then a record of the exchange in the Department. "The Secretary and I have discussed this matter," Ingersoll said. "We both felt that this is no time to make a change."

The Deputy Secretary suggested I take back the letter and

report to Taipei accordingly. This came as a surprise, for it is a well-established diplomatic practice that a government may change its ambassador whenever it deems it fit or necessary, and the receiving government, unless it has strong reservations about the person named as the new envoy, gives agrement as a matter of course. At the time I submitted my resignation there were normal diplomatic relations between Washington and Taipei, and Washington would not have had any objections to my would-be successor, who was certainly no stranger to the United States. The real reason, it seemed perfectly clear, was to be found somewhere else.

This sudden development put me in a most embarrassing position. How was I going to explain to Taipei that, at the moment, Washington wanted no change in ambassadors? I therefore suggested to Ingersoll that he might agree to instruct Leonard Unger, U.S. Ambassador in Taipei, to explain this situation to my government. To this Ingersoll readily agreed and it was done at once.

I knew that unless a miracle happened I would have to stay on in Washington until the U.S. Government decided to change its present course or normalize its relations with Peking, whichever came first.

I must say in retrospect that the whole thing could have been handled better by Taipei. In advance of presenting my resignation to Ingersoll, our Foreign Office could have inquired discreetly, either through the U.S. embassy in Taipei or through me in Washington, about the U.S. Government's willingness to receive a new ambassador from the Republic of China. As a result of what actually transpired, though, our Foreign Office had to rescind its order for my recall. In his message to me, Minister Shen Chang-huan told me that the matter had been shelved indefinitely. Premier Chiang Ching-kuo was thoughtful to have sent me a personal telegram that urged me to carry on as usual. But the harm had been done already. Because I obviously no longer enjoyed the confidence of my own government, the Department of State and the White House had even less reason to be courteous to me. For four years, until the end of 1978, I was thus a lame duck ambassador.

Our Foreign Office should have known that our relations with the United States were very delicate and that for quite some time people in the State Department had been thinking of down-grading Washington's diplomatic ties with Taipei by re-calling Ambassador Leonard Unger and replacing him with a charge d'affaires. It was said that when Roger Sullivan, a career diplomat, was sent to Taipei in 1977 to serve as the deputy chief of mission, the Department of State had exactly that kind of exigency in mind. As it turned out, however, Washington decided to wait. Sullivan went back to the Department of State to serve as Deputy Assistant Secretary for East Asian and Pacific Affairs and Unger was told to stay on till the rupture of ROC–USA relations at the end of December, 1978.

If 1974 was memorable in the U.S. as the year of Watergate, 1975 was memorable to many different peoples for many different reasons. To those in Southeast Asia it was the year of disaster for the three Indochina states—Cambodia, Vietnam, and Laos. The Cambodian Government surrendered to the Khmer Rouge Communists on April 16; the South Vietnamese Government surrendered to the North Vietnamese Communists on April 30; and, shortly afterwards, nominally neutral Laos was absorbed without a fight into the Communist bloc.

For the American people the year was marked by President Ford's signing of the Helsinki Agreement, which endorsed the postwar boundaries of Europe, and his visit to Peking, the second incumbent U.S. President to pay homage to the Chinese Communists. More poignantly, it was the year of the *Mayaguez* incident—Ford's ordering of a bombing attack on Cambodian ships and shore installations in retaliation for the capture by the puny Cambodian Navy of a U.S. warship—and the beginning of the Vietnamese refugee exodus. Overwhelmed by a sense of guilt at having abandoned the South Vietnamese in their hour of peril, the U.S. Government tried to make amends by admitting thousands upon thousands of Vietnamese refugees.

Back in the early '70s, Cambodia under Prince Sihanouk largely minded its own business. True, it had been powerless to expel the North Vietnamese who occupied an eastern strip of its territory, but people elsewhere in the country lived in peace until a U.S.-supported coup, headed by Lon Nol, turned the whole country into a battlefield. When the U.S. Government decided to withdraw from Vietnam, it pulled the rug out from under Lon Nol at the same time. This led to the establishment of the Pol Pot regime and the subsequent Cambodian bloodbath.

The United States had an even stronger commitment to the continued security and well-being of the people of South Vietnam. After all, it was the United States that had arranged the so-called cease-fire and peaceful settlement between the two Vietnams with the understanding that, should the North Vietnamese violate the cease-fire agreement, the United States would take strong measures against them. But in the spring of 1975, when the North Vietnamese launched their final offensive, the U.S. Congress withheld appropriations to meet the crisis that were being sought by the Ford administration. As a result, the South Vietnamese forces became demoralized and, practically overnight, lost their will to fight. The situation reminded us of what the U.S. Government had done to us in 1948–49, when it cut off both economic aid and military supplies. Our government forces, still holding the Chinese Communist insurrectionists to areas north of the Yangtze River, became demoralized and, in no time at all, the entire Chinese mainland fell behind the Iron Curtain.

In reporting to my government on the Vietnam debacle and its consequences, I emphasized that the U.S. Government's refusal to help an ally and friend in the struggle for survival should be taken as a fresh warning. Treaty or no treaty, the

United States no longer could be counted on to honor its commitment to our defense and security. I also pointed out that, in the short run, the loss of South Vietnam would slow down the process of Washington's "normalization of relations" with Peking but that, in the long run, it would necessarily weaken the position of all non-Communist countries in the area and affect their chances for continued existence as free peoples.

It should be noted that only a few months after the fall of Saigon, both Thailand and the Philippines, two pro-U.S. countries in Southeast Asia, established diplomatic relations with Peking. Malaysia, as a matter of fact, had done so a year before, in the mistaken hope that the Peking regime would desist from aiding and abetting Malaysian terrorists. (By the summer of 1982, Singapore and Indonesia were the only two members of the Association of Southeast Asian Nations—ASEAN—who continued to hold out. Singapore, with 85 percent of its population of Chinese origin, has not ignored Peking's existence, as shown in Prime Minister Lee Kuan-yew's visit to the mainland in 1978; but the Prime Minister has said that Singapore would be the last one in ASEAN to take the step of formal recognition. And Indonesia, with the memory of Peking's unsavory role in the 1965 coup d'etat still vivid, has been in no hurry to resume diplomatic relations, waiting until it could feel certain that Chou En-lai's successors would not try again to subvert the existing regime in Jakarta.)

Nineteen seventy-five was also a year of great sorrow for people of the Republic of China as well as for all freedom-loving Chinese throughout the world. Their national leader, Chiang Kai-shek, died in his sleep on April 5. Although the *Gimo* had been known to be in poor health for two or three years, his death still came as a great shock and the whole nation went into deep mourning at the news. Thousands upon thousands of people paid homage to their beloved President as his body lay in state in Taipei's Sun Yat-sen Memorial Hall. On April 16, the day of the funeral, more than two million people, many of them weeping and on their knees, lined the sixty-two kilometer-long route of procession to Tzu Hu, where his remains would be kept until the day when they could be moved to the Chinese mainland for proper interment.

Because of the time difference, April 5 in Taipei was April 4 in Washington. That afternoon, as my wife and I were taking our grandchildren to the circus, we heard the sad news on the car radio. I asked my security guard to accompany the youngsters to the show, but my wife and I returned to our residence right away. I summoned my principal aides to an emergency meeting. A room in the embassy was quickly set aside for ceremonial purposes. Black-bordered notices went out to all embassies that represented countries having full relations with us. A steady stream of people came to sign the book of condolences.

Then, on April 16, there was a memorial service in the Washington Cathedral, only a few steps from Twin Oaks. Evangelist Billy Graham gave the sermon and General Albert Wedemeyer, Commander of U.S. Forces in China in the latter part of the allied war against Japan, offered the eulogy. The cathedral was packed. Carl Albert, Speaker of the House, a number of congressmen, Governor Averill Harriman, Marshall Green, and a few State Department people came. But no officials high in the Ford administration turned up. As a matter of fact, the administration tried to play down President Chiang's death by sending Earl Butz, Secretary of Agriculture, as the U.S. representative to attend the funeral in Taipei. Apparently it wanted the American people to forget that President Chiang was the last of the Big Four allied leaders of World War II. Only when Senator Barry Goldwater threatened to go to Taipei on his own and not as a member of the Butz delegation did the White House relent and send Vice-President Nelson Rockefeller instead.

I went to New York to see Rockefeller off, and I was present at Andrews Air Force Base outside Washington to welcome him back. I also called on him officially to thank him on behalf of my government for attending the *Gimo's* funeral. He said he had been terribly moved by what he had seen and could not think of another world leader whose death could bring forth such a massive outpouring of grief as he had witnessed in Taipei.

Because my presence was required at the memorial service in Washington on the same day, naturally I could not go back to Taipei for the funeral. I wrote Madame Chiang a letter of condolence in which I told her that in my adult life I had cried only twice before, and that was at the time of my parents' deaths. But when news came of the Chief's death, I unashamedly cried, as if I had lost my own parents all over again.

A year later I called on Madame Chiang in New York. She was staying with some relatives to receive medical treatment for her own illness, which she had neglected because of the Chief's poor health. She told me that on the day the Chief died she had been sitting beside him as usual in the afternoon. He was resting in bed, his eyes closed. Suddenly he opened his eyes. His right hand reached out to touch her and he asked her not to leave him. Then he closed his eyes again. Madame Chiang recalled that on all previous afternoons he had sent her away to get some rest herself. She believed that somehow the President had known that the time had come for him to go.

The *Gimo* died ten days before the fall of Cambodia and twenty-four days before the surrender of Saigon. Thus he was spared the great anxiety and agony he would have suffered had he outlived those tragic events.

President Chiang was in good health when I saw him on my first return to Taipei for consultations in March, 1972. In July the same year, while resting at Lishan, a high peak in central Taiwan, he caught a bad cold that subsequently developed into pneumonia. His doctors quickly arranged for him to be moved to the Veterans' Hospital in Taipei. He responded to medication and slowly recovered, but he never completely regained his strength. For many months thereafter he remained in the hospital, which is the best-equipped in the country. Through round-the-clock care by specialists and nurses his condition became stabilized. He stayed generally alert and Chiang Ching-kuo visited him at least twice a day to brief him on important happenings in the country and around the world.

But in the spring of 1975 the President suffered another attack of pneumonia. His doctors again managed to pull him back from death, but he had to stay under the watchful eyes of his doctors, who took turns administering to his needs and comforts. The day before he died a specialist gave him a cardiac examination and found his heart in better condition than it had been in many months.

According to a bulletin signed by the three attending doctors, the President suddenly suffered an acute heart attack at 10:20 P.M. on Saturday, April 5. He failed to respond to treatment and died at 11:50 P.M.

That very morning President Chiang had been alert and doing well. When Chiang Ching-kuo visited with him, he repeatedly asked him to take care of his own health. As that happened to be the anniversary of the death of Chang Po-lin, a well-known Chinese educator, the President reminded the Premier to be sure to attend the memorial service scheduled for that morning. When Chiang Ching-kuo looked in again in the afternoon, the President was taking a nap and everything seemed normal and under control, but he did not wake up again.

The President came from sturdy farming stock in Chekiang's rural area. In his youth he acquired the habits of orderliness and cleanliness and his military training furthered his physical discipline. He learned meditation as he grew older. Twice a day the *Gimo* would sit still in a straight-backed chair with his eyes closed for fifteen or twenty minutes. This way he was able to give himself a complete rest, both physically and mentally. He stuck to a daily routine week after week and month after month without much variation. He ate moderately and never smoked or drank. He said several times within my hearing, when I was his secretary–interpreter, that he was confident he could reach ninety at least. He fell short of the mark by only two and a half years.

President Chiang left a will for the nation. He had dictated it to his secretary, Chin Hsiao-yi, on March 29, 1975, one week before he passed away. When the draft was presented to him, he put it aside without signing it. As he lay on his deathbed, Vice-President C.K. Yen and the heads of all five branches of the government were hurriedly summoned to his residence, where they signed the last testament as witnesses. Premier Chiang Ching-kuo signed not as a son but in his capacity as the head of the Executive *Yuan* (Council) of the Central Government.

In his will President Chiang said that he began to follow Dr. Sun Yat-sen's revolutionary ideals when still a school boy. Since then there had been not a single moment when he had strayed from Dr. Sun's teachings and from the Christian faith, which he had accepted as an adult.

"My life-long career has been devoted to the realization of the Three Principles of the People (Nationalism, Democracy, and People's Livelihood), recovery of the Chinese mainland, rebirth of our cultural heritage and adherence to Democracy," he stressed. He called on all Chinese people at home and abroad to share a common sense of duty and determination in marching toward their revolutionary goals. "Be diligent! Be courageous! Do not relax on your vigilance and preparedness!" This was his last, fatherly advice to the free Chinese.

When the undertakers were preparing the President's remains for the last rites, a copy of Dr. Sun's *Three Principles of the People*, a Bible, a copy each of *Streams in the Desert* and of *Lyrics by Tang Poets* were among the items put in his casket. They had been his favorite reading materials.

Chapter X

The Biggest Shows in Town

Gerald R. Ford of Michigan, Minority Leader of the House of Representatives at the time he was selected to replace Spiro Agnew as Vice-President, became President of the United States in August, 1974, upon the resignation of Richard Nixon. He was widely acclaimed as the right man to bind up the wounds inflicted on the nation's body politic by the devastating Watergate scandal. But foreign policy had never been one of Ford's strengths, and his dependency on Kissinger was greater than Nixon's ever was. On relations with Peking, as on other diplomatic issues, he permitted himself to be led by Kissinger.

When I first went to Washington in the spring of 1971, Ford was one of the first congressional leaders I called on. He was very courteous and sympathetic. He had visited Taiwan in the early '50s and was therefore quite familiar with our struggle for survival. I called on him the next year, following his visit to the Chinese mainland in the company of the late House Majority Leader Hale Boggs of Louisiana. He was quite disturbed by what he had seen on the trip—the Communist way of training the youths, the spartanism, the great regimentation, etc. He said it made him shudder to think of the kind of competition his grandchildren would be up against by the end of the century.

Once Ford assumed the vice-presidency his aides began to draw a ring of protection around him. The ring grew tighter after he moved into the White House and he became inaccessible, at least to me. During his short term in office I met him only three or four times, and then only at receptions at Blair House or at white-tie affairs in the White House. We shook hands, smiled at each other, and exchanged a few words. It seemed he was on guard even when he met me on such occasions.

That Ford would make a trip to Peking in 1975 was agreed upon during Kissinger's visit to the Chinese mainland in November 1974. Before he himself made the journey, Ford sent several congressional groups to Peking. By far the two most important persons to go there were Carl Albert and John J. Rhodes, Speaker and Minority Leader of the House, respectively. They went before the end of March and returned to Washington in early April. I saw Albert before their departure and Rhodes after their return. From our discussions I was able to piece together the following story.

The idea for a trip had come from Ford and Kissinger, but it was the Chinese Communists who picked out these two men, stipulating that no other congressmen be included on this particular trip. They were to travel in a U.S. plane to Shanghai, where a Chinese Communist plane would pick them up and fly them to Peking. As to their itinerary and point of exist— whether Shanghai or Canton—they would know only after their arrival in Shanghai.

To prepare Albert and Rhodes for the trip the Department of State held two briefings, with emphasis on ongoing relations between Washington and Peking since Nixon's February, 1972, visit. They were not given any guidelines or suggestions as to what they should say or try to find out while they were on the mainland. It was entirely up to them to decide and to use their own discretion.

The Albert–Rhodes visit would be followed by visits from other Capitol Hill groups, all for the purpose of informing the Chinese Communists that Congress, like the executive branch of the U.S. Government, was also interested in improving relations with the Peking regime.

I asked the Speaker whether he and the Minority Leader would be able to pay a short visit to the Republic of China on Taiwan after their trip to the Chinese mainland. Albert said there simply wouldn't be time. He revealed that they had declined a similar suggestion from the Soviet Union because they wanted to impress on their hosts in Peking that they were going to see them alone on this trip.

It may be recalled that Albert had led a congressional group to Taiwan during the summer of 1971 after Kissinger's secret mission to Peking. At the time, there was considerable opposition to the trip from the Department of State, which argued that the timing was most inappropriate. Albert, however, ignored the suggestion. This time, though, he was not receptive to the idea of another visit to Taiwan after a trip to Peking.

Albert did not think that Ford would do anything surprising when he went to Peking in the fall—certainly there were no indications that he would. According to Albert, all Ford wanted to do was to let the Chinese Communists know that his administration intended to carry on Nixon's policy of normalizing relations with Peking but that this would have to wait until after the presidential election the following year. The Speaker also pointed out that he and Ford had been in the House of Representatives together for more than twenty years and he knew Ford very well. He assured me that Ford, an honorable man, would not establish diplomatic relations with the Chinese Communists at the expense of the Republic of China.

Albert and Rhodes visited only Peking, Shanghai, and

Canton. Their itinerary, drawn up by their hosts without consulting them, included visits to people's communes, factories, and schools. They found the Chinese people hardworking and courteous. This they attributed to their long cultural heritage rather than to the Communist system under which they lived. The people were unusually quiet, betraying no emotion, as they went about their daily chores. They were all clad in dark blue garments. Albert and Rhodes did not remember seeing any smiles, except on children's faces, throughout their visit.

In Peking they met neither Mao Tse-tung nor Chou En-lai. The former was out of town, they were told, while the latter was in the hospital. When they asked about Chou's illness, their hosts quickly changed the subject.

The only two high-ranking Chinese Communists that Albert and Rhodes met in Peking were Deputy Premier Teng Hsiao-ping and Minister of Foreign Affairs Chiao Kwang-hwa. Their meeting with Chiao lasted much longer whan the one with Teng.

Chiao accused the U.S. Government of failure to normalize relations in accordance with the principles stipulated in the Shanghai Communique. The two congressional leaders replied that, had this been the case, they wouldn't now be visiting Peking.

Asked for his views on how relations between Washington and Peking could be improved, Chiao said that all the U.S. Government had to do was to copy the Japanese formula of recognizing Peking and de-recognizing Taipei.

The two congressional leaders retorted: "But we are not Japan. We have our own principles to uphold and our own position to maintain. Furthermore, we have very good relations with the Republic of China and we would like to see the peace now existing in the area continue undisturbed."

At this Chiao became quite agitated and said: "In that case, we can wait!"

But Albert and Rhodes did not wish to let Chiao off the hook so easily. They asked him what would happen if the United States should be compelled to withdraw from the Taiwan area and another power—they meant the Soviet Union—should move in to fill the vacuum. Chiao's answer was that Peking would decide what to do if this should happen.

There were a million Soviet troops massed along the northern Chinese border. What was Peking going to do about them? Chiao said: "We are not afraid of them. After all, what could a million Soviet troops do to a nation of 850 million people?"

Why had the Soviet Union placed such a sizable force on the Chinese border? Chiao's reply surprised his two American visitors: "They are there because their real enemy is the U.S. Seventh Fleet."

Albert found it hard to suppress his laughter when he heard this. He pointed out to Chiao that following the conclusion of the Vietnam war, the United States no longer had any ground forces anywhere near mainland China. There is a saying in America that a whale and an elephant cannot have a fight because one lives in water while the other moves on land.

What would the Chinese Communists do in case the Soviet Union should launch a military attack? Chiao did not provide any answer, merely mumbling something to the effect, "We'll cope with it when the situation arises."

Albert and Rhodes were told by officials at the U.S. liaison office in Peking that the Chinese Communists were still digging trenches and tunnels in various places, especially in areas close to their northern frontiers. This showed, they concluded, that despite the bold front put up by Chiao and other Communist leaders, mainland China had a morbid fear of the Russians.

Chiao was very critical of U.S. policy in the Middle East. It tipped completely in favor of Israel, he contended, with the result that it created an opportunity for the Soviet Union to move into the area. The two congressmen felt that Chiao was looking at the problem from Peking's own concept of what constituted its global interests. When they asked Chiao whether Peking sought the role of spokesman for the Third World, he answered in the negative.

Shortly before the Albert–Rhodes visit, Peking had raised quite a hue and cry over the cancellation of a Chinese Communist chorus's tour of the U.S. The program, prepared especially for the tour, had contained a number entitled "The Liberation of Taiwan." The U.S. sponsors of the tour suggested a deletion, but Peking insisted on its retention. As a result, the tour was cancelled at the last minute. Chiao raised the subject in his conversation with Albert and Rhodes, alleging noncompliance by the U.S. side with the Shanghai Communique. He argued that since the United States did not challenge Peking's position that there is only one China and that Taiwan is a part of China, the Communist chorus had every right to include "The Liberation of Taiwan" in its repertoire for the U.S. tour.

As it happened, Albert remembered that during the Philidelphia Symphony's visit to the Chinese mainland it had had to alter its program owing to Chinese Communist objections. The U.S. sponsors of the Communist chorus were merely exercising the same right. To Albert's way of thinking, the U.S. sponsors had had a good case; they did not want to see what was purported to be a matter of cultural exchange adulterated by a song high in political propaganda content. Chiao apparently was not so persuaded, but he dropped the matter and did not mention it again during their strained discussions.

I asked Rhodes the same question that I had put to Albert about the likelihood of Ford recognizing Peking when he went there in the fall. The Minority Leader, like the Speaker of the

House, responded with a "Most unlikely!" The reason was simple: With the presidential election coming up, Ford could ill afford to touch off a controversy within his own party by moving precipitously on the China problem. At a time when Ronald Reagan's voice was becoming more and more audible, Ford would need all the support he could muster in the Republican Party to win the nomination. As borne out by subsequent events, the two congressional leaders' analysis was substantially correct.

Ford went to Peking in November, 1975, more than a year after he had accepted the invitation, with plans to visit Indonesia and the Philippines on the same trip. There was reason to believe the Chinese Communists were not too happy with this arrangement, but under the circumstances they had little choice but to accept it. Privately, however, they probably held Kissinger responsible for having reduced the importance of the visit.

Through the usual diplomatic channel the U.S. Government assured us beforehand that, although a number of measures to improve contacts might be agreed upon, nothing dramatic would happen during Ford's stay in Peking that would affect the existing bilateral relations between Washington and Taipei. Just the same, my government reiterated its opposition to any such trip by high U.S. government officials because it was bound to harm the interests of the Republic of China.

At his December 4 news conference in Peking, Kissinger was reported to have said in reference to the question of Taiwan: "We will work out the modalities on the Japanese model over a period of time." When asked whether the U.S. Government had decided on the Japanese model, Kissinger was somewhat evasive, saying: "I think that will have to be decided when the normalization in fact takes place." It had been reported that during Ford's visit the Chinese Communists expressed the hope that the United States would consider using the Japanese formula, whereby Washington could establish diplomatic relations with Peking while retaining nonpolitical ties with Taiwan through a quasi-official or an unofficial organization to be set up for the purpose.

Judging by Kissinger's statement on December 4, clearly neither he nor Ford had rejected Peking's suggestion out of hand. This of course strengthened the Chinese Communists' belief that the U.S. Government eventually would agree to sever its diplomatic relations and terminate its treaty commitment with the Republic of China.

On December 9, 1975, Philip Habib, Assistant Secretary of State for East Asian and Pacific Affairs, arrived in Taipei to brief our government leaders on what had transpired during Ford's visit to Peking. Habib described Ford's visit as a confirmation of the Nixon visit and Kissinger's numerous visits since July, 1971. He said that the bulk of Ford's time spent on discussions with Chinese Communist officials had been taken up with an exchange of views on the international situation; very little time had been spent on matters pertaining to bilateral relations. Washington and Peking were as one in opposing hegemonistic attempts by any country or group of countries anywhere in the world, but they disagreed on many other issues, including the question of Korea.

Habib was the highest U.S. State Department official to visit Taipei since March, 1972, when Marshall Green had paid a visit following Nixon's trip to Peking. Though separated by an interval of almost four years, both visits were meant to reassure our people that the U.S. Government, while seeking to improve relations with the Chinese Communists for reasons of global strategic interests, would be mindful of the position of the Republic of China.

But the only message Habib brought to Taipei was that there had been no change in Washington–Peking relations since the Shanghai Communique and that the U.S. Government anticipated no dramatic developments in the foreseeable future. This had begun to sound like a broken phonograph record.

The question of when and how the U.S. Government was going to normalize its relations with the Chinese Communists remained to be decided, but Habib assured us that the U.S. Government would act carefully and responsibly when it came to matters concerning the security, prosperity, and well-being of our people. This soon became a standard expression of Department of State officials in responding to all questions about Washington–Peking and Washington–Taipei relations, and it remained so until the eve of Carter's announcement of December 15, 1978.

Habib's report deepened the impression in Taipei that in the event of Ford's election in 1976, he would proceed to normalize relations with Peking before the end of 1978. Had Ford actually "promised" during his visit to sever U.S. diplomatic ties with the Republic of China and establish them with mainland China? According to Teng Hsiao-ping, Peking's Deputy Premier, speaking in September, 1977, Ford had done just that. But the President himself maintained that all he had told his hosts was that there was such a "possibility." He'd added that "any change toward normalization must be predicated on the peaceful solution of the Taiwan–mainland China situation." But Ford did not comment on Teng's statement that the President had promised to take such a step if he won the 1976 presidential election.

Having been a journalist in my younger days, I have made it a point of cultivating friendly relations with news media people wherever I go. This stood me in very good stead in Washington, D.C., where the press corps is composed of some of the world's brightest and ablest practitioners of that craft. Many of them knew my professional background and, when we met for lunch or a drink, did not feel they were with a foreign ambassador but with a fellow craftsman. I was on a first-name basis with quite a few of them and found the contacts very helpful in carrying out my ambassadorial duties.

In mid-May, 1975, one month after the fall of South Vietnam, I had lunch with one member of the Washington press corps. He told me, among other things, that despite the Indochina setback, and largely due to Kissinger's persistence, the Ford administration's policy on normalization of relations with Peking was still on course, but the speed had been reduced. It was this man's belief that Ford's trip to Peking, originally scheduled for the middle of the year, was being postponed to the end of November or the beginning of December. Had it not been for the Vietnam disaster, he said, Ford most likely would have picked an earlier date for the visit so that he could dispose of the China question sufficiently ahead of the presidential election to avoid its becoming a campaign issue.

This journalist had accompanied Kissinger on several trips to Peking, including the one in November, 1974, when Kissinger had not been received by Mao Tse-tung and had had only a brief hospital visit with Chou En-lai. He considered all this the Chinese Communists' way of indicating their displeasure at the lack of movement by Washington on the Taiwan question. Kissinger, however, denying Taiwan was the issue, said Peking was unhappy about something else, although he didn't elaborate; it might have had something to do with Peking's quest for assurance that the United States would give more than mere lip service in the event of a Soviet attack on the Chinese mainland. Yet the journalist, recalling his two previous trips to Peking with Kissinger, noted that although the Chinese Communists had continued to speak openly of the Soviet threat, they were somewhat less strident about it. He suggested this was probably because they had made sufficient progress in nuclear weapons development to reduce the danger of a Soviet preemptive assault.

(It was also this newsman's judgment that during Nixon's visit to Peking in 1972, the President had arrived at a private understanding with the Communists that he would complete the "normalization of relations" within five years, if not sooner.

He believed that one of Nixon's conditions was that recognition must wait until after the death of President Chiang Kai-shek. This came as a surprise to me. Frankly, I hadn't thought Nixon capable of personal consideration for anybody once he had made up his mind on something.)

The Republic of China's relations with the United States remained in an unsatisfactory condition throughout 1976, despite the death of Chou En-lai in January and of Mao Tse-tung in September and the purge of the so-called "Gang of Four" in October. Washington never made the promised reassessment of the situation on the Chinese mainland—reports from various reliable sources indicated that staff work connected with normalization of relations was still going on in the White House and the State Department. A source close to Ford confided his feeling that if Ford failed to win the Republican Party's nomination in August, he would move quickly to normalize relations with Peking, thereby gathering to himself the credit for having finished off what Nixon had started. If Ford won the nomination, the same source said, then he would delay taking action. If he lost the election in November, he would resolve the China question before leaving the White House. On the other hand, if Ford succeeded in being elected in his own right, he might wait just a bit before taking the final step. But with Kissinger carrying on as his Secretary of State, Ford could be expected to normalize relations with Peking no later than the end of 1978.

There were also reports in the summer of 1976 that one group of State Department officials was opposing the idea of recognition of Peking before a new administration—be it Republican or Democrat—took office the following January. These people felt that the United States should wait at least until Mao Tse-tung had died to see how the succession problem worked itself out.

All these reports were, I admit, difficult to verify, but at the time they did give us cause for serious concern and unremitting vigilance.

The biggest show in town in 1976 was the American Bicentennial celebration, and I have already described the sadly constricted role the Republic of China was forced to play. The second biggest attractions of 1976 were the two national conventions—the Democratic one in New York in July and the Republican one in Kansas City in August—and my wife and I went to both of them. Compared with the two Miami conventions of 1972, which were held in tight security because of the anti-Vietnam war demonstrations, the two in 1976 were tame affairs indeed. All the excitement was in the convention hall itself. I have heard it said that one could stay home and watch the convention on TV and get full coverage. But then one would have missed all the briefings, tours, and receptions that were put on for the benefit of foreign diplomats, who were all accorded VIP treatment. I know from personal experience how helpful the conventions are in allowing one to gain an understanding of the American system of government. Despite their circus-like atmosphere, the party conventions are actually part of the U.S. political process. True, no outsider can ever get in on secret caucuses, where political deals of one kind or another reportedly are made and unmade. But to be there is to be able to check the accuracy of newscasts and press reports. Another advantage is that one has a chance to meet people who are active in U.S. politics but are not resident in Washington, D.C. These are mostly businessmen, who contribute to campaign funds and, therefore, have a good deal of say in party platforms and policies. In my opinion, foreign diplomats who stay away from American party conventions miss more than they realize.

In New York the Carter forces had no problem in clinching the nomination for their candidate. But in Kansas City it was a different story. The Ford–Reagan contest was so evenly matched that it was not resolved until a few minutes before balloting actually took place. Then Reagan stole the show with an eloquent speech conceding defeat. As a gesture of party unity, Ford made the expected call on Reagan, but he stopped short of asking the Governor to join his ticket. He picked Senator Robert Dole of Kansas as his running mate.

One notable thing about Kansas City was that Kissinger, architect of Nixon's and, therefore, Ford's foreign policy, was conspicuous by his absence. As a matter of fact, he did not appear until the last day, when he arrived by special plane from Washington, accompanying—so the story went—a number of foreign diplomats who wished to hear Ford give his acceptance speech and to take part in the festivities to follow. There was another theory, according to which Ford kept Kissinger away until he had won the nomination, lest Kissinger's presence stiffen the Reagan supporter's resistance to his candidacy, so opposed were they to Kissinger.

The Chinese Communists were busy throughout 1976 with their own internal problems. Chou En-lai, who had survived numerous crises, died in January. In May came the so-called Tienanmen Incident, when thousands upon thousands of young people rioted after they found that flowers placed at a square in Peking in memory of Chou had been removed secretly during the previous night. Teng Hsiao-ping, who had been rehabilitated only a short while before and largely through Chou's intercession, was once again stripped of his party and political posts. This was done at the insistence of Chiang Ching, who was preparing to take over the reins of power at a moment's notice. In September of the same year Mao Tse-tung died, leaving Hua Kuo-feng the nominal party boss. The following month, with the help of Wang Tung-hsin, Mao's security chief, and Chen Hsi-lien, Commander of the Peking Military Region, and a few others, Hua crushed the "Gang of Four" in a countercoup.

With the Americans engrossed in celebrating their Bicentennial during the first half of the year and preoccupied with the presidential election in the second half, and with the

Chinese Communists busy with their power struggle, there was no movement whatsoever on the question of "normalization of relations" between Washington and Peking in 1976.

Chapter XI

False Promises

Jimmy Carter was sworn in as the thirty-ninth President of the United States on January 20, 1977. Two days later he and Mrs. Rosalynn Carter gave a reception in the White House for foreign ambassadors and their ladies. My wife and I shook hands with the First Couple. They were, of course, all smiles. While waiting to be photographed with them, I told the new President that I had had the pleasure of calling on him in Atlanta in 1972, when he was Governor of Georgia. He grinned and mumbled a polite reply. In no time at all we were ushered into an adjoining room where drinks and refreshments were being served. This was the only time I met President Carter, though I saw him on TV and on Capitol Hill, when he delivered a State of the Union message or something of comparable importance—occasions to which members of the diplomatic corps are invited, thereby providing a President with an international audience.

I never saw Carter again face-to-face, and not because I didn't ask for an audience. In fact, I had specific instructions from my government to see him early on in his administration. Somehow the State Department, through which such requests must be processed, had difficulty in getting the message through to the White House. I had also asked to see Vice-President Walter F. Mondale. Unlike Agnew and Rockefeller, two of his predecessors, who were most congenial whenever I asked to see them, Mondale sent word that I ought to see the Secretary of State first. I was given the same runaround when I sought an appointment with Vance. The message was very clear: The top three in the new administration simply did not wish to see me. I was told that I would soon have an opportunity to see the Secretary at a group reception for ambassadors from the East Asian and Pacific region. But that wasn't quite what I had in mind. At one point the country desk in the State Department informed me that Deputy Secretary of State Warren Christopher would be glad to see me instead. I declined politely on principle, saying that I would gladly call on Mr. Christopher anytime but with the understanding that this would not take the place of my request to see Vance in person. I ended up seeing neither of them for quite some time.

A State Department official once asked me why I insisted on seeing the Secretary of State. Was it my purpose to have a direct confrontation? My reply was that I was merely carrying out my instructions. Besides, I knew for a fact that Ambassador Unger in Taipei had easy access to our high government officials, including both the Foreign Minister and the Premier. Reciprocity being a basic principle in diplomacy, I thought it was well within my right as the fully accredited Ambassador from an allied nation to ask to see the Secretary himself on important matters. Whether he cared to receive me was something else. When nothing happened after this encounter, I stopped pressing, aware it would be an exercise in futility. But I never withdrew my request.

Hwang Cheng, chief of the Chinese Communist liaison office in Washington, on the other hand, met Vance in Kissinger's office at the State Department a week before the new administration came in. Carter received Hwang in the White House on February 8, a week after becoming President.

Once I made a point of remarking to Philip Habib, Under-Secretary of State for Political Affairs, that in diplomacy, symbolism and substance should be given equal weight and that people in the Orient are particularly sensitive to diplomatic snubs and slights, be they intentional or otherwise. Still nothing happened. Apparently the Carter administration had already decided to downgrade U.S. relations with the Republic of China, regardless of how we felt about it.

In his campaign oratory and even in some of his postelection speeches, Carter generally took the high ground in foreign policy. He promised to inject morality into diplomacy. He championed human rights. He assured all friends and allies of his determination to honor U.S. treaty commitments. For a while Carter's public expressions aroused in the hearts of some of our people the hope that the incoming Democratic administration might reevaluate the China policy initiated by the preceding Republican administration and take a more cautious approach to the question of normalization of relations with Peking. Note was made of the fact that Carter never mentioned the Shanghai Communique in his campaign speeches. While it would have been unrealistic to expect him to repudiate it, he might at least refrain from building it up as if it were a solemn treaty between two countries instead of a mere declaration by two politicians. After all, in his second TV debate with Ford on October 6, 1976, Carter had said:

> I would certainly pursue the normalization of relation-
> ships with the PRC . . . But I would never let that
> friendship stand in the way of preservation of the inde-
> pendence and freedom of the people on Taiwan.

And in a news conference in Kansas City on October 15, 1976:

> We are bound by a treaty to guarantee the freedom of
> Formosa, Taiwan, The Republic of China. I would like to
> improve our relationships—diplomatic relationships with
> the PRC, mainland China, hopefully leading to normali-
> zation of diplomatic relations sometime in the future.
> But I wouldn't go back on the commitment that we have

had to assure that Taiwan is protected from military takeover.

And then in a *Time* magazine interview on December 28, 1976:

I don't know yet if there is any urgency about resolving the differences that exist between the mainland and Taiwan. I would go into that very cautiously. We have a defense pact with Taiwan, the ROC, and we see the need to have a good relationship with the PRC. I don't know to what degree [Taipei and Peking] want to accommodate our commitments and at the same time search for a way to resolve their differences.

The three statements make interesting reading. In the first one, while seeking to improve relations with Peking, Carter said he would not do so at the expense of the independence and freedom of the people on Taiwan. In the second one he said the United States had a treaty to guarantee the security of Taiwan. In the third one he admitted he was faced with a dilemma—a defense pact with Taiwan and the need for good relations with Peking. He pleaded for more time so that he could "go into it very cautiously."

It was also noteworthy that Carter referred to us as "Formosa," "Taiwan," "Republic of China" in the same breath in his first statement, but subsequently and more and more often as "Taiwan," "ROC," or "people on Taiwan" and "people of Taiwan."

Vance, on the other hand, was more concise in his public utterances. On January 8, 1977, following the first meeting with Hwang Cheng, he told reporters:

Insofar as our bilateral relations with China are concerned, they continue to be guided by the Shanghai Communique. I think that's all I should say at this moment. At some time I would say I probably will be going to Peking. I have no definite date for anything like this now.

On January 21, Vance testified before the Senate Foreign Relations Committee, which was holding confirmation hearings on his appointment as the new Secretary of State, and he had this to say about China:

> First, I believe that our policy with respect to the PRC should be one which is based on the guiding principles, bilaterally, that were set forth in the Shanghai Communique. And I myself believe that our goal should be the normalization of relations with the PRC. As to the pace and mode of achieving that goal, as far as I am concerned, there should be further talks and studies, and it is already in process within our national security system. With respect to the question of Taiwan, one of the factors we have to take into consideration in dealing with the question of the pace and the mode is the security of the people of Taiwan.

On January 31, after assuming his post, Vance told a news conference:

> Let me point out we are only at the end of our first week. I have stated that insofar as our bilateral relations are concerned, we will proceed on the basis of the principles enunciated in the Shanghai Communique. With respect to the pace and mode of reaching normalization, this is a matter which we have under intensive review. I would hope that we can complete that review in the not-too-distant future, and I think there really is nothing more that I can say at this point. I do support very strongly the goal of normalization of relations.

Then, on February 3, he told A.P. and UPI reporters:

> I believe that normalization of relations with the People's Republic of China should be our ultimate goal. As I have previously said, I believe that the pace at which one proceeds and the modalities which might be used, require further careful study, and I further believe that in considering that, we must also consider the question of the security of the people on Taiwan.

Vance gave the U.S. quest for normalization of relations added meaning and significance when he spoke before the U.N. General Assembly on March 17:

> We will continue our efforts to develop further our relationships with the People's Republic of China. We recognize our parallel strategic interests in maintaining stability in Asia and we will act in the spirit of the Shanghai Communique.

In none of these statements did Vance mention the diplomatic relations that existed between the United States and the Republic of China or the USA–ROC Mutual Defense Treaty that bound the two countries as allies.

In May, Vance went to Moscow, carrying with him Carter's new proposal for strategic arms limitations. It was turned down. Shortly after the Secretary's return to Washington, it was announced that his trip to Peking, originally scheduled for November, had been moved up to August—reportedly as a reminder to Moscow that there was a "China card" in Washington's hand.

At the National Foreign Policy Conference for editors and broadcasters on June 28 to 29, Vance was asked whether he would touch on China policy during his address to the Asia Society on July 29. He replied: "We are still in the process of formulating our position with respect to normalization of relations with the People's Republic of China . . . The final decision will not be taken until shortly before I go to China at the end of August." He further disclosed that he would also be discussing a variety of subjects "which will be global in nature, and regional as well as our bilateral relationship."

In mid-July we learned from usually reliable sources that the Carter administration had already completed its China policy studies. The same sources said that the National Security Council had submitted its report to Carter and that it listed several options on the question of normalizing relations with Peking but did not recommend which one to adopt.

In his Asia Society speech Vance emphasized that the United States would remain in Asia to continue to play its important role in the maintenance of peace and stability in the region. He said his country would seek normal and friendly relations with Asian adversaries on the basis of mutual benefit and mutual respect and would, at the same time, be paying attention to the condition of human rights in these countries. The United States, he continued, would attach great importance to its security arrangements with Japan and the Republic of Korea. He promised that the projected withdrawal of American ground forces from South Korea would be handled in such a way as to avoid affecting its security. He also stressed the importance of relations between the United States and Japan and Washington's wish to maintain close bilateral relations with members of ASEAN.

On Washington–Peking relations Vance spoke at considerable length. Besides emphasizing the importance of these relations he pledged that the United States would conclude no treaty directed against Peking, would recognize and respect the independence and unity of the People's Republic of China, and would continue to abide by the principles set forth in the Shanghai Communique for normalization of relations with the PRC. He also declared his concurrence with the communique statement that there is but one China and that Taiwan is a part of China.

Nowhere in the speech did Vance make mention of the Republic of China; it was as if it didn't exist at all. Once he made an indirect reference to us in reiterating the U.S. hope for a peaceful solution of the so-called Taiwan question. Several senators had seen an advance copy of Vance's speech and had noticed this omission. They were alarmed and immediately voiced their objection to the State Department, asking that this be corrected before its release, but they were ignored. The omission was obviously deliberate.

On the very day of Vance's Asia Society speech in New York, Carter received five *Time* magazine correspondents in Washington. One of the questions put to him was: "Can you tell us something about how to deal with Taiwan? Is there a chance that, say, by next year we might have recognized the People's Republic of China?" Carter's answer was most significant: "There is a chance we might have recognized the People's Republic. I would like to see us have normal relations with the People's Republic of China. However," he added quickly, "we don't feel any urgency about the normalization of relationships with China, although it is one of my goals. But in the process we are certainly interested in the peaceful lives of those who live on Taiwan and we hope that those two goals are not incompatible . . . We don't want to be in a position of abandoning the commitment to the peaceful existence of the people of Taiwan." He was obviously still hoping to find a face-saving way out of the dilemma. It was noteworthy too that Carter did not refer to us as the Republic of China, nor did he mention the Mutual Defense Treaty. Compared with his earlier statements about the security and well-being of our people, his position on the Taiwan question was visibly weakening.

The day after Vance's speech and Carter's interview, Carter met for about two hours with Mondale, Vance, Brzezinski, and Holbrooke. According to a White House announcement, this was a preliminary planning meeting for Vance's trip to Peking in August and included a review of U.S. Asian policy that covered a wide range of issues. It is believed that no final decision was reached at the meeting. Some National Security Council staffers had hoped for a decision before Vance's Asia Society speech and were said to have been greatly disappointed at the delay.

Vance went to Peking in the latter part of August, 1977, for what were described as "exploratory talks." On August 27, while the Secretary of State was still on his way back to the United States, Carter was asked by newspaper editors from outside the Washington area what, precisely, was to be "explored" in Peking. In answer, Carter disclosed that a long agenda had been prepared before Vance went to Peking:

It covered a wide range of interests, different areas of the world, the Middle East, Africa, obviously the Western Pacific, peace in Korea, the SALT II talks, a comprehensive nuclear test ban, the relationship between ourselves and the People's Republic of China if recognition is not initiated, the terms under which we could normalize relationships with the People's Republic of China on the mainland and also honor our long-standing commitment that the people in Taiwan could live in freedom.

According to Carter, "Vance spent an extended period of time talking to Premier Hua Kuo-feng. He spent several hours talking to the Vice-Premier and Vice-Chairman of the party Teng Hsiao-ping. And he also spent a couple of hours talking to Huang Hua, his counterpart as Foreign Minister."

The first official hint that Vance's visit had failed to result in any agreement came when Carter said:

I don't feel under any constraint in this instance to act precipitously just to get an agreement . . . I feel like I have got time. I feel at this moment at least that I have got overwhelming support and trust from the American people and I believe we ought to act from a position of strength and soundness.

Carter indicated that Vance's reports to him were very encouraging. "But," he added,

we do not intend to act hastily. When we do make a decision about China, if we make one of recognition, it is undoubtedly going to be well into the future and it will be based on what I consider to be in the interests of our country and one which I think the American people will support.

Before Vance's departure it had been widely believed in Washington that he was going to Peking to negotiate with the Chinese Communists the terms for establishing diplomatic relations. This brought on a storm of protest from Chinese Americans and, naturally, an even greater storm of protest from people in Taiwan. Letters, telegrams, and phone calls by the thousands poured into the White House, the State Department, and various senators' offices, voicing opposition to the Vance mission. At the last minute, reportedly, Carter changed the purpose of the Vance trip from one of negotiation to one of exploration. What had really happened to cause this eleventh-hour change in Carter's instructions to Vance, if indeed there was a change, will not be known until the President or Vance writes his memoirs.

I saw Richard Holbrooke, the new Assistant Secretary of State for East Asian and Pacific Affairs, shortly after his return from Peking as a member of the Vance delegation. He didn't say much, but admitted that the question of Taiwan had been discussed. Since no agreement was sought, none was reached, he said. He repeated the same Carter State Department line: While the Carter administration was committed to normalizing relations with Peking, the pace and modalities—that is, the actual terms—remained undecided.

It is quite possible that Holbrooke, who had stopped over in Taipei to brief our government leaders, wasn't being frank, because Carter had earlier described the Vance mission as "satisfactory" and had even reported some progress. I asked Holbrooke to arrange for me to see Vance. It took several weeks for such a meeting to materialize, and then only after several senators—some of whom were members of the Foreign Relations Committee—had pointedly asked the Secretary of State whether he had seen me and, if not, why not? He finally saw me not so much to accommodate me as to pacify them.

In Peking on September 6, Teng Hsiao-ping told an A.P. correspondent that Vance's trip not only had failed to make progress on the question of "normalization of relations" but had actually caused it to move backward. This outburst caught Washington officials completely by surprise. Neither Carter nor Vance had expected to be contradicted so openly by someone with whom the Secretary of State had just spent "several hours" talking about important matters.

When I was finally ushered into Vance's office on September 10, he was quite courteous. I thanked him for receiving me, without mentioning my earlier unsuccessful request to see him in January. He sat down, holding in his hands some notes at which he glanced several times during the meeting, but he didn't tell me anything Holbrooke hadn't told our officials in Taipei or me. He said the only point he had emphasized with Teng was that in order to normalize relations both sides must make some concessions.

Teng had claimed in his interview with the A.P. correspondent that he had rejected Vance's proposal to upgrade the U.S. liaison office in Peking to an embassy and to downgrade the U.S. embassy in Taipei to a liaison office on the ground that this would still mean government-to-government relations between Washington and Taipei. I asked Vance whether this was true. Without answering me directly he said this was one of the modalities he had discussed with Teng.

A few days after my session with Vance I visited Georgetown University's Center for International and Strategic Affairs to see Kissinger, Vance's immediate predecessor, just to check on what he had heard about the Secretary of State's visit to Peking. He had no wish to criticize the Carter administration for the way it had been handling the normalization issue, but Kissinger did point out that in his numerous trips to Peking the Taiwan question invariably appeared on the agenda, yet each time it was quickly passed over for something else. In other words, there had been no serious discussion on this question because both sides agreed there were other and more important or urgent matters to talk about.

My conclusion after listening to Kissinger was that Vance had gone beyond what Kissinger felt was necessary, actually discussing with Teng such specific proposals as the swapping of embassies and liaison offices. Would Kissinger have done it differently if Ford had won in 1976 and he himself had stayed on as Secretary of State? It is hard to say.

Dr. Zbigniew Brzezinski's trip to Peking on May 20-23, 1978, was the clearest single tip-off about Carter's decision to recognize the Peking regime at the expense of U.S. relations with the Republic of China on Taiwan. The mission of the National Security Advisor was announced on April 26 by both the White House and the State Department—an unusual procedure that was arranged to overcome Vance's reported opposition. The fact that State Department officials went out of their way to say for the record that Vance had "recommended" the Brzezinski trip tended to confirm that report.

According to some in Washington at the time, Vance objected to the timing more than the substance of Brzezinski's trip, contending that it could complicate SALT II negotiations with the Soviet Union. Vance's backing down indicated Brzezinski's growing influence in the administration.

To allay apprehension in Taiwan and possible objections on Capitol Hill, Assistant Secretary Holbrooke made the statement: "This is not a normalization trip. It is a consultation trip on a broad range of issues." He did not anticipate any movement toward normalization of relations with Peking as a result of Brzezinski's visit. But as subsequent developments proved, it was Brzezinski's mission that finally started the ball rolling till it reached its goal on December 15, 1978.

Like Kissinger, Brzezinski had dealt with European matters for most of his academic career and had no background in Asian affairs. Yet also like Kissinger, he wished to use Communist

China "as a means of tweaking the Soviet Union." The name of the game, based on geopolitical considerations, was "playing the China card."

When we learned that Brzezinski's arrival in Peking was scheduled for May 20—the date of our new President Chiang Ching-kuo's inauguration—we immediately got in touch with the State Department officials concerned and also Michael Oksenberg, a China specialist in the National Security Council. While the former expressed regret over this coincidence, the latter remained unmoved. Oksenberg, who had probably worked out the itinerary, merely said there was no way to move Brzezinski's arrival date either forward or backward because of something Vance or Mondale would be doing around that time. "We are boxed in" was what Oksenberg said to me when I went to see him. He didn't even say "Sorry."

Was this a deliberate snub? Or was it unintentional but unavoidable? Some of my colleagues in the embassy thought it deliberate. But I was more inclined to the view that it was largely a case of ignorance and false pride. Oksenberg, or whoever had sketched the Brzezinski itinerary, simply did not know that the day had special significance for the 17 million people in the Republic of China. When his attention was called to this unhappy coincidence, he was simply too proud to admit that he hadn't known it was the date of our presidential inauguration. Of course we had no way of knowing whether he went back to Brzezinski and suggested a change. At any rate, this soon became widely known. A number of congressmen even made reference to the "error" in their speeches and statements. But the White House turned a deaf ear to all criticism on this matter and Brzezinski went to Peking as originally scheduled.

This incident caused a great deal of resentment in Taiwan and in Chinese communities in the United States. Though our government officials kept quiet about it, all free Chinese took this as a great insult. They saw in Washington's insensitivity in this case further evidence of the Carter administration's hardening of feelings toward our government and our people. Harder blows could be expected to fall fairly soon!

Because of Brzezinski's trip to Peking I called first on Holbrooke and then on David Newsom, who had only recently succeeded the ailing Habib as the Under-Secretary of State for Political Affairs, to ascertain (1) whether Brzezinski's real mission was to discuss normalization of relations and if so, what sort of concessions the administration had in mind to make; and (2) to remind them both that during Kissinger's days as the National Security Advisor he as a rule gave me a briefing after each of his trips to Peking and that I hoped Brzezinski would agree to follow the same practice. Both Holbrooke and Newsom, as had Oksenberg before them, assured me that Carter's National Security Advisor would receive me after his return to Washington. Nothing happened however. Despite my repeated requests, Brzezinski never received me. If he had no intention of seeing me, why had all three of them—Oksenberg, Holbrooke, and Newsom—told me that he would? Certainly none of the trio would have given me that assurance without Brzezinski's knowledge and approval. His failure to keep his word lay his colleagues open to the charge of making false promises.

At the Japan Society in Washington two days after the announcement, Brzezinski delivered what was described as an important Asia policy speech. He devoted a major portion of his lengthy talk to Japan and U.S. relations with Korea, Australia, New Zealand, Thailand, Indonesia, and the Philippines, but there was no mention of either the Republic of China or the then existing Mutual Defense Treaty between Washington and Taipei. This was widely interpreted as Brzezinski's way of signaling Peking that the Carter administration was ready to establish diplomatic relations on Peking's terms.

It may be recalled that President Carter, in a speech at the University of Notre Dame the summer before, had emphasized the importance he attached to a more positive and expanding relationship with the People's Republic of China. "We see the American–Chinese relationship as a central element of our global policy, and China as a key force for global peace." he said at the time. "We wish to cooperate closely with the creative Chinese people on the problems that confront all mankind. And we hope to find a formula which can bridge some of the differences that still separate us."

Brzezinski would refer to Carter's Notre Dame speech in his toast at the banquet given in his honor in Peking on the day of his arrival, May 20, 1978, assuring his hosts that the United States did not view its relationship with Peking as a tactical expedient. It was, in fact, based on shared concerns and derived from a long-term strategic view—"to resist the efforts of any nation which seeks to establish global or regional hegemony." Furthermore, Brzezinski said:

> We approach our relations with three fundamental beliefs: That friendship between the United States and the People's Republic of China is vital and beneficial to world peace; that a secure and strong China is in America's interest; that a powerful, confident and globally engaged United States is in China's interest . . . Only those aspiring to dominate others have any reason to fear the further development of American–Chinese relations.

And to top it off:

> The President of the United States desires friendly relations with a strong China. He is determined to join you in overcoming the remaining obstacles in the way to full normalization of our relations within the framework of the Shanghai Communique. The United States has made up its mind on this issue.

In a toast at the banquet on the last day of his visit, May 23, Brzezinski said he had found his talks with his hosts "useful, important and constructive." He elaborated:

> They were useful because we reviewed in a candid
> fashion our respective views on international affairs.
>   They were important because the review revealed
> that we hold basically similar views on most inter-
> national questions.
>   They were constructive because they will facilitate the
> normalization of our bilateral relations in the spirit of
> the Shanghai Communique.
>   I want to repeat that only those aspiring to dominate
> others have any reason to fear the further development
> of American–Chinese relations.

Brzezinski added that "the United States cannot be indifferent to the efforts of others either to seek domination or to exploit regional turbulence."

One theme emerged particularly clearly, according to Brzezinski: "Our shared views outweigh our differences." He also asserted that "as a consequence [of the improved mutual understanding achieved in his talks in Peking] our separate actions can be mutually supportive in the many areas where we have common concerns."

Brzezinski was in Peking for three days. He did not visit any other city on the Chinese mainland, nor did he do any sight-seeing, except for a trip to the Great Wall, where he had a race with his hosts, jesting that whoever got to the top last would be the one to oppose the Russians in Ethiopia. As no news reporters or TV cameramen were allowed to accompany Brzezinski on his trip to Peking, there were no independent eye-witnesses to this unusual race. Quite likely he and his hosts arranged to reach the top of the Great Wall simultaneously, so that no one would be required to oppose the Russians in Ethiopia alone.

From Peking, Brzezinski went first to Japan and then on to Korea to brief the two governments on his discussions in Peking. To Prime Minister Takeo Fukuda he brought a special message from the Chinese Communists: They wanted Japan to sign the proposed treaty of peace and friendship with them as soon as possible.

Tokyo and Peking had established diplomatic relations in September, 1972, when Tanaka was Prime Minister. But negotiations on the conclusion of a treaty to end the state of war that technically still existed between the two governments had been stalled for years over Peking's insistence on the inclusion of an article voicing opposition to hegemony by any country in the area. Japan was resisting on the ground that it might further complicate her already difficult relations with Moscow. Presumably what Brzezinski had to say about Carter's decision on the normalization issue changed Prime Minister Fukuda's mind. Three months later Peking withdrew its objection to the Japanese suggestion to insert in the treaty a separate article to the effect that the treaty is not aimed at any other country. The treaty was finally signed—one of those "separate actions" which Brzezinski had said in Peking in May could be "mutually supportive."

In another such action in June, Peking's Foreign Minister, Huang Hua, went from New York to visit Zaire, the Netherlands, and Turkey to demonstrate Peking's "common concerns" with the United States in Africa, Western Europe, and the Middle East. No one had given any previous thought to what Peking could actually do to help bolster American positions or safeguard American strategic interests in these various regions.

One of the "three fundamental beliefs" Brzezinski had announced in his toast in Peking on May 20 was "that a secure and strong China is in America's interest." But the fact remains that Communist China is neither secure nor strong. It feels terribly insecure because the Soviet Union has maintained a million troops along its border with China since the late 1960s. It is not strong because the country is so backward economically and technologically that it can do hardly more than feed its teeming population. Unless the United States should decide to start an unprecedentedly large aid program and keep it up for at least ten years—if not longer—the Peking regime would not be strong enough to stand up to the Russians in any confrontation.

In view of the American people's mood after the Vietnam war, it would be utterly inconceivable for the U.S. Congress to vote the kind of funds needed to help modernize mainland China.

The Brzezinski visit was followed by two other actions. One was the dispatch of a high-level U.S. Government science and technology mission to Peking headed by Dr. Frank Press, the White House Science Advisor, to lay the ground for cooperative scientific and technological projects. The other was the relaxation of Washington's arms control policy vis-a-vis Peking. While still refraining from selling highly sophisticated U.S.-made weapons, the Carter administration gave its Western allies the go-ahead to sell their arms to the Chinese Communists. This decision, conveyed to Peking by Brzezinski, was said to consist of three points:

1. The United States will not supply weapons to China or the Soviet Union.

2. The United States remains opposed to any sale of "offensive" weapons that could threaten China's neighbors, especially Taiwan or the Soviet Union, or that would be a "destabilizing" factor in Asia.

3. The United States will no longer object to sales of nonthreatening or "defensive" arms to China by its NATO allies.

Chapter XII

Striking a Deal

The year 1978 was scarcely under way before there were signs that most likely this would be the year of decision for the Carter administration vis-a-vis its China policy.

On January 29, following a trip to the Chinese mainland, Senator Edward M. Kennedy of Massachusetts appeared on national TV and urged "normalization of relations" with Peking. He called Communist China a key to peace in Asia "in a unique period of history." If Japan could reach accommodation with Communist China, why not the U.S.?

Another Democrat, Senator Alan Cranston of California, who had visited Communist China at about the same time, urged the same thing upon his return: "the time has come for recognition of Communist China." He thought the United States ought to break with Taiwan.

In February, Leonard Woodcock, chief of the U.S. liaison office in Peking, journeyed back to America for consultations. Speaking to a legislative conference of the United Automobile Workers, of which he had been the President, he said it was "an obvious absurdity" for the United States to have relations with Taiwan "but not with [Communist] China."

As a political appointee with direct access to the White House, Woodcock spoke more freely than would a career diplomat on such a sensitive matter. His off-the-cuff remarks gained added significance in the conspicuous absence of corrections or clarifications from the White House. The State Department contented itself with stating that there has been "no change in policy" and that "the goal is normalization of relations."

Woodcock, who had been in Peking since July, 1977, was obviously disappointed at the lack of progress on the normalization issue following Secretary Vance's exploratory visit to the mainland capital in August, 1977. As the man on the spot, naturally he wanted to see some movement. He said he had no quarrel with President Carter's decision to postpone any decision regarding further moves on (Communist) China. But he said he was convinced that not to have full diplomatic relations with Peking was an "absurdity."

The ex-labor boss's rational was this: "The greatest threat of another world war is in the Northeast Pacific, probably on the Korean Peninsula." He warned that the danger could not be eased "until we take the step for a full and normal relationship between the world's most populous power and the world's mightiest power." He concluded: "I am positive this nation can find the necessary courage to take the obvious step" of establishing relations with Peking.

In his annual statement on U.S. defense issued late in January, 1978, Defense Secretary Harold Brown attached importance to effective relations with Communist China, "not only because China is a strategic counter-weight to the Soviet Union, but also because such relations will strengthen the interest of the People's Republic of China in regional stability."

Then, in May, came Brzezinski's trip to Peking and his banquet toast assuring the Chinese Communists that the President "is determined to join you in overcoming the remaining obstacles in the way of full normalization of relations." Woodcock must have felt that his efforts would soon bear fruit.

On June 13, UPI's Washington correspondent, Nicholas Daniloff, reported that President Carter had told the Trilateral Commission, an influential private foreign policy study group, that he would press for full diplomatic relations with Peking, setting out three conditions for safeguarding the future of Taiwan. Though no deadline had been set, it had been decided to speed up negotiations and to ask for Peking's specific concessions on the Taiwan issue.

The three conditions were, according to Daniloff:

1. that U.S. trade and aid to the Republic of China—including military assistance—continue after the establishment of full diplomatic relations with Peking;

2. that a U.S. trade office be established in Taiwan once the U.S. embassy there had been closed;

3. that Communist China make clear, through a formula yet to be agreed upon, that it would not use force in seeking to reunite Taiwan with the Chinese mainland.

These U.S. "conditions" could not have been intended seriously as "counterproposals" to Peking's three conditions for the establishment of diplomatic relations with the United States—severance of diplomatic relations with the Republic of China, abrogation of the USA–ROC Mutual Defense Treaty, and complete withdrawal of U.S. military forces and installations from Taiwan. Rather, it was Carter's way of telling Peking that it needn't make any real concessions; all it had to do was sit tight and Washington would accept its terms.

As it turned out, this was exactly what did happen later on. When Ambassador Unger told me in Washington in October, 1978, that the U.S. Government had reached the conclusion that it would be useless to insist that Peking make a clear-cut pledge not to use force against Taiwan, I told Taipei that we would soon be witnessing the final denouement.

In the interest of truth, however, it must be said that there had been plenty of circumstantial evidence since the beginning of the year. But at no time had the Carter administration taken us into its confidence. It kept on saying that neither the "timing" nor the "modalities" for normalization were yet decided. Technically, it cannot be accused of telling lies, but in reality it kept us—and the American public—completely in the dark even when Woodcock began serious negotiations in Peking in November–December, 1978. It failed to consult us as promised, and it failed to consult the Senate, as was required by the Dole–Stone amendment of July 25, 1978. When the news became known on December 15, the feeling of shock and betrayal in Taipei was simply shattering. Hundreds of demonstrators appeared before the U.S. embassy to protest the perfidy and to give vent to their indignation. They were largely orderly and peaceful until the Deputy Secretary of State's arrival on December 27. Still, one can't help wondering what would have happened had the United States done this to another country, one in which the local people are more excitable by nature. They might have taken it out directly on American citizens and property.

After the Brzezinski visit to Peking in May, 1978, I and my colleagues in the embassy felt terribly depressed. If the Carter administration hadn't the decency to change the date of the National Security Advisor's arrival in Peking, there no longer was ground for hope that it would be sensitive on any matters concerning us, unless Congress came in as a counterbalancing force and factor. It was exactly this realization which caused the Senate to adopt the Dole–Stone amendment by a 94–0 vote on July 25 and the House of Representatives to adopt the same amendment as its own in October.

In the amendment the Senate staked out its right to prior consultation "on any proposed policy changes affecting the continuation in force of the Mutual Defense Treaty." The amendment became part of the International Security Assistance Act of 1978. Carter signed the Act but, when the time came, chose to ignore its provision calling for prior consultations. Although he hurriedly called a few senators and congressmen to the White House to inform them of what was about to happen three hours before making the fateful announcement on December 15, it was not accepted as the kind of "prior consultation" required under the Act. This failure or deliberate omission on Carter's part caused him serious difficulties on Capitol Hill, especially with the Senate, which tore his so-called Omnibus Bill on Taiwan apart and put together a more comprehensive and rational Taiwan Relations Act of its own to govern future ROC–USA relations.

The historic Dole–Stone amendment reads:

> (1) Whereas the continued security and stability of East Asia is a matter of major strategic interest to the United States;
>
> (2) Whereas the United States and the Republic of China have for a period of twenty-four years been linked together by the Mutual Defense Treaty of 1954;
>
> (3) Whereas the Republic of China has during that twenty-four-year period faithfully and continually carried out its duties and obligations under that treaty; and
>
> (4) Whereas it is the responsibility of the Senate to give its advice and consent to treaties entered into by the United States;
>
> (5) It is the sense of the Senate that there should be prior consultation between the Senate and the Executive Branch on any proposed policy changes affecting the continuation in force of the Mutual Defense Treaty cited above.

Our spirits were somewhat lifted by the Dole–Stone amendment. Even if Carter didn't care for us, he had to be mindful at least of his relations with Congress, especially the Senate side, and to carry out the spirit as well as the letter of the amendment that he had turned into law by attaching his signature to the International Security Assistance Act.

Until December 15 we at the embassy had been given no indication of what was about to happen. Even a week before, in a routine check with the State Department, there had been no warning signals of any kind. Otherwise, I would not have been in Phoenix, Arizona, on that day, three-quarters of the way across the American continent.

True, in late November we had picked up one piece of intelligence which indicated there would be an important announcement from the White House before the end of the year. Even earlier, there had been a story floating around Washington to the effect that Carter might announce shortly the date of his trip to Peking, and our first guess was that this must be the "important announcement." Though we didn't rule out the possibility of Carter making a sudden move on the question of normalization, it was considered improbable for the following reasons:

First, with the midterm elections barely out of the way, the Carter administration would need time to tackle the SALT II negotiations—which, after all, were believed to have a higher priority.

Second, with the amendment to the International Security Assistance Act in effect, Carter would be unwise to abrogate the Mutual Defense Treaty without first consulting congressional leadership—and we would have heard the moment the consultation process got under way.

Third, with the Camp David peace talks between Egypt and Israel getting unstuck and Vance still busy traveling in Europe, the Secretary of State would have little time to attend to the China question until 1979 at the earliest.

Fourth, with the U.S. Congress in recess for the Christmas

and New Year holidays and most of the senators and congressmen away from Washington, Carter would hesitate to upset the vacation plans of even a few key members by calling them back to Washington, unless there was a national emergency—and the question of "normalization of relations" with Peking could hardly be regarded as such.

Fifth, hadn't Carter said he is a born-again Christian? He, after all, should have some respect for the season of "peace on earth and good will to all men."

What we had failed to take into consideration was that Peking, after ratifying its treaty of peace and friendship with Japan in October—which led in turn to the conclusion of the Soviet-Vietnam Treaty of Friendship and Cooperation in mid-November—suddenly developed a sense of great urgency in the matter of normalization.

The Teng-Woodcock negotiations in Peking, begun in great secrecy in late November, had made quick progress. There were two key questions from the U.S. side: Would Peking agree to pledge not to attack Taiwan? What would Peking's attitude be if the United States should insist on supplying Taiwan with defensive arms after the switch in recognition from Taipei to Peking?

On the first question, Peking's answer was "no," but it would not contradict Washington if the U.S. should express its hope or even expectation for a peaceful settlement of the Taiwan question. On the second question, Peking *would* voice its opposition, but it would not let the matter of continued U.S. arms sales to Taiwan block the way to normalization.

On the issue of the USA-ROC Mutual Defense Treaty, Peking accepted Washington's decision to serve the one-year notice called for by the treaty in exchange for Washington's promise not to consider new arms sales to Taiwan during the one-year "extension" ending on December 31, 1979.

An agreement was finally reached on December 13, save for the issue of arms sales. Born-again Christian or not, congressional resolutions or not, Carter decided to move right away. Once the decisions had been made in the White House and its National Security Council, Vance was called back to Washington to take nominal charge.

During this critical period the Carter administration kept us completely in the dark. All that was made known to us was that Woodcock had been in frequent touch with the Chinese Communist authorities. With the help of postevent press dispatches and syndicated columns, one could reconstruct how the deal in Peking was made.

- Things began to move in earnest after Brzezinski's visit to Peking in May, 1978.

- On September 19, Carter received Chai Tse-ming, Peking's liaison office chief in Washington, and told him that, in the event of "normalization of relations," the United States must maintain commercial and cultural relations with Taiwan. Peking must promise not to use force against Taiwan, and the United States must continue arms sales to Taiwan.

- In early October the Carter administration picked January 1, 1979, as the target date for the "normalization of relations" with Peking. In late November the United States produced its first draft announcement, and Peking submitted its version in early December.

- In late October, Teng Hsiao-ping told a group of Japanese visitors that Peking was in no hurry on the Taiwan question and that it could wait ten years, a hundred if necessary. In retrospect, Teng must have indicated to Washington his predisposition toward a compromise on the question of Taiwan.

- Rowland Evans and Robert Novak, co-authors of a syndicated column bearing their names, were in Peking on November 27. They heard Teng Hsiao-ping close his two-hour interview with them "with a seemingly wistful desire to visit Washington someday." And according to the two journalists, Teng summoned Woodcock on December 5, advising him that the Peking government would look the other way at U.S. arms sales to Taiwan. He also told Woodcock that "he [Teng] would—though very reluctantly—cause no uproar over an extra year of the U.S.-Taiwan defense treaty."

- During the Teng-Woodcock negotiations the Carter administration accepted all three of Peking's demands without much resistance, insisting on only two points: that the U.S. be allowed to continue arms sales to Taiwan, though these would be kept at a restrained level; and that the U.S. be allowed to abrogate the Mutual Defense Treaty with the ROC properly by serving the required one-year notice. Teng bargained hard and obtained U.S. consent to suspend new arms sales to Taiwan until the end of December, 1979, when the treaty officially expired. This last was supposed to be secret, but it was leaked to the news media during congressional hearings on the Taiwan Relations Act early in 1979.

- Teng received Woodcock on December 13 and told him that Peking was ready to normalize relations with the United States on the basis of American terms. The following day, on Carter's instructions, Woodcock made a last and unsuccessful effort to secure Peking's stated agreement to continued U.S. arms sales to Taiwan. Brzezinski, in Washington, sent for Chai on the morning of December 15 and the two "agreed to disagree" on this issue. With the last obstacle thus removed, Carter decided to break the news at 9:00 P.M. Washington time.

- Continuing U.S. arms sales to Taiwan was one of the most delicate and difficult issues in almost six months of secret negotiations with Peking, according to Don Oberdorfer and Edward Walsh's story in the *Washington Post* two days after Carter's announcement.

Hua Kuo-feng, at his press conference in Peking on December 16, insisted that Taiwan remained a part of China and that Peking firmly opposed the U.S. plan to provide defensive arms for the island. He acknowledged that Peking had endorsed the normalization deal with full knowledge that the United States would continue to make arms available to Taiwan.

According to Jay Mathews, the *Washington Post's* correspondent in Hong Kong, the finessing of the arms issue was a nice diplomatic ploy, allowing the United States to preserve Taiwan's military security while Peking averted its eyes. Nevertheless, said Mathews, the arrangement could cause trouble in the future.

• Toward the end the Carter administration made no really serious effort to wring any promise from Peking not to use force against Taiwan once "normalization of relations" had been accomplished.

After a talk with Ambassador Unger, when he was in Washington for consultations in early October, 1978, I got the strong impression that the Carter administration already had decided not to press the matter anymore because it believed that Peking never would agree to give such a pledge and that, for a number of years to come, Peking would lack the capability for such a move. Why, then, insist that Peking give such a pledge?—that seemed to be the administration's rationale.

How will the United States assure the peace and security of Taiwan? It is based on Carter's judgment that the Chinese Communists will not try to take over Taiwan by force. This is a dangerous assumption. Peking has absolutely refused to make a public commitment not to use force against Taiwan.

Commenting on this matter, one informed U.S. source said: "We made it clear that we expect a peaceful resolution of the Taiwan issue and the word 'expect' means much more than 'hope.'"

There is reason to believe this subtle distinction was entirely lost on Peking.

One thing which remains a mystery to many of us who were in Washington at the time is why Carter did it in such a great hurry? Had Teng Hsiao-ping set any time limit to normalization of relations? Was Teng caught in a serious political struggle and, therefore, in need of U.S. support to sustain his power and influence in Peking's hierarchy? Had he told Woodcock to inform Carter that unless normalization became a reality before the end of December, he might lose control of the situation at home? Or was it because the Soviet–Vietnam treaty of November had put Peking at such a great disadvantage that Teng felt it imperative to redress the balance by coming to terms with Washington? Did he put it to Carter on a now-or-never basis? Was it possible, on the other hand, that Carter, when Israel and Egypt were unable to reach an accord in November, felt he needed something dramatic to shift the American people's attention from the Middle East? Or was it because he had run into strong Soviet opposition in SALT II negotiations and wanted to prod the Russians by establishing diplomatic relations with Peking at that particular juncture? It would have taken something very, very urgent to make Carter run the risk of offending the Senate.

• The negotiations in Peking reached the final stage on December 11–13. Carter announced the outcome on December 15 (Washington time). Rarely has the United States handled such an important matter in such hurried and haphazard a fashion.

Chapter XIII

The Other Shoe

December 15, 1978, was a Friday. My wife and I were in Phoenix, Arizona, on the third day of a visit planned a month earlier. We had a busy morning calling on local dignitaries and being interviewed on local TV stations. Having missed our luncheon engagement, we returned to our hotel and had a quick bite, then went to our room. There I found a message waiting for me. It said: "Please call Mr. Chen at the embassy. It is urgent." I immediately dialed our embassy number in Washington. Minister Chen Tai-chu, my deputy, was very excited when he came to the phone. He said Vice-Minister Frederick Chien had just called from Taipei and had asked for me. As I was away, Minister Chen had taken the call. The gist of the message was this: "Ambassador Unger had just seen President Chiang. The situation was very bad. Ask Ambassador Shen to return to Washington at once." There were no details. I sensed something big and bad was about to be announced. But what could it be? Earlier in the month we had heard that Carter might announce his intention to visit Peking sometime early in 1979. Could that be it?

I knew that Senator Barry Goldwater of Arizona was in town, so I called his Phoenix office. His staff told me they were also looking for him, because the White House wanted to know whether the Senator could get back to Washington in time for an early evening meeting at the White House. An hour or so later the Senator called me back. He told me that he had checked with his office in Washington. People there didn't have much to tell him, except that all three TV networks had been alerted for an important announcement by the President at 9:00 P.M. Washington time, and the subject matter was believed to be China.

I immediately phoned S.K. Hu, the other Minister in the embassy, to see what he had heard from his contacts on Capitol Hill. Yes, a number of senators and congressmen, including some away in their home districts for Christmas, had been summoned to meet Carter in the White House early that evening, but no one knew exactly what the President had to tell them. Hu also told me that Washington was full of rumors, most of them unfavorable to us. He was afraid that the second shoe was about to drop.

A little later Minister Chen phoned. He had just received word from the State Department asking that he see Warren Christopher, the Deputy Secretary of State, at 8:00 P.M. Washington time. The appointment was later advanced by half an hour to 7:30.

With the help of a friend in Phoenix, I began to check with the airlines for two tickets to get us back to Washington. One airline had a late night flight, but there were no vacancies. All it could promise was to give us the first two cancellations, if any. We decided to take a chance.

Before leaving for Arizona, we had made plans to go on to California, where some engagements had already been set up for me to see a number of professors and academicians in Los Angeles and San Francisco who were interested in the China question. Of course all these engagements had to be cancelled on short notice.

Our last few hours in Phoenix were most harassing. News media representatives, including journalists based in Washington, found out where I was and the phone in my hotel room rang incessantly. All wanted statements. I declined by saying that any official statement must come first from Taipei. Besides, I did not know what Carter was going to say, so there was no point in my saying anything at that moment. A local TV station, where I had been interviewed in the morning, even sent a reporter–cameraman team to my hotel just in case I should change my mind.

Shortly after 6:00 P.M. Phoenix time (8:00 Washington time) Minister Chen called again. He had just come back from Christopher's office, where he was shown the texts of two statements Carter was going to make from the White House at 9:00 Washington time. Christopher had asked him whether he had any questions. He asked for clarification on a couple of points, but they were all technical in nature. Soon he meeting ended.

We stayed in the Phoenix hotel room and waited for Carter to come on the tube. After that we had a Chinese dinner a friend had kindly brought us. Then we quietly moved to the same friend's house, where we waited until it was time for us to leave for the airport. There had been no assurance we could get on the flight, but thanks to the sympathetic help of the airline's executive-on-duty we were given two seats in the first-class section normally reserved for crew members. We got back to Washington's Dulles International Airport before dawn, Saturday morning.

In his televised news conference Carter first read the joint communique on the establishment of diplomatic relations between the United States and the PRC as of January 1, 1979, and then the U.S. statement on the same subject.

In the joint communique, released simultaneously in Washington and Peking, the United States recognized the Government of the PRC "as the sole legal government of China," and "within this context the people of the United States will maintain cultural, commercial, and other unofficial relations with the people of Taiwan."

Both parties reaffirmed the principles agreed on by the two sides in the Shanghai Communique and again emphasized that:

> Both wish to reduce the danger of international military conflict.
>
> Neither should seek hegemony in the Asia Pacific region or in any other region of the world, and each is opposed to efforts by any other country or group of countries to establish such hegemony.
>
> Neither is prepared to negotiate on behalf of any third party or to enter into agreements or understandings with the other directed at other states.
>
> The government of the United States of America acknowledges the Chinese position that there is but one China and Taiwan is a part of China.
>
> Both believe that normalization of Sino–American relations is not only in the interest of the Chinese and American peoples but also contributes to the cause of peace in Asia and the world."

The joint communique also announced that the USA and the PRC "will exchange ambassadors and establish embassies on March 1, 1979."

In the unilateral statement Carter said the USA would notify Taiwan of its decision to terminate diplomatic relations as of January 1, 1979, and the USA–ROC Mutual Defense Treaty as of January 1, 1980. In the future the American people and the people of Taiwan would be maintaining commercial, cultural, and other relations without official government representation and without diplomatic relations. American laws and regulations, wherever necessary, would be readjusted to permit the maintenance of such nongovernmental relationships in the new circumstances after normalization with the PRC.

On the question of "the security and well-being of the people of Taiwan," a subject on which Carter and other U.S. government officials had spoken so piously and earnestly before normalizing relations with Peking, the U.S. statement had only this to say:

> The United States is confident that the people of Taiwan face a peaceful and prosperous future. The United States continues to have an interest in the peaceful resolution of the Taiwan issue and expects that the Taiwan issue will be settled peacefully by the Chinese themselves.

The U.S. statement ended by expressing the belief "that the establishment of diplomatic relations with the People's Republic of China will contribute to the welfare of the American people, to the stability of Asia, where the United States has major security and economic interests, and to the peace of the entire world."

Having delivered himself of the two written statements, Carter gave the following oral explanation for his decision:

> Yesterday our country and the People's Republic of China reached this final historic agreement.
>
> On January 1, 1979, a little more than two weeks from now, our two governments will implement full normalization of diplomatic relations.
>
> As a nation of gifted people who comprise about one-fourth of the total population of the earth, China plays already an important role in world affairs—a role that can only grow more important in the years ahead.
>
> We do not undertake this important step for transient, tactical or expedient reasons. In recognizing the People's Republic of China that it is the single government of China, we are recognizing simple reality. But

far more is involved in this decision than just recognition of a fact.

Before the estrangement of recent decades, the American and the Chinese peoples had a long history of friendship. We have already begun to rebuild some of those previous ties. Now, our rapidly expanding relationship requires the kind of structure that only full diplomatic relations will make possible.

The change that I am announcing tonight will be of great long-term benefit to the peoples of both our country and China—and, I believe, to all the peoples of the world.

Normalization—and the expanded commercial and cultural relations that it will bring—will contribute to the well-being of our own nation, to our national interest, and it will also enhance the stability of Asia.

These more positive relations with China can beneficially affect the world in which we live and the world in which our children will live.

We have already begun to inform our allies and other nations and the members of the Congress of the details of our intended action. But I wish also tonight to convey a special message to the people of Taiwan—I have already communicated with the leaders in Taiwan—with whom the American people have had and will have extensive, close and friendly relations.

This is important between our two peoples.

As the United States asserted in the Shanghai Communique of 1972, issued on President Nixon's historic visit, we will continue to have an interest in the peaceful resolution of the Taiwan issue.

I have paid special attention to ensuring that normalization of relations between our country and the People's Republic will not jeopardize the well-being of the people of Taiwan.

The people of our country will maintain our current commercial, cultural, trade and other relations with Taiwan through non-governmental means. Many other countries in the world are already successfully doing this.

These decisions and these actions open a new and important chapter in our country's history, and also in world affairs.

To strengthen and to expedite the benefits of this new relationship between China and the United States, I am pleased to announce that Vice Premier Teng has accepted my invitation and will visit Washington at the end of January. His visit will give our governments the opportunity to consult with each other on global issues and to begin working together to enhance the cause of world peace.

These events are the final result of long and serious negotiations begun by President Nixon in 1972, and continued under the leadership of President Ford. The results bear witness to the steady, determined and bipartisan effort of our country to build a world in which peace will be the goal and the responsibility of all nations.

The normalization of relations between the United States and China has no other purpose than this—the advancement of peace.

It is in this spirit, at this season of peace, that I take special pride in sharing this good news with you tonight.

When he had completed his talk, and unaware that the TV microphones were still on, Carter could be heard saying to himself: "Now a round of applause from all over the country." Apparently he was very pleased with the "good news" he had just given everybody for the Christmas holidays. How mistaken he was, for he was greeted instead with cries of "perfidy," "betrayal," and "sell-out," not only by free Chinese everywhere, but also from Americans in all walks of life. The denunciation was widespread and spontaneous and lasted for many weeks. While few would have objected to improving Washington's relations with the Chinese Communists, the majority of the American people, as demonstrated in numerous opinion polls and surveys, were strongly opposed to having it done at the expense of the Republic of China, an ally and friend of many, many years. Furthermore, the way the Carter administration had handled the matter instantly cast doubts on the dependability of the United States as an ally.

Meanwhile, over in Taipei, Ambassador Leonard Unger had been alerted by the State Department to stand by for an important message which would soon be on its way. It was then close to midnight, Taipei time. Unger was attending a staff Christmas party. He immediately left the party and went to the embassy's telecommunications center. There he waited. Over the teleprinter came the texts of the joint communique and the US. statement, plus instructions that he deliver both to President Chiang Ching-kuo no earlier than two hours before they were to be announced simultaneously in Washington and Peking. What surprised Unger was not so much Washington's decision to establish diplomatic relations with the PRC—he'd been expecting that to happen some day—but its timing; he too had thought it would not take place until sometime the following spring. What really upset him, however, was that he was asked to withhold the information from President Chiang until almost the last minute. This was simply too harsh a way to break the news to the leader of an allied government. He protested to the State Department, using—he later confided to a friend—"unprintable words and expressions" to make his point. He asked for permission to give President Chiang an earlier (by a few hours) notice. Permission finally came, but grudgingly, and with the proviso that President Chiang keep the news to himself and his close associates until it was officially announced.

Then and only then did Unger contact James Soong, President Chiang's secretary–interpreter and concurrently Deputy Director of the Government Information Office, to ask him to set up an appointment right away. By then it was well past midnight. President Chiang Ching-kuo was already in bed. Soong sensed it must be something of great urgency, so he went to the

President's residence instead of using the phone. At 2:30 A.M. Taipei time, Unger's official car drove up to President Chiang's unpretentious residence on the outskirts of Taipei. The meeting lasted less than fifteen minutes. President Chiang lodged a strong protest with the U.S. envoy. As soon as Unger had left, he summoned Premier Sun, Foreign Minister Shen, and other senior officials concerned to an urgent conference. Members of the Standing Committee of the Kuomintang Central Committee were called to an emergency session at 8:00 in the morning. At 10:00 A.M. on December 16 (9:00 P.M. Washington time, December 15), President Chiang issued the strongest statement in the history of ROC–USA relations:

> The decision by the United States to establish diplomatic relations with the Chinese Communist regime has not only seriously damaged the rights and interests of the government and people of the Republic of China, but also has a tremendously adverse impact upon the entire free world. For all the consequences that might arise as a result of this move, the Government of the United States alone should bear the full responsibility.
>
> In the last few years, the United States Government has repeatedly reaffirmed its assurances to maintain diplomatic relations with the Republic of China and to honor its treaty commitments. Now that it has broken the assurances and abrogated the treaty, the U.S. Government cannot expect to have the confidence of any free nations in the future.
>
> The United States in extending diplomatic recognition to the Chinese Communist regime, which owes its very existence to terror and oppression, is not in keeping with her professed position of safeguarding human rights and strengthening the capabilities of democratic nations to resist totalitarian dictatorships. Such a move is tantamount to dashing the hopes of the hundreds of millions of people enslaved on the Chinese mainland for an early restoration of freedom. Viewed from whatever aspects, the move by the United States constitutes a

great setback to human freedom and democratic institu-
tions. It will be condemned by all freedom-loving and
peace-loving people throughout the world. Recent international events have proven that the United States' pur-
suit of "normalization" with the Chinese Communist
regime did not protect the security of free Asian
nations. It has further encouraged Communist subversion and aggressive activities and hastened the fall of
Indo-China into Communist hands. The Government
and people of the Republic of China firmly believe that
lasting international peace and security can never be
established on an unstable foundation of expediency.

Regardless of how the international situation may
develop, the Republic of China as a sovereign nation will
carry on in the light of her glorious tradition by rallying
all her people, both civilian and military, at home and
abroad, to continue to make progress in social, economic
and political fields. The Chinese Government and people
will remain faithful to their national objectives and dis-
charge their international responsibilities, thereby
demonstrating their full confidence in the future of the
Republic of China. Our late President Chiang Kai-shek
had repeatedly instructed our people to be firm and
strong and to face adversity with dignity and to press
on till the task of national recovery and reconstruction
is completed. The Government and people of the
Republic of China are determined to do their utmost in
their fight against Communist tyranny and aggression
and in cooperation with other free peoples and democratic countries. Henceforth, we shall remain calm and
firm, positive and hard-working. All our citizens are
urged to work fully with the Government, one heart
and one soul, united and determined to tide over this
difficult moment in our history. Under whatever circumstances, the Republic of China will neither negotiate
with the Chinese Communist regime, nor compromise
with Communism. Our nation will never give up its
sacred dual task of recovering the Chinese mainland and

delivering our compatriots there from Communist enslavement. This firm position of ours will remain unchanged for all time to come.

Carter's December 15 announcement was a great blow to me. It was utterly unthinkable that he would do a thing like that without taking us into his confidence. All along, U.S. officials had been telling us that they would consult us first. What they did was to give our President seven hours' notice. Although the writing had been on the wall, so to speak, ever since Nixon's visit to Peking in February, 1972, I had been hoping against hope that the United States would at least insist on maintaining government-to-government relations with us after normalizing relations with Communist China and on exacting Peking's promise not to attack Taiwan.

As I told Joy Billington of the *Washington Star* during an interview, my mission was to preserve and strengthen the relations between our two countries. What happened on December 15 meant that I had failed completely in my mission. Foreign Minister Shen Chang-huan immediately resigned, and I was prepared to accept my share of the responsibility.

That interview appeared in the *Washington Star* on December 19. Many of my friends, who knew how long and hard I had worked to delay, if not prevent, the day of de-recognition, came to see me in person or phoned, trying to convince me that I hadn't failed and that I had carried out my mission with dignity and perseverance. My mission, they said, had been a hopeless one from the very beginning, and my job was comparable to that of a rear guard, whose sole duty is to delay the enemy's advance long enough for the main force to fall back to prepared positions so that it can regroup to fight another day. In that sense, my friends asserted, my mission wasn't such a failure after all: I had held the "fort" for seven years and eight months.

I thanked them for their kindness but told them there was no other way for me to look at my mission. It was a failure!

Chapter XIV

Last Two Weeks

Before dawn on Saturday, December 16, my wife and I returned to Dulles Airport outside Washington after a sleepless flight from Phoenix. We were met by our son, Carl, and my secretary, C.Y. Chang. As the embassy's DPL sedan sped to Twin Oaks, I made a quick mental review of the major events during my long tour of duty in the U.S. One scene after another flashed by, just like a movie. My main feeling was one of immense sadness as I contemplated the break-off in two more weeks of diplomatic relations that had lasted for many decades and had been further strengthened by a Mutual Defense Treaty. All our earnest efforts to maintain these relations had now been nullified by Carter's decision to recognize Peking as the sole legal government of China as of January 1, 1979.

What had I, as Ambassador, done wrong? What should I have done but somehow failed to do to prevent this rupture? Had I really done my best? Would the people back home even understand? What had we, as a nation, done to deserve this harsh treatment? What did the U.S. hope to get out of this switch? I was still deeply wrapped in thought when the car turned into the driveway leading to my official residence.

At 9:00 I called together all my principal colleagues at the chancellery for an emergency meeting. Everybody looked depressed. What we had feared most had finally happened. I tried to cheer them up. I assured them that though this meant the end of our diplomatic relations with the United States, other relations would remain. The only treaty—although undeniably the most important—to be terminated was the Mutual Defense Treaty, but fifty-nine other treaties and agreements would remain in effect to ensure continuous commercial and cultural relations. I asked them to be calm and work doubly hard to do whatever was necessary to make the painful transition as smooth and businesslike as possible.

All embassy files, except those necessary to keep on hand, were either to be destroyed or shipped back to Taipei before the end of December. All office bank accounts and cars were to be transferred to individual members of the embassy staff. These precautionary measures were taken just in case the Chinese Communists should lay claim to our bank accounts and other assets the moment their diplomatic relations with Washington began. In view of the State Department's attitude toward our diplomatic properties—the decision, which Deputy Secretary of State Warren Christopher confirmed, that all our pre-1949 diplomatic properties in the U.S. should go to Peking—our precautionary measures were absolutely necessary.

On Monday, December 18, I sent for all our lawyers and for friends in the legal profession. After a careful discussion it was decided to ask Taipei for permission to transfer rights to our diplomatic properties, including Twin Oaks and the chancellery building on Massachusetts Avenue, to the Friends of Free China Association, a nonprofit corporation of which Senator Barry Goldwater and Thomas Corcoran, a well-known and highly respected lawyer in Washington, are Board Co-Chairmen. The transfer papers, properly notarized, were filed with the District of Columbia on December 22, nine days before our diplomatic relations with the U.S. were to end. A few days later we also deeded over to the same association our military attache's office building. Those properties, in the eyes of all free

Chinese, have a high symbolic value and, therefore, must be kept out of Peking's clutches.

In the last few years the Chinese Communists have had a windfall from our diplomatic properties in Tokyo, Bangkok, and Manila, not to mention those in London, Paris, and elsewhere. In all cases they simply took over what we had left behind. This time we decided to make an exception to the "rule." After all, these were our properties, and we had every right to dispose of them any way we saw fit. If the Chinese Communists wanted them badly enough, they could go to court, but without any assurance of winning.

George Meany, President of AFL–CIO, called on me at the chancellery on December 18 to express his disapproval of the way the Carter administration treated us. American news media got wind of the visit. The labor leader, however, did not talk to them. Two days later he issued a strong statement that attacked Carter's decision to recognize Peking as "a betrayal of the president's own human rights policy . . . We can understand—although not approve—the applause from the business community, which is in search of quick profits, no matter what the cost in human rights."

On Friday, December 22, H.K. Yang, our Vice-Minister for Political Affairs, arrived in Washington to help during the transition period. To enable him to deal with State Department officials, he was later given the title of "President Chiang Ching-kuo's Personal Representative." This relieved me of many of my official duties. Only then did I begin to think of matters pertaining to our imminent departure. My instructions were to leave Washington before our diplomatic relations ended on December 31, 1978. A number of our friends on Capitol Hill tried to arrange for Carter to receive me in person. I appreciated their thoughtfulness but told them not to move heaven and earth for my sake. In view of Carter's decision on normalization, such a meeting, even if it could be brought about, would be more helpful to him in his relations with Congress than it would be to us in assuaging our feelings of national outrage.

The American Security Council, a private organization that believes in "peace through strength," asked me to appear at a news conference on USA–ROC relations. I was to share the platform with Republican Senator Dole of Kansas and Republican Senator Orrin G. Hatch of Utah and a couple of other congressmen. On the morning of December 20, a few hours before the event, I received a phone call from Taipei asking me to stay away from the conference, and at about the same time the State Department called Minister Chen. I immediately contacted Senator Dole, asking to be excused. He asked me what had happened. "Haven't you heard of such a thing as diplomatic illness?" I asked. He quickly understood what I was talking about and asked me how many tablets of aspirin I was taking. "At least two," I said.

But I did attend a testimonial dinner given jointly by the Heritage Foundation and several other organizations on the eve of our departure. It was held in the Russell Senate Office Building on Capitol Hill and attended by well over a hundred people. Senator and Mrs. Carl Curtis were the official host and hostess, with Edwin J. Feulner, President of the Foundation, the master of ceremonies. Speakers of the evening included Representative Edward J. Derwinski (R.–Ill.); William A. Rusher, Publisher of the *National Review;* Thomas G. Corcoran, lawyer; and Dr. Walter Judd, a Republican and former congressman from Minnesota.

It was not a happy occasion. Listening to all the distinguished speakers, I was greatly moved by their kind words. When I was called on to respond, I had a hard time controlling myself, but I managed to keep my voice even and steady despite the great agitation inside of me. I told everybody of my great affection and admiration for the United States and its people, built up over a period of more than four decades of association. I told them that I had first come as a graduate student and later spent four years (1943–47) on the Pacific Coast as a regional representative of our wartime Ministry of Information. Before I took up the ambassadorial post in May, 1971, I had visited the United States on numerous occasions, either traveling alone or accompanying high officials in my own government, including the late Vice-President Chen Cheng and the incumbent President Chiang Ching-kuo. In my seven years and eight months as Ambassador, I had traveled extensively in the United States and met hundreds of people, some of whom later became personal friends. The American people have many good traits, most notably their openness, kindness, and warmth. Everywhere we went, my wife and I were received with courtesy and hospitality. We had come to look upon the United States as our second home. All three of our children and their families are in the United States. We, therefore, feel nothing but friendship for the American people.

I thanked everybody for their kindness and goodwill, which, I believed, was intended both for me and my family and for my country. I said: "I shall leave the United States with a heavy heart. I am very sad but not bitter. I am disappointed but not despairing. My faith in the American people, in their sense of decency, their sense of fair play and their sense of righteousness, shall remain unchanged."

The dinner over, we said goodbye to our hosts and all the participants. As we left the building and before we got into our car, we looked up. The sky was clear and a few stars were visible. I uttered a sigh of relief. Our personal ordeal would soon be over!

I had a busy morning on December 29, the day of our departure. I called at the chancellery to bid farewell to my staff. I thanked them for their cooperation and asked them to remain calm and work harder than ever in the difficult days ahead. Suddenly I received word that Senator Goldwater was on his way to Twin Oaks to say goodbye to me. Again, as in the case of Mr. Meany's visit, the media people got wind of it. They were all waiting when the Senator walked into my official residence. We spent a few minutes chatting together. Then he spoke to the reporters.

"This is a very sad day in American history," Senator Goldwater began. "The Chinese Ambassador is leaving because our President has acted in an illegal way. I hope to see the day when it will be reversed."

He conceded that it would be well-nigh impossible to overturn Carter's decision to recognize the Chinese Communists—"given the make-up of the Senate Foreign Relations Committee." But he announced that he would take legal action to try to reverse Carter's decision to terminate the Mutual Defense Treaty, and he vowed he would continue to fight a kind of rear guard legislative war against the administration. "We can be stingy when it comes to funds for anything having to do with Red China, and we can be generous when it comes to giving arms to Taiwan."

Goldwater said: "The President not only broke the law (in ending the Mutual Defense Treaty), he thumbed his nose at the constitution and defied the Senate." Here the Senator obviously was referring to the Senate Amendment to the International Security Assistance Act, which said, "It is the sense of the Congress that there should be prior consultation between the Congress and the Executive Branch on any change affecting the U.S.-R.O.C. treaty."

Zbigniew Brzezinski, the White House's National Security Advisor, defended Carter's failure to consult with the Senate, claiming that the negotiations with Peking could not have been conducted successfully in public. Appearing before the Foreign Policy Association, Brzezinski stated: "I think the American people are mature enough to realize that you cannot conduct negotiations and at the same time advertise every single step in the negotiation process. This would simply prevent negotiations." But he didn't explain why the Carter administration had failed to consult with the Republic of China on Taiwan, an ally and friend and also a party directly concerned with Carter's decision. All we got was a seven-hour notice!

Fourteen U.S. lawmakers—six senators and eight representatives—joined Senator Goldwater in his suit, which named President Carter and Secretary of State Vance as defendants. They charged Carter and Vance with violating U.S. law and ignoring precedents for terminating treaties when they failed to give Congress a chance to vote on any possible termination of the U.S.-Taiwan treaty.

"Just as the president alone cannot repeal a law," Goldwater pointed out, "he cannot repeal a treaty, which itself is a law. He first must ask Congress, or at least the Senate, which was a partner with him in ratifying a treaty, for approval to cancel it."

The White House cited the treaty's own one-year notification provision as ground for its right to terminate it. But Goldwater and his congressional colleagues claimed in their suit that where the treaty said that "either party" could terminate the treaty by giving a one-year notification, it did not mean that a President could do that unilaterally. The suit cited a provision of the Vienna Convention on the Law of Treaties that defined the term "party" as "a state which had consented to be bound by the treaty—and for which the treaty is in force."

The suit claimed that "under past practice," presidents have acted with the Senate or the whole Congress to end treaties. Of the forty-eight treaties that have been terminated, the suit noted, thirty have been ended by congressional legislation, eight by joint House and Senate resolutions, two by Senate resolutions, and four were superseded by new treaties or laws. Another four have been ended by presidents, "but under circumstances where it became impossible to perform the obligations specified in those treaties, and thus went unchallenged."

The lawmakers asked the U.S. District Court in Washington, D.C., to declare that Carter cannot unilaterally end the Mutual

Defense Treaty with the Republic of China and that any decision to terminate it must be approved by Congress. The case went all the way up to the U.S. Supreme Court, where it ended in dismissal in December, 1979.

Following Carter's December 15 announcement and before leaving Washington, I made only two visits to the State Department. I saw Holbrooke on December 18, though I forget who initiated the visit and, at any rate, we didn't have much to talk about. But I did ask him what had happened to his repeated promises that the U.S. Government would consult us before making the final decision to normalize relations with Peking. His explanation was that Woodcock's discussions in Peking happened so fast there simply wasn't time to consult us. Besides, he said, as our position was well known, consultation between Washington and Taipei would have caused only further delay in coming to terms with the Chinese Communists on a matter of such great importance to the United States. I could not detect even the slightest hint of regret by Holbrooke that the U.S. Government had willfully violated one of the basic principles of diplomacy: good faith and mutual respect. The United States had treated some of her enemies with greater consideration!

The only piece of solid information Holbrooke gave me in that unhappy meeting was that Carter had decided to send Warren Christopher to Taipei for a two-day visit, December 27–29, during which, it was hoped, the two parties would be able to work out a modus operandi for maintaining unofficial relations after January 1, 1979. I told Holbrooke I would like to see Christopher before he left Taipei. Christopher was planning to spend the Christmas holidays with his family in California before going on to Taipei, so it was arranged for me to call on him on December 23. As Vance was out of town at the time, my call on the Deputy Secretary of State was also in the nature of a leave-taking at the end of my mission. I was usually a good listener, but on this occasion I did most of the talking. I told him I had come to say goodbye with a very heavy heart. All my efforts to maintain diplomatic and defense relations between our two countries had been in vain. The U.S. Government, for reasons best known to its policy-makers, had finally done the unthinkable. I was certain that one day they would realize what a mistake they had made. But great harm had already been done to the Republic of China, an ally and friend for long, long, time. I was prepared to think that the U.S. Government had done it in the honest belief that this would yield immense geopolitical as well as economic benefits. In time, all this would prove to be nothing but a mirage. Now that what did not have to happen had happened, there was no point crying over the spilt milk. We should instead look forward to the future. On this, Christopher said, he couldn't agree with me more.

I pointed out that we didn't have to worry too much over our commercial and cultural relations, because they could be expected to go on very much by themselves anyway. What we really needed to work out was how to provide for Taiwan's future security now that the U.S. Government had decided to terminate the Mutual Defense Treaty as of January 1, 1980. This was particularly important, since the U.S. Government had failed to obtain any assurance from the Chinese Communists that they would not use force against Taiwan. True, Carter had said the U.S. Government would continue to provide Taiwan with defense weapons, but these would be only on a selective and restrained basis. For many years, though, the U.S. Government had been keeping us on a very tight leash in the matter of arms supplies. Unless Carter meant what he had said and took necessary steps to assure us of a continuous flow of weapons for our defense, our security situation could quickly deteriorate and cause miscalculation by Peking, thereby increasing the danger of war in the Taiwan Straits. I didn't think the U.S. Government would like to see this happen.

I said I was quite familiar with the argument prevalent in U.S. official circles that the Chinese Communists, aside from their strained relations with the Soviets, did not as yet have the capability to invade Taiwan. But we, the government and people of the Republic of China on Taiwan, could not afford to be complacent on a matter concerning our very security. I hoped that in his forthcoming discussions in Taipei he could reassure our leaders about the U.S. Government's readiness to back up its professed interest in the maintenance of peace in the Taiwan Straits with concrete proposals on the continued supply of arms needed for our defense.

I also told Christopher that Carter's December 15 announcement had aroused widespread indignation in Taiwan. Our people not only felt betrayed, but insulted. Feelings were running high. I urged him not to use any high-pressure tactics in negotiating with our officials on future relations. Above all, I hoped he would not feel that he had to come back from Taipei with an agreement in his pocket. He would probably run into some demonstrations in Taipei, but I assured him that my government would see to his personal safety and that of his colleagues.

Christopher complimented me on my representation, which he thought was one of the most lucid he had ever heard from a foreign ambassador calling on him. He thanked me for my thoughtful comments and suggestions. He said he sympathized with me for what I had gone through during all these difficult years. He admired me for the dignified manner with which I had carried out my mission. With the exception of our diplomatic relations, which would end on January 1, 1979, and the Mutual Defense Treaty, which would end a year later, all other treaties and agreements between our two countries would remain in effect. The U.S. administration would take all necessary steps to set up an unofficial organization so that commercial, cultural, and other relations could go on without interruption.

I told Christopher I would be leaving the United States with a heavy heart but would always think of the American people as friends. On that note I rose, shook hands, and left the State

Department building for the last time as Ambassador of the Republic of China.

The Christopher mission arrived in Taipei the evening of December 27. It was met by Frederick F. Chien, the Second Vice-Minister of Foreign Affairs (the First Vice-Minister, H.K. Yang, was already in Washington). Chien set the tone for the three-day discussions by saying to the U.S. Deputy Secretary of State: "I meet you here at this time with a heavy and pained heart."

Chien reminded Christopher of the long history of friendly ties between the two countries, the common concepts and interests of the two peoples, and the fact that "We have always treasured the Sino–American diplomatic relationship and have faithfully honored our treaty commitments." He regretted the U.S. Government's December 15 decision to sever diplomatic relations and terminate its Mutual Defense Treaty with the Republic of China—"an action which has disrupted the traditional friendship and harmonious relations between our two countries and has seriously impaired the peace and security of the Asian–Pacific region."

"Your visit here," Chien continued, "should be the first step in your government's efforts to mitigate the disastrous damage wrought by this mistake. I expect that during your stay in Taipei, you will gain a clear understanding of the position of our government and the feelings of our people."

Then he emphasized the following points:

- The Republic of China is prepared "to meet this new challenge with increased determination" to achieve its national goal by ceaseless efforts, which will contribute to the peace and stability of the Asian–Pacific region and the world.

- In view of the U.S. Government's expressed hope of maintaining cultural, economic, trade, and scientific and technological relations with the Republic of China, "We feel most strongly this could be carried out only on a government-to-government basis."

- Since the assurance of freedom and human rights is in the traditional American spirit, and since President Carter has stressed that human rights are the soul of U.S. foreign policy, "it seems ironic" that his administration should be the one "to establish relations with the Chinese Communists and recognize the most tyrannical regime in the world."

- Since the United States has repeatedly expressed its intention to remain a Pacific power and is concerned with the security of the Western Pacific and the Republic of China, and since it has now decided to terminate the Mutual Defense Treaty, the U.S. Government ought to clarify what specific and concrete measures it would take to ensure the stability and peace of this region.

President Chiang Ching-kuo received Christopher and his party on December 29. He told them that future relations between the two countries should rest on five principles—reality, continuity, security, legality, and governmentality:

1. The existence of the Republic of China is an international *reality*. It does not change just because some country decides to recognize the Chinese Communist regime. The United States, therefore, should continue to recognize and respect the legal status and international personality of the ROC.

2. It is unfortunate that the two countries have broken diplomatic ties, but the two peoples should *continue* to strengthen their cooperation and promote their friendship.

3. As the situation in this area remains unstable, and the danger of Communist invasion and subversion is ever present, it is hoped that "the United States can continue

to provide effectiveness guarantees of our security and remain committed to the sale of defensive weapons we need to ensure the peace and *security* of the Western Pacific area, including the R.O.C."

4. Following the severance of diplomatic relations, "the private interests of both Chinese and American citizens require the protection of definite *legal* provisions as well as government policy guidance. The United States has stated that after the termination of the Mutual Defense Treaty, it will continue to be concerned about the peace, security and prosperity of this region, and that it will continue to supply the R.O.C. with defensive weapons. The United States has also said that except for the Mutual Defense Treaty, all of the more than 50 other treaties and agreements will remain in full force and effect. These commitments and pledges and the establishment of proposed government-to-government representation and all other relations can be effectively carried out and preserved only by legislation."

5. "The Government of the United States had declared that it will continue to sell defensive weapons to the Republic of China and maintain cultural, economic, trade, scientific, technological and travel relations. Considering these activities of mutual benefit and of such a complex nature, it is impossible for any private organization or any individual to carry them out. To facilitate the continuation and enhancement of our relationship, it is essential that *government-to-government* representation be established in Taipei and Washington to administer all relations." (All emphases added.)

Because of the thirteen-hour time difference between Washington and Taipei, I had learned before we left Washington on December 29 of the frightening experience Warren Christopher and his party suffered at the hands of youthful demonstrators. So incensed were these youths by Carter's move that they took to the streets the day the Christopher delegation arrived. They stopped Christopher's car outside Taipei's International Airport, pelted it with tomatoes, eggs, and mud. A few more agitated ones wielding wooden sticks even tried to smash the car windows. Fortunately, police appeared on the scene in time and in large enough numbers to rescue the motorcade. As a Chinese, I can well understand what provoked the demonstrators to show their feelings, but I simply can't condone the violence involved, and it tended to tarnish our image at a time when we could least afford it. I was relieved when I learned that my government had quickly apologized and taken steps to guarantee the personal safety of Christopher and his party.

The negotiations went on as scheduled but were inconclusive because of the divergence of views. While Taipei wanted future relations to be conducted on a government-to-government basis, Washington insisted on having unofficial relations only. The impasse persisted until the middle of February, 1979, with Washington maintaining its position that the American Institute in Taiwan is a nongovernmental body incorporated in the District of Columbia and Taipei claiming that the functions our Coordination Council for North American Affairs had been created to perform were of an official character. There the matter lay when the U.S. Congress passed the Taiwan Relations Act in March, 1980.

On December 29, our final day in Washington, my wife and I sat down for our last luncheon there with members of the family—two married daughters, Joyce and Cynthia; our son, Carl, his wife, Anne, and our grandson Francis; as well as my niece Billie and her husband, David Tong. Joyce, Cynthia, and Billie had come to Washington from California, New Jersey, and Pennsylvania, respectively, to be with us at a time of great sadness. They also helped us pack our books, clothing, and other personal effects that had accumulated over the years. All our children looked depressed, and we tried to cheer them up by promising to come back to visit them at the earliest opportunity. But deep down in our hearts we realized it would be quite some time before we would see them again.

The luncheon over, embassy staff members and their families started coming in, until the main reception room was packed with men, women, and children, forming a semicircle facing the entrance. Minister Martin Wong, one of my two special assistants, broke down before he had uttered more than two or three sentences. This immediately cast further gloom over the gathering. In my farewell remarks I tried to control myself, but failed. All around me people were in tears. Some of my women colleagues sobbed openly. The whole atmosphere was like a funeral. I apologized for letting my emotion get the better of me and urged everybody to remember what our late beloved leader, President Chiang Kai-shek, had said: "Be calm and strong in time of adversity." I asked everybody to turn indignation into strength and to rally to the support of our new national leadership. I asked them not to despair; the fate of our nation lay in our own hands. The meeting broke up. My wife and I shook hands with everybody as they began to file past us. Some were still crying. Then it was time to say goodbye to our household staff—the butler, the cook, the maid, the chauffeur, the gardener, and their families. Some of them had been working at the embassy for many years. They were sad at our leaving. The womenfolk wept, especially the maid and the cook's wife. So did their children, of whom both my wife and I were very fond.

American media representatives, TV crewmen, and news photographers were present during all this time. It was decent of them to stay aside as silent observers when all this was going on. In a sense, it was a family affair. But I finally did consent to say a few words to them. I told them that as the Republic of China and the United States had been friends and allies for many years, I never thought our relations would end this way.

"With our effort, our hard work, we thought we had earned

the right to live the way we want without being made part of a bargain," I said. Referring to the U.S. decision to recognize Peking and break diplomatic relations with the Republic of China as of January 1, 1979, I said: "It was unusual, unnecessary and it may yet prove to be totally unwise for the U.S. Government to do a thing like this."

One Washington paper described my remarks as "a parting shot at the Carter administration." Actually, I offered them more in sadness than in anger.

Finally, we embraced our own children. They all tried to look brave. Our four-year-old grandson, Francis, was in his mother's arms. He was too young to understand what was happening around him. He was quiet, however, having been told that his *Yeh-yeh* and *Nai-nai*, his grandpa and grandma, were going back to Taipei, a place far, far away. In deference to our wishes, none of our children went to the airport. We thought it would be better that way. And we were right.

There were many people, Americans and Chinese, waiting for us by the time we arrived at Dulles. The crowd kept on growing until it filled one whole section of the spacious waiting lounge. Some even carried banners and placards. Admiral John McCain, former CINCPAC chief, and Mrs. McCain, Thomas Corcoran, Anna Chennault, Admiral Thomas Moorer, the former Chairman of the Joint Chiefs of Staff, and Dr. Diosdado Yap were among those to see us off. Some of our fellow-countrymen, besides pledging their continued support to our government, sang patriotic songs and led all our well-wishers in a cheer, "Long live the Republic of China!" I was told later that General Albert Wedemeyer, who was Commander of U.S. forces in the China Theater in World War II, also went to the airport but arrived after we had boarded the plane. David Newsom, Under-Secretary of State for Political Affairs, and Harvey Feldman, chief of the ROC desk at the State Department, also arrived late, but they came on board to say farewell. That was the last courtesy the U.S. Government extended to us for our sincere and dedicated efforts to preserve and promote friendly relations between our two peoples!

As the airliner winged its way to the Pacific Coast, my wife and I leaned back in our seats, held hands, and said nothing. We found it very comforting that our eldest daughter, Joyce, who had rushed to Washington to be with us, was on the same flight. She sat across the aisle and looked at us every now and then. Recognizing that we were absorbed in deep thought, she understood that we wanted to be left alone for a while.

Five hours later we arrived in San Francisco. Our Consul-General, Chung Hu-ping, and a few others were there to meet us. So were Albert Hsu, our son-in-law, and our two grandsons Mark and Michael. Earlier, Mark, the elder, had asked his father what had happened. "Did grandpa lose his job?" His father answered, "Yeah, something like that." It shows how quickly and correctly a seven-and-a-half-year-old could size up a seemingly complicated situation.

As expected, I was approached by American media representatives. One of them asked me how I felt. I said: "I have been greatly puzzled by why the Carter administration did this to us. Here are two men having a fight. Instead of helping the little guy who was having a hard time defending himself, your President sided with the big bully. This is contrary to the American people's traditional attitude of helping the underdog. It is hardly worthy of the United States to kick us down the steps just to curry favor with the Chinese Communists for geopolitical reasons. It is downright un-American. If this is the way your government treats those who are and wish to remain your friends, may God help America!"

I confess I was outspoken, but dep down in my heart I have nothing but goodwill for the American people. As a matter of fact, this was the essence of the farewell message I taped at the request of all three TV networks. I appealed to the American people to let their congressmen know how they felt about the way the Carter administration had handled the so-called China issue and urged them to do everything in their power to mini-mize the harm already done to the free Chinese on Taiwan by enabling them to defend their way of life against possible as well as probable hostile actions by the Chinese Communists. I made more or less the same points in my interview with the *U.S. News and World Report* for the January 8, 1979, issue.

We spent two days with Joyce and her family in Saratoga, California. After the two hectic weeks this was indeed a most welcome respite for me and my wife. We took off from San Francisco on December 31 on China Airline's 747 SP, flying nonstop to Taipei. The same afternoon Vice-Minister Yang lowered our national flag at Twin Oaks in Washington on my behalf. Thus ended the tour of duty of the Republic of China's last Ambassador to the United States. The last, that is, until Washington changes its China policy at some future date.

In January, 1981, my wife and I returned to Washington for the first time since the United States had terminated diplomatic relations with the Republic of China. It was in more sense than one a sentimental journey, because we had come to attend the inauguration of Ronald Reagan, who had kept a second term in the White House from the man who had done us in two years earlier.

Our request for tickets had been made to Ed Feulner, Presi-dent of the Heritage Foundation, who was visiting Taiwan in the month before the election. I had the feeling in my bones that Reagan would win. And, whatever the outcome, we would plan a trip to the States to visit our children and grandchildren, whom we missed very much.

January 20, 1981, was a cold but sunny day in Washington. We got up early, had a hearty breakfast, and left our hotel for the swearing-in ceremony in a limousine. I was wearing a morning coat and my wife was rather more warmly dressed.

When the ceremony was over and participants and spectators alike had begun to disperse, I saw Henry Kissinger coming from the opposite direction. We met on the Capitol steps. As if nothing had changed and no time at all had passed, we greeted each other somewhat warmly, shook hands, and exchanged quick glances—a brief encounter, totally unexpected and completely unrehearsed.

As each of us was about to go his own way, Kissinger said: "Mr. Ambassador, I have written about you." He was alluding to the few references to me in his *White House Years*, and, since he obviously meant this as a compliment, I thanked him. For just a moment I was tempted to rejoin, "and I have written about *you*," but resisted. He would be reading what I had to say about him soon enough.

Chapter XV

TRA Under the Carter Administration

On January 1, 1979 official relations between the Republic of China and the United States ended. Insofar as the Carter administration was concerned, the Republic of China ceased to exist and henceforth there were only "the people on Taiwan" with whom the United States would continue "commercial, cultural and other relations" on an unofficial basis. For this purpose, the Carter administration submitted a so-called Omnibus Bill to the U.S. Congress on January 26, 1979. The bill merely clarified the application of U.S. laws to the "people on Taiwan" in light of the changed diplomatic situation and provided for the continued conduct of programs and transactions with the "people on Taiwan." It also contained a number of provisions on administrative, financial and related subjects to carry on this non-governmental relationship with the "people on Taiwan." In particular, it proposed to establish a private organization, later known as the American Institute in Taiwan, to be incorporated into the District of Columbia, to carry on the relationship with and through on instrumentality to be established by the "people on Taiwan." (This was the Coordination Council for North American Affairs subsequently established in Taipei with offices in the United States.) The Bill bore every mark of a hastily-done job!

Fortunately, the U.S. Congress, dissatisfied with Carter's failure to consult it as required by law, felt sympathetic toward the "people on Taiwan" about the turn of events and were shocked by the Carter administration's inadequate consideration for the future security of Taiwan and its people. Thus Congress proceeded to write a Taiwan Relations Act of its own, which was finally approved by the House of Representatives on March 28, 1979 and by the Senate the very next day. But Carter waited until April 10 before he signed it, and then waited again until June 20 before he signed the Executive Order.

The Congress-written Taiwan Relations Act represents a vast improvement over the administration-proposed version. The Act (Section 2(b) declares: "It is the policy of the United States—

(1) to preserve and promote extensive, close, and friendly commercial, cultural, and other relations between the people of the United States and the people on Taiwan as well as the people on the China mainland and all other peoples of the Western Pacific area;

(2) to declare that peace and stability in the area are in the political, security, and economic interests of the United States, and are matters of international concern;

(3) to make clear that the United States decision to establish diplomatic relations with the People's Republic of China rests upon the expectation that the future of Taiwan will be determined by peaceful means;

(4) to consider any effort to determine the future of Taiwan by other than peaceful means, including by boycotts, or embargoes, a threat to the peace and sincerity of the Western Pacific area and of grave concern to the United States;

(5) to provide Taiwan with arms of a defensive character; and

(6) to maintain the capacity of the United States to resist any resort to force or other forms of coercion that would jeopardize the security, or the social or economic system, of the people on Taiwan.

The Act (Section 3(a)) commits the United States to "make available to Taiwan such defense articles and defense services in such quantity as may be necessary to enable Taiwan to maintain a sufficient self-defense capability. It also stipulates (Section 3(b)) that "the President and the Congress shall determine the nature and quantity of such defense articles and services based solely upon their judgment of the needs of Taiwan, in accordance with procedures established by law. Such determination of Taiwan's defense needs shall include review by United States military authorities in connection with recommendations to the President and the Congress."

In addition, the Act (Section 3(c)) directs the President "to inform the Congress promptly of any threat to the security or the social or economic system of the people on Taiwan and any danger to the interests of the United States arising therefrom." Of particular significance, the Act in the same section stipulates that "the President and the Congress shall determine, in accordance with constitutional processes, appropriate action by the United States in response to any such danger."

According to the Act (Section 4(a) and (b)), the absence of diplomatic relations or recognition shall not affect the application of U.S. laws with respect to Taiwan; shall not affect the authority of the President or any agency of the U.S.

Government to conduct and carry out programs, transactions and other relations with respect to Taiwan; shall not abrogate, infringe, modify, deny or otherwise affect in any way any rights or obligations involving contracts, debts, or property interests of any kind under the U.S. laws "heretofore or hereafter acquired by or with respect to Taiwan;" shall not affect in any way the ownership of or other rights or interests in properties, tangible and intangible, and other things of value, owned or held on or prior to December 31, 1978, or thereafter acquired or earned by the governing authorities on Taiwan."

Furthermore, the Act (Section 4(b)) assures the people on Taiwan of continued supply of nuclear fuels, of same treatment as before for purposes of immigration and nationality, of the capacity to sue and be sued in U.S. Courts, and the waivering of requirement, whether expressed or implied, under the U.S. laws, with respect to maintenance of diplomatic relations or recognition.

The Act (Section 4(c)) provides: "For all purposes, including actions in any court in the United States, the Congress approves the continuation in force of all treaties and other international agreements, including multilateral conventions, entered into by the United States and the governing authorities on Taiwan recognized by the United States as the Republic of China prior to January 1, 1979, and in force between them on December 31, 1978, unless and until terminated in accordance with law." It says (Section 4(d)) that nothing in this Act may be construed as a basis of supporting the exclusion or expulsion of Taiwan from continued membership in any international financial institution or any other international organization."

Under Section 10(b) of the Act, the U.S. President "is requested to extend to the instrumentality established by Taiwan the same number of offices and complement of personnel as were previously operated in the United States by the governing authorities on Taiwan recognized as the Republic of China prior to January 1, 1979."

Before the Carter administration severed diplomatic relations with the Republic of China at the end of December 1978, the Republic of China had its embassy in Washington D.C. and 11 consulates-general in New York, Boston, Atlanta, Houston, Chicago, Kansas City, Seattle, San Francisco, Los Angeles, Calexico and Honolulu, plus three consulates in Portland (Oregon), Guam and American Samoa. The consulates-general in Atlanta and Kansas City and the consulate in Portland (Oregon) were all established during my tour of duty in Washington. But in the negotiations which Vice-Minister Yang conducted with the State Department in January and February 1979, the latter insisted that CCNAA could have only eight offices, besides the main office in Washington D.C. As a result, the Republic of China had to close down its consulates-general in Boston, Calexico, and Kansas City and the consulates in Portland (Oregon), Guam and American Samoa. During the remainder of the Carter administration, the State Department turned a deaf ear to R.O.C.'s requests for reopening these six offices as allowed in the Taiwan Relations Act.

The first indication that the executive branch of the Carter administration had its own ideas regarding the implementation of the Taiwan Relations Act came in August 1979. During his visit to Peking, Vice-President Walter Mondale informed his Chinese Communist hosts that in order to pave the way for the conclusion of an official Washington-Peking air transport agreement, the Carter administration had decided to abrogate the R.O.C.-U.S.A. Air Transport Agreement of 1946 and to replace it with an informal and unofficial one between the AIT and the CCNAA. When he made the announcement at a news conference in Canton, the immediate reaction was that this was another of the Carter administration's deliberate moves to please its new friends in Peking and to further harm its former allies in Taiwan. How could it justify its decision under the Taiwan Relations Act, which, in Section 4(c), clearly provides that all treaties and other international agreements including multilateral conventions entered into between the U.S.A. and the R.O.C. prior to January 1, 1979 and in force on December 31, 1978, shall continue in forcé unless and until terminated in accordance with law? What was particularly disturbing was that the Carter administration reached the decision without consulting Congress.

At the hearings held by the Asia–Pacific Sub-Committee of the Senate Foreign Relations Committee on September 27, 1979, Richard Holbrooke, Assistant Secretary of State for East Asian and Pacific Affairs, under persistent questioning by numerous senators, disclaimed that the State Department had a policy to turn all existing treaties and agreements with the Republic of China into informal and unofficial ones. He, however, admitted that the State Department did intend to revise a number of the treaties and agreements between the U.S.A. and the R.O.C. although the bulk of the 59 treaties and agreements would be permitted to remain in force.

On November 13 the AIT, on instructions of the State Department, suddenly notified its counterpart, the CCNAA in Taipei, of U.S. intention to terminate the above-mentioned air transport agreement a year hence. On November 16, Taiwan's delegate initiated a draft agreement in return for a U.S. under-taking to withdraw its termination notice when the new agreement was signed between the AIT and CCNAA.

On March 5, 1980, the new air transport agreement was signed but the question remained unsolved: Should the new agreement be considered as a "successor" to the agreement of 1946 or as its "substitute?" Taipei was inclined to the former view while Washington took the latter view. So far, the new agreement has only an English version. The State Department under the Carter administration took a strong exception to the Taiwan-prepared Chinese version because it described the new agreement as one between *Chung*, meaning China, and *Mei*, meaning the United States, and also because it used "the

69th year of the Republic of China" instead of 1980 as the year of its signing.

Of crucial importance to the R.O.C. was the continued supply of arms and military equipment necessary for its defense. But this provision got off to a bad start. As part of its agreement with Peking permitting the U.S.A.-R.O.C. Mutual Defense Treaty to remain in effect until December 31, 1980, the Carter administration yielded to the latter's demand not to consider any new arms sales to Taiwan for one year. This was meant as a secret understanding. But somehow it leaked out to the news media. This became known as the one-year moratorium. Though it did not affect items agreed upon in previous sales and items already in the pipeline, it caused a great deal of apprehension in Taipei that the moratorium might be extended under Peking's pressure.

Then on January 3, 1980, the day before Carter's Defense Secretary Harold Brown left for Peking, the State Department announced that the U.S. Government would sell to Taiwan about US$280 million worth of weapons, including anti-tank and anti-aircraft missile systems. They were "selected defensive items" to be used to protect Taiwan. The new arms included:

1. One battalion of—I—Hawk anti-aircraft missiles;
2. Shipborne "Sea Chapparal" anti-aircraft missiles and a fire-control system for naval ships;
3. TOW anti-tank missiles which can be carried by helicopters;
4. Rapid-fire 76mm anti-aircraft gun systems.

On the whole, the announcement came as good news. But there nevertheless was general disappointment because the list lacked the more advanced combat planes which Taiwan had requested for many years.

The Carter administration left undecided whether it would agree to sell to the Republic of China an improved version of F–5Es which the latter had been co-producing under license with the Northrop Aircraft Company during the past five or six years. This improved version, temporarily named F–5X, was still on the drawing board at the end of 1980. At one point, the Carter administration took the position that since it did not have this type of fighters in U.S. inventory, it would not consider making them for export only. A few months later, there were signs that it might reconsider this matter. At any rate, the Republic of China had been left in continued suspense till the end of the Carter administration.

On the other hand, the Carter administration was inching its way toward supplying Peking with arms. It began by withdrawing its objections if its European allies should decide to sell military supplies to Peking. During his visit to Peking in early January 1980, Defense Secretary Brown indicated to his hosts that the U.S. might agree to transfer defense-related American industrial know-how to Red China. On March 11, 1980, the State Department gave general approval for U.S. manufacturers to sell Peking six categories of military equipment.

Included in the six categories were communications equipment, certain kinds of early warning radar, training equipment, trucks and certain types of helicopters and cargo aircraft. But, officially it held on to its policy of not selling any lethal weapons to Peking.

When Keng Piao, Peking's vice-premier in charge of its military modernization program, visited Washington in late May and early June 1980, he held further discussions with Brown. Soon afterwards the U.S. Defense Department announced that it would authorize U.S. companies to build electronics and helicopter factories on the Chinese mainland.

It may be recalled that before 1972, the United States, together with its European allies, Australia and Japan, prohibited the sale to Peking of any equipment which potentially could be used for military purposes. As a matter of fact, the ban against Peking was even stricter than the one against Moscow insofar as items of dual use (civilian and military) were concerned. In 1978, the year he decided to recognize Peking, Jimmy Carter modified this policy by agreeing to release to Peking on a case-by-case basis items of dual-use while maintaining the same ban against Moscow. One conspicuous example was the sale of a U.S. manufactured receiving station which could be hooked up with an American earth satellite already in orbit gathering data on crop conditions in various parts of the world and also collecting valuable information on other potentially important matters.

Then came the Soviet invasion of Afghanistan in December 1979. On January 4, 1980, the U.S. Government banned the transfer of any high technology to the U.S.S.R. At the same time, it let it be known that, first, Peking could buy U.S. high technology of dual use without having to go through the usual long procedures otherwise required if it is on a case-by-case basis, and secondly, it removed earlier restrictions on the sale of such military equipment as trucks, radar, telecommunications, helicopters and other items specially designed for military use.

Prior to Keng Piao's visit to Washington, the U.S. Government's official policy was not to sell arms to the Peking regime, which, incidentally, for lack of foreign exchange, was not out to buy arms in any large quantity anyway. It was more interested in acquiring U.S. technology instead. This would be a matter of mutual convenience because neither Washington nor Peking in the summer of 1980 wanted to alarm Moscow with any large-scale transfer of actual weapons. Even if and when such a transfer should become feasible, Washington could claim that they were only defensive weapons. But should there be further deterioration in Washington–Moscow relations one day, then it would presumably be another story altogether.

To the free Chinese in Taiwan the question of U.S. arms sales to Peking has very serious implications, because they could be used against Taiwan one of these days. For one thing, the Chinese Communists have never disowned their intention to conquer Taiwan. For another, they have never promised not to use force against Taiwan. Even as things stand, they have not only the intention but also the capability to attack Taiwan. Their air force consists of more than 6,000 combat planes of various types, of which 1,800 are deployed within a 500-mile radius of the mainland coast facing Taiwan. Their navy has 2,510 ships of various types, including 96 submarines. As to their army, it is the largest one in the world, totalling 3.4 million men. Although a third of Peking's ground forces are deployed along the Sino–Soviet border, it has all along maintained 900,000 forces in Southeast China in the area south of the Yangtze River and east of the Canton-Hankow Railway.

Against this formidable array of hostile forces on the other side of the Taiwan Straits, the Republic of China had only 350,000 officers and men in its grough forces, organized into three army corps, a small navy of some 200 ships none of which is bigger than destroyers, with a personnel complement of 70,000 men (including two divisions of marines), and a small air force consisting of mostly F–104s and F–100s and about 200 F–5Es.

For its adequate defense, Taiwan needs high performance fighters to neutralize the Chinese Communist air force's superiority in numbers; modern missiles for its naval vessels; more improved missiles for its integrated air defense; new type anti-submarine planes and helicopters; electronic equipment for counter-missile operations; and new tanks and armored personnel carriers to strengthen the mobility as well as firepower of its ground forces.

The thinking behind these requirements seems quite clear; Taiwan's best bet is: 1) to deny the Chinese Communist air force the control of the skies above the Taiwan Straits; 2) to stop the Chinese Communist invation fleet from crossing the Taiwan Straits; and 3) to destroy the enemy forces if they landed on Taiwan's beaches or air-dropped onto its countryside before they could consolidate their positions. Those planning Taiwan's defense hope that the last exigency would never arise, because once the Chinese Communists should succeed in controlling the Taiwan Straits both in the air and on water, they would be able to reinforce their invasion forces until they seized control of Taiwan altogether. It is the considered view of people in Taiwan that if the U.S. Government should move closer to Peking militarily, it would increase the risk of war in the Taiwan Straits.

One of the arguments used by policy-makers in Washington has been that the Chinese Communists, in view of their strained relations with Moscow, would unlikely start a war in the Taiwan Straits for this would give the Soviets a chance to invade Sinkiang or Manchuria at both ends of their long border. They have chosed to ignore the fact that the Chinese Communists pushed the Indians out of disputed areas on the Sino-Indian border in 1962 and invaded North Vietnam in 1979, and in neither case did they have to take troops away from the Sino-Soviet border. Judging by their present military deployment, they have enough forces in the coastal area in Southeast China to launch a lightning attack against Taiwan.

Another of Washington's arguments for its policy of arming Peking was the supposition that Peking would remain at logger-heads with Moscow indefinitely. What if it should decide to patch up with Moscow? After all, hasn't it offered to negotiate with Moscow on how to improve their state-to-state relations, as distinguished from party-to-party relations, after the termination of their Treaty of Friendship and Alliance in April 1980? Some students of the Moscow–Peking split believed that there was nothing to prevent a rapprochement if the Soviets should one day decide to treat the Chinese Communists more as an equal instead of as a vassal or a satellite and divide Asia into spheres of influence between the two of them? For basically the two Communist powers have much more in common with each other than either one of them has with the United States or other members of the free world. In other words, there is nothing permanent in their existing enmity and it would be ill-advised for the United States to assume that the Moscow-Peking estrangement will remain unchanged forever.

The question of continued U.S. arms supplies to the Republic of China on Taiwan, therefore, involves more than the security of the 18 million free Chinese on the island but the possibility of a war in the Taiwan Straits, which, once it gets started, may turn into an international conflict with unpredictable consequences to the balance of power between the free nations on the one hand and the Communist bloc on the other.

During the first year of the Taiwan Relations Act, the U.S. administration failed to consult with either the Senate or the House of Representatives on its implementation. In a public hearing held in mid-May, 1980, Senator John Glenn (D–Ohio) chairman of the Senate sub-committee on East Asian and Pacific Affairs, openly voiced his dissatisfaction with the lack of consultation between the administration and the Congress on matters pertaining to Washington's new non-governmental relations with the Republic of China, with particular reference to matters of arms sales. He complained that the U.S. policy on arms sales seemed to be dictated by the Chinese Communists. Kenneth Fasick, director of the international division of the General Accounting Office, said the executive branch had made little effort to explain to the Congress what specific plans there might be for future arms sales to the Republic of China.

It was clear that, left by itself, the Carter administration could not be expected to implement the Taiwan Relations Act fully and faithfully. The Republic of China's only hope was that the U.S. Congress which under the said Act, has the right to consultations as well as the power of holding public hearings on Washington–Taipei's new relations, would exercise that right.

Chapter XVI

Since Reagan
Took Over

Ronald Reagan's election as the 40th President of the United States on November 5, 1980 was greeted with a great deal of enthusiasm in both governmental and non-governmental circles in the Republic of China. The incoming president has made no secret of his friendly feelings for the free Chinese. Several times during his campaign he faulted Jimmy Carter for the way he established diplomatic relations with Peking. Since he moved into the White House, an improvement has already been noticed in contacts between the two countries. His administration has proved to be much more cordial and much more considerate in dealing with R.O.C.'s unofficial representatives in Washington. Consultations have become more frequent and more business-like. Above all, there has been no deliberate attempt to humiliate the Republic of China and its people.

During the summer of 1980 when the U.S. presidential campaign was fast reaching its climax, Reagan criticized Jimmy Carter for having shabbily treated the Republic of China in December 1978. He promised to upgrade U.S. relations with the free Chinese in Taiwan when and if he should win the election. This immediately created a controversy within the Republican Party itself because one faction reportedly was in favor of maintaining close relations with Peking for geopolitical reasons. The Chinese Communists attacked Presidential candidate Reagan's China policy. To allay mainland China's sensitivity, Reagan asked Bush to visit Peking to assure the Chinese Communists that when and if elected, Reagan would not restore official relations with the Republic of China. Upon Bush's return from Peking, Reagan held a news conference in Los Angeles on August 25 when he stated his position on the question of Taiwan as follows:

> "I intend that U.S. relations with Taiwan will develop in accordance with the law of our land, the Taiwan Relations Act. This legislation is the product of our democratic process, and is designed to remedy the defects of the totally inadequate legislation proposed by Jimmy Carter."

Continuing, Reagan said:

> "By accepting China's three conditions for normalization, Jimmy Carter made concessions that President Nixon and Ford had steadfastly refused to make. I was and am critical of his decision because I believe he made concessions that were not necessary and not in our national interest. I feel that a condition of normalization—by itself a sound policy choice—should have been the retention of a liaison office on Taiwan of equivalent status to the one which we had earlier established in Peking. With a persistent and principled negotiating position, I believe that normalization could ultimately have been achieved on this basis. But that is behind us now. My present concern is to safeguard the interests of the United States and to enforce the law of the land.

> "It was the timely action of the Congress, reflecting the strong support of the American people for Taiwan, that forced the changes in the inadequate bill which Mr. Carter proposed. Clearly, the Congress was unwilling to

buy the Carter plan, which it believed would have jeopardized Taiwan's security.

"This Act, designed by the Congress to provide adequate safeguards for Taiwan's security and well-being, also provides the official basis for our relations with our long-time friend and ally. It declared our official policy to be one of maintaining peace and promoting extensive, close, and friendly relations between United States and the 17 million people on Taiwan as well as the one billion people on the China mainland. It specifies that our official policy considers any effort to determine the future of Taiwan by other than peaceful means a threat to peace and of 'grave concern' to the United States.

"And, most important, it spells out our policy of providing defensive weapons to Taiwan and mandates the United States to maintain the means to 'resist any resort to force or other forms of coercion' which threaten the security or the social or economic system of Taiwan.

"This Act futher spells out, in great detail, how the president of the United States, our highest elected official, shall conduct relations with Taiwan, leaving to his discretion the specific methods of achieving policy objectives.

"The Act further details how our official personnel (including diplomats) are to administer United States relations with Taiwan through the American Institute in Taiwan. It specifies that for that purpose they are to resign for the term of their duty in Taiwan and then be reinstated to their former agencies of the U.S. Government with no loss of status, seniority or pension rights.

"The intent of the Congress is crystal clear. Our official relations with Taiwan will be funded by Congress with public monies, the expenditure of which will be audited by the comptroller general of the United States, and congressional oversight will be performed by two standing committees of the Congress.

"You might ask what I would do differently. I would not pretend, as Carter does, that the relationship we now have with Taiwan, enacted by our Congress, is not official.

"I am satisfied that this Act provides an official and adequate basis for safeguarding our relationship with Taiwan, and I pledge to enforce it. But I will eliminate petty practices of the Carter administration which are inappropriate and demeaning to our Chinese friends on Taiwan. For example, it is absurd and not required by the Act that our representatives are not permitted to meet with Taiwanese officials in their offices and ours. I will treat all Chinese officials with fairness and dignity.

"I would not impose restrictions which are not required by the Taiwan Relations Act and which contravene its spirit and purpose."

The Carter administration, following its severance of diplomatic relations with the Republic of China, resorted to various schemes to humiliate the government and people on Taiwan. Mr. Reagan gave the following examples:

1. It forbad R.O.C. representatives in Washington to meet their U.S. counterparts in the latter's offices and vice versa.
2. It stopped R.O.C. military officers from receiving training in the United States or attending U.S. service academies.
3. It abrogated the Sino–American Civil Aviation Agreement in effect since 1946 and replaced it with an unofficial one. This was done in response to demands from the Chinese Communists.
   (Had it not been for strong voices of opposition in U.S. Congressional circles, the Carter administration would probably have proceeded to change the other Sino–American treaties and agreements into unofficial ones, too, which under the Taiwan Relations Act, were to remain in force.)
4. It unilaterally imposed a one-year moratorium on arms supplies to the Republic of China even though

it was stipulated in the Taiwan Relations Act that Taiwan should continue to be provided with arms of a defensive character.

5. It tried to ban all imports from Taiwan labeled "Made in the Republic of China" until it was forced to rescind the order after opposition began to mount in U.S. Congress.

It must be said that since it took over in January 1981, the Reagan administration has given free Chinese representatives in Washington greater access to American officials although they still have to meet outside each other's offices. It has not tried to replace any of the other existing Sino–American treaties and agreements with unofficial ones, nor has it taken any steps not called for under the Taiwan Relations Act to embarrass the government and people of the Republic of China.

True, the Reagan administration has yet to permit the Republic of China to have as many regional offices in the U.S. as it had before the severance of diplomatic relations, but it has not closed the issue.

Insofar as the Republic of China was concerned, the most important matter, however, has remained one of continued sale of sophisticated aircraft and other defense weapons—a matter on which the Reagan administration had yet to make a decision.

In mid-June 1981 Secretary of State Alexander M. Haig Jr. made a three-day visit to Peking. He told his Chinese Communist hosts that the Reagan administration had decided in principle to sell them lethal arms. He disclosed at a news conference that (1) the Reagan administration would remove the so-called Munitions List Restrictions that had hitherto prohibited arms sales to Communist China and that (2) any arms sales would have to be approved on a case-by-case basis after consultations with the U.S. Congress and possibly other nations.

Secretary Haig also told the Chinese Communists that President Reagan intended to treat Red China as a friendly nation with which the United States is not allied but with which it shares many interests. The success of his trip, Haig added, "foreshadows the prospect that President Reagan's administration will be marked by a major expansion in friendship and cooperation between Peking and Washington."

Haig also disclosed that he had extended an invitation from President Reagan for Premier Chao Chi-yang to visit the United States in 1982 and that Chao had accepted. He said Chao also repeated his invitation to President Reagan to visit mainland China and this would be discussed further at a later date.

Back in Washington on the same day, President Reagan told his first news conference since the attempt on his life on March 30 that despite the decision to lift U.S. restrictions on selling weapons to Red China, "I have not changed my feeling about Taiwan. We have an Act . . . called the Taiwan Relations Act that provides for defense equipment being sold to Taiwan . . . and I intend to live up to the Taiwan Relations Act."

Liu Hua-ching, the deputy chief of staff of the Chinese Communist armed force, was supposed to visit the United States in August 1981 to explore specific arms purchases but the trip was postponed. At the time there were two theories for the delay. One was that the Reagan administration, in view of the voices of caution uttered by people in the United States and also among ASEAN member countries, decided to slow down the matter. The other was that the Chinese Communists, concerned over the possible sale of U.S. sophisticated defense items to the Republic of China, suggested a postponement in Liu's mission so as to bring pressure to bear on Washington not to honor its commitment under the Taiwan Defense Act.

At any rate, up to the end of October 1981, the Reagan administration had taken no action on the sale of weapons either to Peking or to Taipei. In the minds of some policy-makers in Washington, there was a direct link between the two. In the summer of 1981, it was even considered that Washington might sell arms to both Peking and Taipei on the understanding that those to be sold to Peking would be enough to help restrain Soviet expansion but not enough to provoke a Soviet attack on Chinese mainland, and that those to be sold to Taipei would be enough to improve Taiwan's defense capability but not enough to tip the balance of arms in the Taiwan Straits against Peking. Insofar as Taipei's request for sophisticated aircraft was concerned, the mid-summer thinking in Washington circles, was, "I would be surprised if anything is done within a year at least," as one State Department official put it at the time.

The Republic of China's request for more advanced aircraft was made in 1980 but the Carter administration did not act upon it even though the latter had earlier approved a sales presentation, which was duly made. Since the Reagan administration came into power, the Republic of China had not repeated the request, the understanding being this was not necessary just because there was a change of government in Washington.

Sources close to the U.S. State Department said in mid-June 1981 that Taiwan has not been able to justify the request for sophisticated aircraft on defense grounds. They pointed to the seemingly quiet situation in the Taiwan Straits and accused Taipei of seeking political rather than military support in its confrontation with the Chinese Communists. They have deliberately closed their eyes to the fact that the F–5Es which constitute the bulk strength of Taiwan's air force are becoming obsolete in the 1980s and in need of replacements. In view of the long time-lags usually involved before newer planes could be made available and before crews could be trained to fly them, an early decision by the Reagan administration was being anxiously awaited in Taiwan in the fall of 1981. A mere continuation of U.S. arms sales consistent with the previous level of annual sales of US$700 million to US$80 million would exclude sophisticated jets and other high-performance defense weapons such as surface-to-air and ship-to-ship missiles, which will be needed for the defense of Taiwan in the 1980s.

On July 15, 1981, six months after Reagan entered the White House, President Chiang Ching-kuo made the following statement on Sino–American relations:

> "All of us are greatly concerned about recent development'
> in the relations with the United States. On the basis of
> what President Reagan has said and done since his
> inauguration, I think he is a statesman of ideals,
> principles and moral courage. He is an anti-communist.
> He believes that Communism and its influence is the
> greatest scourge of humankind. His dedication to the
> assurance of justice has won the respect of people of
> vision throughout the world.
>   "We must be aware that the U.S. Government faces
> many urgent problems, all waiting to be solved. We
> should, therefore, stick to our established policy and
> principle and move ahead little by little with maximum
> patience and total perseverance. I am certain that the
> mutually beneficial relationship between the two
> countries will improve as time goes by."

This statement showed President Chiang's understanding of the host of urgent problems facing President Reagan. It also indicated his own "maximum patience and total perseverance" while waiting for President Reagan to act on the question of U.S. arms sales to the Republic of China.

In mid-September 1981, he told Keith Fuller, president-general manager of the Associated Press, that Sino–U.S. relations are now based on "a foundation of faith." He again described President Reagan as "a man of principles," stating his sincere hope that Reagan would adhere to what he had said on improving relations between the R.O.C. and the United States, and on implementing the Taiwan Relations Act.

Toward the end of September 1981, President Chiang told Marvin Stone, editor of the *U.S. News and World Report* that "mutual trust was gradually being restored between the Republic of China and the United States."

In answer to Stone's question "How do you see relations developing under President Reagan?" President Chiang said,

"President Reagan is a political leader of principles and ideals. He has a strong sense of justice and morality. Since his inauguration he has shown determination and courage in external and internal affairs and a strong distaste for Communism. The relations between the Republic of China and the United States are based on mutual benefit and mutual trust is gradually being restored. This improvement is expected to continue."

In the above-mentioned three statements, President Chiang was clearly trying to send a message to President Reagan expressing his implicit faith in the U.S. Chief Executive's good faith, sincerity and friendliness toward the free Chinese on Taiwan. At the same time, he could also be sending President Reagan a subtle reminder that he was still waiting for some news from Washington. But there was a glimmer of hope that before too long there might be some movement on this matter. This came from President Reagan's meeting with the Chinese Communist premier Chao Tze-yang on October 21, 1981 during the North-South Summit Conference at Cancun, Mexico.

According to U.S. news dispatches from Cancun, published in Taipei papers on October 22, President Reagan and Chao discussed at length the continued sale of American arms to Taiwan and Reagan was reported to have told Chao that the United States would maintain its obligations to Taiwan as stipulated in the Taiwan Relations Act.

President Reagan was said to have told Huang Hua, Peking's foreign minister, the same thing, in their 40-minute conversation in the White House on October 30. Secretary of State Haig, emerging from his three-hour-long meeting with Huang the same day, confirmed that the question of U.S. arms sales to Taiwan was among the topics they had discussed and that Huang had threatened to reduce the level of representation between Peking and Washington if the Reagan administration should honor its commitment toward the Republic of China as stipulated in the Taiwan Relations Act.

It may be recalled that earlier in the year Peking had used the same threat when the Dutch government was considering the sale of arms, including two submarines, to the Republic of China. It didn't work in the case of the Netherlands, a small country. Will the Reagan administration succumb to Peking's brandishment? Most unlikely. There the matter lay at the end of October, 1981.

Epilogue

By the end of 1981, the Nationalist Chinese faith in Ronald Reagan may be said to have remained largely intact, but not for long.

On January 4, 1982, Richard Allen, national security advisor to President Reagan, resigned. He was noted for his friendly attitude toward Taiwan. Replacing him was William P. Clark, a total stranger insofar as the Republic of China was concerned.

On January 11, 1982, the Reagan administration informed Taipei of its decision not to sell it any advanced aircraft, but that it would replace Taiwan's F–5E fighters with comparable aircraft. This was clearly a concession to Peking which was also informed of this decision since it had made an issue of this matter by threatening to downgrade relations with Washington.

But Peking refused to be mollified. Instead it kept up its pressure on the Reagan administration. This caused Reagan to take the unusual step of writing three personal letters to Chinese Communist leaders. The first two letters dated April 5, 1982 were addressed to Teng Hsiao-ping, a vice-chairman of the Chinese Communist Party, and to Chao Tse-yang, Peking's premier.

Reagan's letter to Teng contained two key paragraphs. The

first one reads: "The United States firmly adheres to the positions agreed upon in the joint communique on the establishment of diplomatic relations between the United States and China. There is only one China. We will not permit the unofficial relations between the American people and the people of Taiwan to weaken our commitment to this principle."

This was tantamount to giving Peking a veto power on future Washington–Taipei relations. He also suggested that a visit to Peking by Vice-President Bush at the end of April "could be a useful step in deepening the understanding between our two countries."

The second key paragraph was even more mischievous. It reads as follows: "We fully recognize the significance of the nine-point proposal of September 30, 1981 and the policy set forth by your government as early as January 1, 1979. The decisions and the principles conveyed on my instructions to your government on January 11, 1982 reflect our appreciation of the new situation created by these developments."

In his letter to Chao, Reagan also referred to "the nine-point initiative," adding that "in the context of progress toward a peaceful solution, there would naturally be a decrease in the need for arms by Taiwan."

Then on May 3, 1982, Reagan wrote a third letter, this one addressed to Hu Yao-pang, chairman of the Chinese Communist Party, in which Reagan said "Vice-President Bush is visiting China as my personal emissary," adding that "among the issues the Vice-President will discuss (in his April 23–May 9 visit to Peking) is the question of U.S. arms sales to Taiwan."

Reagan emphasized that "our policy will continue to be based on the principle that there is but one China. We will not permit the unofficial relations between the American people and the Cinese people on Taiwan to weaken our commitment to this principle."

Reagan concluded the letter by saying, "It is my hope that you and I will have an opportunity to meet soon."

The wording and phraseology used in Reagan's three letters bore unmistakable marks of input by the State Department. Secretary Alexander Haig had made no secret of his intention to appease Peking at any cost for geo-political reasons, even if it meant the sacrifice of Taiwan's security interests.

Vice-President Bush was followed by Senate Majority Leader Howard Baker. The latter visited Peking May 30–June 10 at the invitation of the Standing Committee of the National People's Congress. Later, in his report to Bush, Baker summed up his impressions by saying that before he went to Peking he had thought that Peking was seriously prepared to downgrade its relations with Peking if the U.S. should continue to sell arms to Taiwan. But after the visit he felt that the issue was not as critical and difficult as he had imaged.

Baker's report apparently set the tone for subsequent negotiations between Washington and Peking. Meanwhile the State Department had drafted a "Shanghai Communique No. 2" for Reagan. It was reported that Reagan didn't like certain parts and sent the draft back to the State Department for revisions to make it more palatable to the Chinese Nationalists in Taiwan.

Peking sought two things from Washington: a cut-off date for such arms sales to Taiwan, and U.S. acceptance of its claim of sovereignty over Taiwan. Meanwhile it refused to renounce the use of force against Taiwan.

Then came Haig's dramatic resignation (or dismissal) on June 25. He was succeeded by George Shultz, whose confirmation hearings on Capitol Hill caused further delay and the so-called "Shanghai Communique No. 2" was not issued until August 17.

Now what was Peking's nine-point proposal of September 30, 1981 which Reagan, and Haig before him, thought so significant or important? The said proposal was made in the name of

Marshal Yeh Chien-ying, chairman of the Standing Committee of Peking's National People Congress. It was conceived as a "proposal for the peaceful re-unification of Taiwan with the Chinese mainland."

The date September 30, 1981 was carefully chosen. It was the eve of the 32nd anniversary of the People's Republic of China, and only 10 days before the 70th anniversary of the Revolution of 1911 which Peking was to observe for the first time.

The proposal was not addressed to the government of the Republic of China which Peking does not recognize, but to the Kuomintang, the Chinese Nationalist Party, which is the party in power in Taiwan.

Yeh proposed that talks be held between the two parties "on a reciprocal basis so that the two parties will cooperate for the third time to accomplish the great cause of national re-unification."

Yeh specifically proposed "the exchange of mail, trade, air and shipping services, and visits by relatives and tourists as well as academic, cultural and sports exchange."

"After the country is re-unified" he said, "Taiwan can enjoy a high degree of autonomy as a special administrative region and it can retain its armed forces. The Central Government will not interfere with local affairs on Taiwan."

Furthermore, Yeh said: "Taiwan's current socio-economic system will remain unchanged, so will its way of life and its economic and cultural relations with foreign countries."

Yeh added that "people in authority and representative personages of various circles in Taiwan may take up posts of leadership in national political bodies and participate in running the state."

What completely gave Yeh away was his offer of financial help if Taiwan's local finance should be in difficulty, forgetting the fact that the US$2,500 per capita income of people in Taiwan was ten times that of people on the mainland.

Twice before, in the 1920s and 1930s, the Kuomintang, the then leading party on the mainland, accepted the cooperation of the Chinese Communist Party first in its campaign against regional warlords and later in the national war of resistance against Japanese aggression, only to have the Communists turn against the government. Now that the tables are turned and the Communists are in control of the mainland, there is not the slightest possibility for them to abide by any agreement with the Kuomintang, which is the weaker party.

Then there was the object lesson of Tibet. The Communists promised to treat Tibet as a special administrative region and to respect its autonomy in 1953 only to seize it by force in 1959, causing the Dalai Lama, Tibet's political as well as spiritual leader, to flee across the Himalayas into India with 100,000 of his faithful followers.

In view of those happenings, could anyone blame the Kuomintang or the government it heads in Taiwan, for not meeting Yeh's nine-point proposal with enthusiasm? There is a saying that if a man is fooled once he can blame the other fellow for trickery but if he permits himself to be taken in the second time, he has only himself to blame. For the Kuomintang it would be the third time if it should accept Yeh's proposal. The Communists will have only themselves to blame for the lack of any response from Taiwan. Their bad faith in the two previous instances has killed all possibility for accommodation now or in the foreseeable future.

Taiwan, therefore, took Yeh's proposal as nothing but a trick and a call for surrender. However it made the tactical error of rejecting it too soon and too completely, thereby giving the outside world the impression of being the more recalcitrant one in this so-called Taiwan problem.

It wasn't until many months later and only after numerous

friends had pointed out the unfavorable image the Chinese Nationalists had thus created of themselves that the R.O.C. government authorities began to bestir themselves. When their response to the Chinese Communists' "peace offer" finally came, it took the form of a speech by Premier Sun Yun-suan at his reception on June 11 for Chinese and American scholars meeting in Taipei for the Annual Sino–American Conference on mainland China.

Sun began by declaring that Free China proposed to unify China on the basis of Dr. Sun Yat-sen's (founding father of the R.O.C.) Three Principles of the People: Nationalism, Democracy and People's Livelihood. He said these Principles, intended to establish a country of the people, by the people and for the people, have already succeeded in Taiwan. He called on the Chinese Communists to give up their "four persistences": hewing to the socialist road, Communist Party leadership, dictatorship of the proletariat, and ideological fealty to Marxism, Leninism and Mao Tse-tung thought.

Sun noted that the Communists had already followed the Republic of China's example in:

1. Recognizing the greatness of Dr. Sun Yat-sen and the success of his Three Principles;

2. Imitating R.O.C. export processing zones;

3. Seeking foreign capital for the expansion of exports;

4. Giving priority to agriculture in economic development; and

5. Allowing some aspects of individual economy to exist on the mainland.

The Chinese mainland has been compelled to change, Sun noted. "If the political, economic, social and cultural gaps between the Chinese mainland and Free China continue to narrow, the conditions for peaceful reunification could gradually mature. The obstacles to reunification will be reduced naturally with the passage of time."

Sun concluded by declaring that China's unification "should be based on the free will of the Chinese people as a whole."

Compared with Taipei's previous "absolutely not" stand, Sun's announcement was seen as a significant step forward. It didn't say Taipei would actually sit down with the Chinese Communists in the foreseeable future. But it did not foreclose such a possibility indefinitely. It merely said that conditions for peaceful reunification had not yet matured. How long will it take for conditions to mature? It's anybody's guess. Another 30 years? The general belief is that by then the disparity in living standards between Taiwan and the mainland will in most probability have further widened instead of narrowed. For the Chinese Communists know that as long as they hold on to communism they can never expect to win the race of peaceful competition with Taiwan and that is why they have never agreed to renounce the use of force. For this reason and for many others, Taiwan needs to maintain a strong defense capability for years and decades to come.

In the Communique of August 17, 1982, the United States made a major concession to Peking on the question of arms sales to Taiwan. Paragraph Six states "that it does not seek to carry out a long-term policy of arms sales to Taiwan. That its arms sales will not exceed either in qualitative or quantitative terms the level of those supplied in recent years since the establishment of diplomatic relations between the United States and (Red) China and that it intends to reduce gradually its sales of arms to Taiwan, leading over a period of time to a final resolution."

This is clearly a contravention, both in letter and in spirit, of the Taiwan Relations Act which stipulated: "The United States will make available to Taiwan such defense articles and defense services in such quantity as may be necessary to enable Taiwan to maintain a sufficient self-defense capability."

In his statement on the Communique, Reagan claimed that the U.S. policy is fully consistent with the Taiwan Relations Act, adding that arms sales will continue in accordance with the act and with the full expectation that the approach of the (Red) Chinese government to the resolution of the Taiwan issue will continue to be peaceful."

Meanwhile, through appropriate channels, Reagan made the following points known to the Republic of China:

The United States:

1. Has not agreed to set a date for ending arms sales to Taiwan;

2. Has not agreed to hold prior consultations with the Chinese Communists on arms sales to Taiwan;

3. Will not play any mediation role between Taipei and Peking;

4. Has not agreed to revise the Taiwan Relations Act;

5. Has not altered its position regarding sovereignty over Taiwan; and

6. Will not exert pressure on Taiwan to enter into negotiations with the Chinese Communists.

In its rather mildly-worded statement on the Communique, the R.O.C. government reiterated its position that "it considers null and void any agreement involving the rights and interests of the government and people of the Republic of China" and expressed the hope that "the U.S. government will not be taken in by the Chinese Communists' plot to seize our base of national recovery and to divide the free world." These last five words refer to the Chinese Communists' objective of further isolating the Republic of China from the free world in general and from the United States in particular, as a step toward their ultimate destruction of Taiwan.

Though the United States failed to satisfy either Peking or Taipei, it has succeeded in reducing, however temporarily, the tensions which the Chinese Communists had deliberately created ever since the beginning of the Reagan administration in the hope of wrestling some major concessions from Washington regarding Taiwan.

When at long last, the Reagan administration announced its decision on August 19, two days after the release of the Shanghai Communique No. 2, to allow Taiwan to continue the co-production of 60 more of the improved 7-5Es, Peking protested but did nothing to downgrade its diplomatic representation as it had threatened to do over the arms sales issue.

The Reagan administration said in January 1982 that it would allow Taiwan to continue co-producing the 7-5E jet fighters with the Northrop Corporation, while refusing to sell it more sophisticated fighters such as the F-5Gs and the F16J79, a simpler version of the F-16. Even then it waited till August 19 before it formally notified Congress of its decision. The long delay was caused by the secret negotiations leading up to the said Communique, which seeks to reduce both qualitatively and quantitatively the sale of U.S. arms to Taiwan. This provoked charges from a number of U.S. Congressmen that Reagan had reneged on his campaign promise of 1980 and violated certain provisions of the Taiwan Relations Act of 1979.

No sooner was the August 17 Communique signed than Washington and Peking openly aired their different interpretations of some of its provisions. Peking said it had not agreed to the renunciation of force as it deemed Taiwan part of its territory and therefore will not tolerate any outside interference as to the means it is going to use to reunite Taiwan with the mainland. The U.S., on the other hand, claimed that it tried to hold Peking to the latter's "fundamental policy" of striving for a peaceful resolution of the Taiwan question "as indicated in (Red) China's message to compatriots in Taiwan issued on

January 1, 1979 and the nine-point proposal put forward by (Red) China on September 30, 1981.

In the next round of the Washington–Peking dispute, the Chinese Communists can be expected to start a movement in the United States for the abrogation or revision of the Taiwan Relations Act. They will never deviate from their ultimate objective to put Taiwan under their absolute control. They realize they will not be able to do it as long as Taiwan has access to U.S. arms. That is why they have become so insistent on U.S. agreeing to a cut-off date on U.S. arms sales to Taiwan and U.S. recognition of their claim of sovereignty over Taiwan. They can be expected, therefore, to keep up their pressure on Washington indefinitely until the U.S. gives up.

Even a cursory review of the China policy of recent U.S. administrations—from Nixon's reopening to China in 1977, Ford's readiness to oblige Peking in 1976, Carter's normalization of relations with Peking and de-recognition of the Republic of China in 1978 and the abrogation of the Sino–American Mutual Defense Treaty in 1979, to Reagan's decision in August 1982 to reduce arms sales to Taiwan—over a period of time until "its final settlement of the question"—will lead one to the inevitable conclusion that the United States over a period of 10 years has been selling its loyal friend and long-time ally, the Republic of China, down the river, a bit at a time, but down the river just the same.

Appendix

The Taiwan Relations Act of March 28-29, 1979

An Act to help maintain peace, security, and stability in the Western Pacific and to promote the foreign policy of the United States by authorizing the continuation of commercial, cultural, and other relations between the people of the United States and the people on Taiwan, and for other purposes.

Short Title

Section 1. This Act may be cited as the "Taiwan Relations Act."

Findings and Declaration of Policy

Section 2. (a) The President having terminated governmental relations between the United States and the governing authorities on Taiwan recognized by the United States as the Republic of China prior to January 1, 1979, the Congress finds that the enactment of this Act is necessary—

(1) to help maintain peace, security, and stability in the Western Pacific; and
(2) to promote the foreign policy of the United States by authorizing the continuation of commercial, cultural, and other relations between the people of the United States and the people on Taiwan.

(b) It is the policy of the United States—

(1) to preserve and promote extensive, close, and friendly commercial, cultural, and other relations between the people of the United States and the people on Taiwan as well as the people on the China mainland and all other peoples of the Western Pacific area;

(2) to declare that peace and stability in the area are in the political, security, and economic interests of the United States, and are matters of international concern;

(3) to make clear that the United States decision to establish diplomatic relations with the People's Republic of China rests upon the expectation that the future of Taiwan will be determined by peaceful means;

(4) to consider any effort to determine the future of Taiwan by other than peaceful means, including by boycotts, or embargoes, a threat to the peace and security of the Western Pacific area and of grave concern to the United States.

(5) to provide Taiwan with arms of a defensive character; and

(6) to maintain the capacity of the United States to resist any resort to force or other forms of coercion that would jeopardize the security, or the social or economic system, of the people on Taiwan.

(c) Nothing contained in this Act shall contravene the interest of the United States in human rights, especially with respect to the human rights of all the approximately 18 million inhabitants of Taiwan. The preservation and enhancement of the human rights of all the people on Taiwan are hereby reaffirmed as objectives of the United States.

Implementation of United States Policy with Regard to Taiwan

Section 3. (a) In furtherance of the policy set forth in Section 2 of this Act, the United States will make available to Taiwan such defense articles and defense services in such quantity as may be necessary to enable Taiwan to maintain a sufficient self-defense capability.

(b) The President and the Congress shall determine the nature and quantity of such defense articles and services based solely upon their judgment of the needs of Taiwan, in accordance with procedures established by law. Such determination of Taiwan's defense needs shall include review by United States military authorities in connection with recommendations to the President and the Congress.

(c) The President is directed to inform the Congress promptly of any threat to the security or the social or economic system of the people on Taiwan and any danger to the interests of the United States arising therefrom. The President and the Congress shall determine, in accordance with constitutional processes, appropriate action by the United States in response to any such danger.

Application of Laws: International Agreements

Section 4. (a) The absence of diplomatic relations or recognition shall not affect the application of the laws of the United States with respect to Taiwan, and the laws of the United States shall apply with respect to Taiwan in the manner that the laws of the United States applied with respect to Taiwan prior to January 1, 1979.

(b) The application of subsection (a) of this section shall include, but not be limited to, the following:

(1) Whenever the laws of the United States refer or relate to foreign countries, nations, states, governments, or similar entities, such terms shall include and such laws shall apply with respect to Taiwan.

(2) Whenever authorized by or pursuant to the laws of the United States to conduct or carry out programs, transactons, or other relations with respect to foreign countries, nations, states, governments, or similar entities, the President or any agency of the United States Government is authorized to conduct and carry out, in accordance with section 6 of this Act, such programs, transactions, and other relations with respect to Taiwan (including but not limited to, the performance of services for the United States through contracts with commercial entities on Taiwan), in accordance with the applicable laws of the United States.

(3) (A) The absence of diplomatic relations and recognition with respect to Taiwan shall not abrogate, infringe, modify, deny, or otherwise affect in any way any rights or obligations (including but not limited to those involving contracts, debts, or property interests of any kind) under the laws of the United States heretofore or hereafter acquired by or with respect to Taiwan.

(B) For all purposes under the laws of the United States,

including actions in any court in the United States, recognition of the People's Republic of China shall not affect in any way the ownership of or other rights or interests in properties, tangible and intangible, and other things of value, owned or held on or prior to December 31, 1978, or thereafter acquired or earned by the governing authorities on Taiwan.

(4) Whenever the application of the laws of the United States depends upon the law that is or was applicable on Taiwan or compliance therewith, the law applied by the people on Taiwan shall be considered the applicable law for that purpose.

(5) Nothing in this Act, nor the facts of the President's action in extending diplomatic recognition to the People's Republic of China, the absence of diplomatic relations between the people on Taiwan and the United States, or the lack of recognition by the United States, and attendant circumstances thereto, shall be construed in any administrative or judicial proceeding as a basis for any United States Government agency, commission, or department to make a finding of fact or determination of law, under the Atomic Energy Act of 1954 and the Nuclear Non-Proliferation Act of 1978, to deny an export license application or to revoke an existing export license for nuclear exports to Taiwan.

(6) For purposes of the Immigration and Nationality Act, Taiwan may be treated in the manner specified in the first sentence of Section 202(b) of that Act.

(7). The capacity of Taiwan to sue and be sued in courts in the United States, shall not be abrogated, infringed, modified, denied, or otherwise affected in any way by the absence of diplomatic relations and recognition.

(8) No requirement, whether expressed or implied, under the laws of the United States with respect to maintenance of diplomatic relations or recognition shall be applicable with respect to Taiwan.

(c) For all purposes, including actions in any court in the United States, the Congress approves the continuation in force of all treaties and other international agreements, including multilateral conventions, entered into by the United States and the governing authorities on Taiwan recognized by the United States as the Republic of China prior to January 1, 1979, and in force between them on December 31, 1978, unless and until terminated in accordance with law.

(d) Nothing in this Act may be construed as a basis for supporting the exclusion or expulsion of Taiwan from continued membership in any international financial institution or any other international organization.

Overseas Private Investment Corporation

Section 5. (a) During the three-year period beginning on the date of enactment of this Act, the $1,000 per capita income restriction in clause (2) of the second undesignated paragraph of Section 231 of the Foreign Assistance Act of 1961 shall not restrict the activities of the Overseas Private Investment Corporation in determining whether to provide any insurance, reinsurance, loans, or guarantees with respect to investment projects on Taiwan.

(b) Except as provided in subsection (a) of this section, in issuing insurance, reinsurance, loans, or guaranties with respect to investment projects on Taiwan, the Overseas Private Insurance Corporation shall apply the same criteria as those applicable in other parts of the world.

The American Institute in Taiwan

Section 6. (a) Programs, transactions, and other relations conducted or carried out by the President or any agency of the United States Government with respect to Taiwan shall, in the manner and to the extent directed by the President, be conducted and carried out by or through—

(1) The American Institute in Taiwan, a nonprofit corporation incorporated under the laws of the District of Columbia, or
(2) Such comparable successor nongovernmental entity as the President may designate
(hereafter in this Act referred to as the "Institute").

(b) Whenever the President or any agency of the United States Government is authorized or required by or pursuant to the laws of the United States to enter into, perform, enforce, or have in force an agreement or transaction relative to Taiwan, such agreement or transaction shall be entered into, performed, and enforced, in the manner and to the extent directed by the President, by or through the Institute.

(c) To the extent that any law, rule, regulation, or ordinance of the District of Columbia, or of any State or political subdivision thereof in which the Institute is incorporated or doing business, impedes or otherwise interferes with the performance of the functions of the Institute pursuant to this Act, such law, rule, regulation, or ordinance shall be deemed to be preempted by this Act.

Services by the Institute to the United States Citizens on Taiwan

Section 7. (a) The Institute may authorize any of its employees on Taiwan—

(1) to administer to or take from any person an oath, affirmation, affidavit, or deposition, and to perform any notarial act which any notary public is required or authorized by law to perform within the United States;

(2) to act as provisional conservator of the personal estates of deceased United States citizens; and

(3) to assist and protect the interests of United States persons by performing other Acts such as are authorized to be performed outside the United States for consular purposes by such laws of the United States as the President may specify.

(b) Acts performed by authorized employees of the Institute under this section shall be valid, and of like force and effect within the United States, as if performed by any other person authorized under the laws of the United States to perform such Acts.

Tax Exempt Status of the Institute

Section 8. (a) The Institute, its property, and its income are exempt from all taxation now or hereafter imposed by the United States (except to the extent that Section 11(a)(3) of this Act requires the imposition of taxes imposed under chapter 21 of the Internal Revenue Code of 1954, relating to the Federal Insurance Contributions Act) or by any State or local taxing authority of the United States.

(b) For purposes of the Internal Revenue Code of 1954, the Institute shall be treated as an organization described in sections 170(b)(1)(A), 170(c), 2055(a), 2106(a)(2)(A), 2522(a), and 2522(b).

Furnishing Property and Services to and
Obtaining Services From the Institute

Section 9. (a) Any agency of the United States Government is authorized to sell, loan, or lease property (including interests thereof) to, and to perform administrative and technical support functions and services for the operations of, the Institute upon such terms and conditions as the President may direct. Reimbursements to agencies under this subsection shall be credited to the current applicable appropriation of the agency concerned.

(b) Any agency of the United States Government is authorized to acquire and accept services from the Institute upon such terms and conditions as the President may direct. Whenever the President determines it to be in furtherance of the purposes of this Act, the procurement of services by such agencies from the Institute may be effected without regard to such laws of the United States normally applicable to the acquisition of services by such agencies as the President may specify by Executive order.

(c) Any agency of the United States Government making funds available to the Institute in accordance with this Act shall make arrangements with the Institute for the Comptroller General of the United States to have access to the books and records of the Institute and the opportunity to audit the operations of the Institute.

Taiwan Instrumentality

Section 10. (a) Whenever the President or any agency of the United States Government is authorized or required by or pursuant to the laws of the United States to render or provide to or to receive or accept from Taiwan, any performance, communication, assurance, undertaking, or other action, such action shall, in the manner and to the extent directed by the President, be rendered or provided to, or received or accepted from, an instrumentality established by Taiwan which the President determines has the necessary authority under the laws applied by the people on Taiwan to provide assurances and take other actions on behalf of Taiwan in accordance with this Act.

(b) The President is requested to extend to the instrumentality established by Taiwan the same number of offices and complement of personnel as were previously operated in the United States by the governing authorities on Taiwan recognized as the Republic of China prior to January 1, 1979.

(c) Upon the granting by Taiwan of comparable privileges and immunities with respect to the Institute and its appropriate personnel, the President is authorized to extend with respect to the Taiwan instrumentality and its appropriate personnel, such privileges and immunities (subject to appropriate conditions and obligations) as may be necessary for the effective performance of their functions.

Separation of Government Personnel for Employment with the Institute

Section 11.　(a) (1) Under such terms and conditions as the President may direct, any agency of the United States Government may separate from Government service for a specified period any officer or employee of that agency who accepts employment with the Institute.

(2) An officer or employee separated by an agency under paragraph (1) of this subsection for employment with the Institute shall be entitled upon termination of such employment to reemployment or reinstatement with such agency (or a successor agency) in an appropriate position with the attendant rights, privileges, and benefits which the officer or employee would have had or acquired had he or she not been so separated, subject to such time period and other conditions as the President may prescribe.

(3) An officer or employee entitled to reemployment or reinstatement rights under paragraph (2) of this subsection shall, while continuously employed by the Institute with no break in continuity of service, continue to participate in any benefit program in which such officer or employee was participating prior to employment by the Institute, including programs for compensation for job-related death, injury, or illness; programs for health and life insurance; programs for annual, sick, and other statutory leave; and programs for retirement under any system established by the laws of the United States; except that employment with the Institute shall be the basis for participation in such programs only to the extent that employee deductions and employer contributions, as required, in payment for such participation for the period of employment with Institute, are currently deposited in the program's or

system's fund or depository. Death or retirement of any such officer or employee during approved service with the Institute and prior to reemployment or reinstatement shall be considered a death in or retirement from Government service for purposes of any employee or survivor benefits acquired by reason of service with an agency of the United States Government.

(4) Any officer or employee of an agency of the United States Government who entered into service with the Institute on approved leave of absence without pay prior to the enactment of this Act shall receive the benefits of this section for the period of such service.

(b) Any agency of the United States Government employing alien personnel on Taiwan may transfer such personnel, with accrued allowances, benefits, and rights, to the Institute without a break in service for purpose of retirement and other benefits, including continued participation in any system established by the laws of the United States for the retirement of employees in which the alien was participating prior to the transfer to the Institute, except that employment with the Institute shall be creditable for retirement purposes only to the extent that employee deductions and employer contributions, as required, in payment for such participation for the period of employment with the Institute, are currently deposited in the system's fund or depository.

(c) Employees of the Institute shall not be employees of the United States and, in representing the Institute, shall be exempt from Section 207 of Title 18, United States Code.

(d) (1) For purposes of sections 911 and 913 of the Internal Revenue Code of 1954, amounts paid by the Institute to its employees shall not be treated as earned income. Amounts received by employees of the Institute shall not be included in gross income, and shall be exempt from taxation, to the extent that they are equivalent to amounts received by civilian officers and employees of the Government of the United States as allowances and benefits which are exempt from taxation under Section 912 of such code.

(2) Except to the extent required by subsection (a)(3) of this section, service performed in the employ of the Institute shall not constitute employment for purposes of Chapter 21 of such Code and Title II of the Social Security Act.

Reporting Requirements

Section 12. (a) The Secretary of State shall transmit to the Congress the text of any agreement to which the Institute is a party. However, any such agreement the immediate public disclosure of which would, in the opinion of the President, be prejudicial to the national security of the United States shall not be so transmitted to the Congress but shall be transmited to the Committee on Foreign Relations of the Senate and the Committee on Foreign Affairs of the House of Representatives under an appropriate injunction of secrecy to be removed only upon due notice from the President.

(b) For purposes of subsection (a), the term "agreement" includes—

   (1) any agreement entered into between the Institute and the governing authorities on Taiwan or the instrumentality established by Taiwan; and
   (2) any agreement entered into between the Institute and an agency of the United States Government.

(c) Agreements and transactions made or to be made by or through the Institute shall be subject to the same congressional notification, review, and approval requirements and procedures as if such agreements and transactions were made by or through the agency of the United States Government on behalf of which the Institute is acting.

(d) During the two-year period beginning on the effective date of this Act, the Secretary of State shall transmit to the Speaker of the House of Representatives and the Committee on Foreign Relations of the Senate, every six months, a report describing and reviewing economic relations between the United States and Taiwan, noting any interference with normal commercial relations.

Rules and Regulations

Section 13. The President is authorized to prescribe such rules and regulations as he may deem appropriate to carry out the purposes of this Act. During the three-year period beginning on the effective date of this Act, such rules and regulations shall be transmited promptly to the Speaker of the House of Representatives and to the Committee on Foreign Relations of the Senate. Such action shall not, however, relieve the Institute of the responsibilities placed upon it by this Act.

Congressional Oversight

Section 14. (a) The Committee on Foreign Affairs of the House of Representatives, the Committee on Foreign Relations of the Senate, and other appropriate committees of the Congress shall monitor—

(1) the implementation of the provisions of this Act;
(2) the operation and procedures of the Institute;
(3) the legal and technical aspects of the continuing relationship between the United States and Taiwan; and
(4) the implementation of the policies of the United States concerning security and cooperation in East Asia.

(b) Such committees shall report, as appropriate, to their respective Houses on the results of their monitoring.

Definitions

Section 15. For purposes of this Act—

(1) the term "laws of the United States" includes any statute, rule, regulation, ordinance, order, or judicial rule of decision of the United States or any political subdivision thereof; and

(2) the term "Taiwan" includes, as the context may require, the islands of Taiwan and the Pescadores, the people on those islands, corporations and other entities and associations created or organized under the laws applied on those islands, and the governing authorities on Taiwan recognized by the United States as the Republic of China prior to January 1, 1979, and any successor governing authorities (including political subdivisions, agencies, and instrumentalities thereof).

Authorization of Appropriations

Section 16. In addition to funds otherwise available to carry out the provisions of this Act, there are authorized to be appropriated to the Secretary of State for the fiscal year 1980 such funds as may be necessary to carry out such provisions. Such funds are authorized to remain available until expended.

Severability of Provisions

Section 17. If any provision of this Act or the application thereof to any person or circumstance is held invalid, the remainder of the Act and the application of such provisions to any other person or circumstance shall not be affected thereby.

Effective Date

Section 18.   This Act shall be effective as of January 1, 1979.